American Architecture 1860–1976

Frederick Koeper

AMERICAN ARCHITECTURE
Volume 2
1860–1976

The MIT Press
Cambridge, Massachusetts

Second paperback edition, 1984

© 1981 by The Massachusetts Institute of Technology
New material © 1983 by The Massachusetts Institute of Technology

This book was set in VIP Aldus and VIP Palatino Bold Italic by DEKR Corporation and printed and bound by Halliday Lithograph in the United States of America.

Library of Congress Cataloging in Publication Data

Whiffen, Marcus.
    American architecture.

    Reprint. Originally published: American architecture, 1607–1976. With new foreword.
    Bibliography: p.
    Includes index.
    Contents: v. 1. 1607–1860—v. 2. 1860–1976.
    1. Architecture—United States. I. Koeper, Frederick. II. Title.
NA705.W473   1983   720'.973   83–5403
ISBN 0–262–73069–3 (v. 1)
        0–262–73070–7 (v. 2)

To Inge

Contents

Contents
Volume 1
1607–1860

Marcus Whiffen

Foreword

In the decades prior to 1860, American architecture had been nourished by European sources. By far the most pervasive was the English influence, such as that exerted by ecclesiastical sponsorship in England of the Gothic Revival style for churches. Germany had a minor role, bearing only on the Romanesque Revival. The French academic tradition as sustained by the Ecole des Beaux-Arts was still only faintly discernible in America in the 1850s—however strong the political and cultural alliances with France during the Revolution. It was not until 1855 that America's first graduate of that famous Paris institution, Richard Morris Hunt, returned to America to begin his career. And Hunt, despite his unique training, was first employed by Thomas Ustick Walter to assist on the new dome for the United States Capitol, a design inspired by St. Pauls in London.

In the first half of the century building assignments requiring professional design services were traditional in nature, namely buildings for government and beneficent institutions, churches, and country houses for the rich. As commerce grew, new categories were added. But even such distinctive examples as Boston's Quincy Market and the Providence Arcade, both of the 1820s, and William Strickland's elegant Merchants' Exchange for Philadelphia in 1836 contained no hint of the scale and urban density that came with the dramatic appearance of the commercial skyscraper of the 1880s. This peculiarly American achievement is traced directly to the use of cast iron in the 1840s for store fronts. East Coast manufacturers quickly filled orders for prefabricated cast-iron parts to satisfy the demand for office loft buildings across the nation. The now ubiquitous hotel appeared in flourishing cities to accommodate the commercial traveller. The first of the type was the Tremont House in Boston in 1828–32; its architect, Isaiah Rogers, chose the Greek Revival style for his innovation. Apart from commerce, another new type appeared before 1860: the modest country or vacation house, given shape by the English doctrine of the Picturesque, a belated arrival, and by American pragmatic sense in planning as well as native carpentry skills. Thus Andrew Jackson Downing's dream of "rural adaptation" began America's architectural idyll, an enduring Arcadian tradition that has produced such disparate examples as the "cottages" of fashionable Newport and Wright's celebrated "Fallingwater."

It would be wrong to view American architecture after 1860 as a mere enlargement of ideas previously laid down. American architecture became markedly different in two distinct shifts, one of which followed in step with Europe. This was the stylistic permissiveness encouraged by the Victorian Gothic and the French Second Empire styles, both established in Europe in the 1850s. However undogmatic the original definitions of these two eclectic styles, American designers took even greater advantage of this freedom, achieving striking originality. In American practice often these two styles were intertwined and interpretations quite free—the most rebellious of all being those of Frank Furness of Philadelphia. The second shift was a matter of maturity: the emergence of the American architect with a distinct, recognizable stylistic signature (one could also make this claim of the English-born Latrobe practicing in America in the early nineteenth century). Most obvious are the assertive design personalities of H. H. Richardson, Louis Sullivan, and Frank Lloyd Wright. What is remarkable is that each of the three was given recognition in Europe, temporarily reversing the usual east-to-west flow of influence. In Wright's case professional recognition, long withheld at home, was immediate abroad.

In the 1930s transatlantic influence, which for two centuries had been retrospective and historical, was to reassert itself in a different kind of importation, this time primarily from Germany. Fugitives from Nazi rule, in particular Gropius and Mies van de Rohe, led the formation of an avant-garde sensibility in America. Here these expatriates found more opportunity for the fulfillment of their ideas, a climate more free from precedent and history. Their concepts of modern architecture, named the International Style, became the staple of American practice. In recent decades the International Style has faced the challenge of widespread criticism and surely it will not survive intact. As might be expected, active debate about its future is not without foreign entanglements, this time primarily with Italy and Japan.

II   *1860–1976*

Frederick Koeper

The mid-century years saw revivalism replaced by a wholly contemporary eclecticism with the French Second Empire and the English High Victorian Gothic as the predominant styles. The interpretative license afforded by these two importations was seen in American buildings of the seventies in independent experiments, variously regarded as bold inventions or regrettable lapses in taste. Then Henry Hobson Richardson returned to historical eclecticism with his Romanesque Revival and created from this base a personal style that reintegrated architectural values and is properly regarded as proto-modern.

The Second Empire Style   The Second Empire Style is marked by a quality of cosmopolitan urbanity. Its first American appearance was in a New York town house on lower Fifth Avenue, the Hart M. Shiff House of 1850. The Danish-born architect, Detlef Lienau, had studied in Paris before emigrating in 1848—well before the accession of Napoleon III, whose reign (1852–70) gave the style its name. The style was popular in every Western country, England being no exception. Visitors to the Paris expositions of 1855 and 1867 saw vast building operations in that city, including major extensions to the Louvre and the impressive boulevards of Baron Haussmann, the emperor's city planner. No new avenues appeared in America, but the gridiron streets of New York accommodated Parisian-type row houses, a number of which were designed by Lienau. As an urban architectural style, Second Empire was just what America needed at a time of unprecedented urban growth. It was more appropriate for the hotels, railway stations, and government buildings that were the product of post–Civil War prosperity than any other style then current. Certainly its connotations of prestige, affluence, and authority, as well as of cosmopolitan Paris itself, together with the fact that it was notably free from the esthetic and moral entanglements that surrounded the High Victorian Gothic, appealed to practical men of commerce and government.

French buildings of the sixteenth century, half medieval, half Renaissance, such as the Louvre and the Tuileries, furnished the Second Empire Style with its two identifying features, the mansard roof and the pavilion motif. The latter is a forward break in the elevation, usually at the center and frequently at the ends as well but always symmetrically disposed, which is acknowledged by a corresponding break in the roof. These features were treated in various manners; for example, the restrained surfaces of the Shiff House contrast with the robust modelling and sculpture of the Philadelphia City Hall, which recalls Charles Garnier's Paris Opéra (1861–74), itself more Neo-Baroque than Second Empire in style.

Accomplished gothicist though he was, James Renwick yielded quickly to mid-century stylistic license, as his use of Egyptian and Romanesque motifs in the 1840s testifies. His were the first two major works in the Second Empire Style: the Corcoran (now Renwick) Gallery of Art in Washington (1859) and Vassar College in Poughkeepsie, New York (1861–65). The banker and art collector, William Corcoran, and his architect-to-be made a trip together to the Paris Exposition of 1855 and, as a belated memento four years later, the Corcoran Gallery rose in showy Parisian style. However, neither its coloration of red brick and brownstone nor its column capitals, which repeated Latrobe's invention for the United States Capitol, were French. For his new college, the brewer-philanthropist Matthew Vassar received from Renwick's hand an enormous but rather plain, four-story brick building, whose extended array of pavilion accents recalls the Tuileries Palace.

Precedent for government buildings in the French style was to be found in recent English architecture, notably the designs submitted in the 1857 competition for government offices in London that were much publicized by the English journals. The controversy between the Goths and the classicists that followed this competition, the so-called "Battle of the Styles," was settled in favor of classicism by the whim of one man, the prime minister. An American example that reflects Lord Palmerston's taste is the New York Capitol in Albany by Thomas Fuller. Described as conforming to a "Renaissance style similar to that of the Louvre in Paris," it was begun in 1867; the original scheme was later modified and completed by Leopold Eidlitz and H. H. Richardson.

The most prolific designer in the Second Empire Style—thanks to his being Supervising Architect of the Treasury from 1865 to 1875—was Alfred B. Mullett. The unmistakable prototype of many of the designs that issued from his office was Boston City Hall (1861–65) by Arthur Gilman with his partner Gridley Bryant (171). Unlike Renwick, Gilman was capable of self-criticism and never mistook fashion for architectural elegance. Boston City Hall is suave and consistent even if without the sculptural richness of the New Louvre.

The Boston City Hall motif of recurrent columns and arched windows on every floor was repeated *ad nauseam* in Mullett's courthouses and post offices, such as those in St. Louis, Philadelphia, Cincinnati, and New York. This repetitiveness, an inescapable characteristic of bureaucratic architecture, has a counterpart in the cast-iron Renaissance facades of the Haughwout Store in New York and

171
Boston City Hall, Boston,
Massachusetts. Arthur
Gilman and Gridley
Bryant, 1861–65.
Exterior.

172
State, War and Navy Building (Executive Office Building), Washington, District of Columbia. Alfred B. Mullett, 1871–87. Exterior.

similar examples of these years. Mullett's buildings, however, were substantially built, usually of granite, with the use of iron limited to interior stairs and skylighted courts; for example, the State, War, and Navy Building in Washington, renamed the Executive Office Building (1871–87) (172). Although technically satisfactory, they are compositionally uninteresting. An exception was the New York Post Office at the tip of City Hall Park, with its crescendo of multiple breaks leading to a center pavilion capped by a bulbous dome supporting an open lantern.

The most opulent of civic monuments in the French mansard style was built not by federal or state but municipal government. Designed by John McArthur, Jr., the marble Philadelphia City Hall was begun in 1871 and completed a decade later when the style was no longer in fashion. This Brobdingnagian building illustrates the fate of Second Empire design in America: it became florid, restless, and fragmented. No longer did substantive wings link pavilion accents; the whole became a bundle of verticals. A great tower, frequent in English Gothic Revival buildings of the time but incongruous with the French sources drawn on here, rises from the hollow square of the building to mark the intersection of Market and Broad streets, the center of William Penn's 1681 city plan, and to support a statue of the seventeenth-century Quaker.

Victorian Gothic

The assertive, at times aggressive, character of High Victorian architecture is achieved, in part, with color. That a church striped from top to bottom in red and yellow should have inspired two young men to become architects hardly seems likely; yet such was the case. The church was All Souls' Unitarian in New York (1853–55); the architects-to-be were Russell Sturgis and Peter Bonnett Wight, both later active Ruskinians. All Souls' was designed by Jacob Wrey

Mould, an inexperienced young man recently arrived from England, where he had studied under the colorist Owen Jones.[1] The contrast between layers of yellowish Caen stone alternating with bands of dark red brick was too violent even for Leopold Eidlitz, an architect sympathetic to Mould's approach, and the public soon labelled the building the "Holy Zebra" (173). Unfortunately economy cut the height of the walls by six feet and the free-standing corner campanile was never built. Part Romanesque, part Byzantine, with its strident polychromy, a foretaste of High Victorian Gothic, and its willful dissonance, felt in the tension of horizontal banding broken by pilaster strips, Mould's church remains an avant-garde example of the mannerisms that formed the "character" of postwar buildings.

High Victorian Gothic was in large part the unintentional creation of John Ruskin, the English writer and critic, who never designed a building. The spell Ruskin cast over American architecture of the sixties and seventies is understandable when one considers the persuasiveness of his prose style and his appeal to nineteenth-century moral values. Despite his popularity in America, he refused an invitation to cross the Atlantic, saying he could not be happy in a land where there were no castles. His books, *The Seven Lamps of Architecture* of 1849 and *The Stones of Venice* of 1851–53, appeared in simultaneous, pirated American editions. These two works, his most influential on architecture, were reprinted throughout the century. Ironically the very architectural style that Ruskin's writings inspired was one he disowned as untrue to his preachings. Ruskin's own opinions were never wholly consistent, but he remained firm in his distinction between architecture and mere building, the former being adorned with "unnecessary features" of decoration. The encrustation of structure was, for Ruskin, the essential problem of architecture and the measure of its success. To his eyes the chromatic decoration of the Gothic palaces of Venice—in particular that model of all perfection, the Doge's Palace—deserved his greatest praise. That Ruskin was opposed to the adoption of Italian Gothic for northern countries did not prevent its adoption in England and, a decade later, in America.

In 1860 Ruskinian Gothic was used for the first time by Mould in his Trinity Church Parish School in New York. More noticed and praised by contemporary critics, however, was Peter B. Wight's National Academy of Design in New York (174). Wight shifted from Romanesque of his 1861–62 competition design, now lost, to Venetian Gothic in the executed building of 1863–65. The Doge's Palace was his obvious model, made more utilitarian by the inclusion of a row of street-level shops along the side. The banding of stone and

173
*All Souls' Unitarian
Church, New York City.
Jacob Wrey Mould, 1853–
55. Exterior.*

174
*National Academy of
Design, New York City.
Peter B. Wight, 1863–65.
Exterior.*

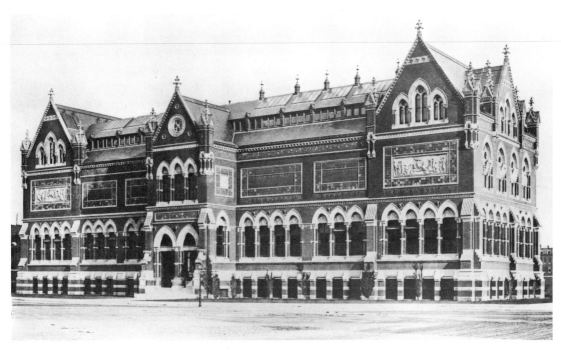

175
*Museum of Fine Arts,
Boston, Massachusetts.
John H. Sturgis and
Charles Brigham, 1870–
76. Exterior.*

176
*Nott Memorial Library
(Alumni Hall), Union
College, Schenectady,
New York. Edward T.
Potter, 1872–75. Exterior.*

brick between the pointed arches of the lower floors and the diagonal patterning of the top story were a response to Ruskin's plea for constructive truth: surface ornament integral with the building.

The proper way to achieve decorative effects in architecture became a debated issue with the growing use of cast iron and terra-cotta in the 1840s in England. Ruskin never approved of the use of cast iron, however easily and cheaply it could reproduce carved ornament; yet he approved of molded terra-cotta as a substitute for cut stone.[2] In America terra-cotta (manufactured in England) was first used in quantity in the Museum of Fine Arts in Boston (1870–76) by the local architects John H. Sturgis and Charles Brigham (175). Sturgis, who maintained an office in England and commuted across the Atlantic, emulated the terra-cotta of the Victoria and Albert (formerly South Kensington) Museum in London of 1867 as well as the design of the New Museum at Oxford by Deane and Woodward, a building in which Ruskin had a proprietary interest and which he intended to be a manifesto of the new style.

Ruskin's eloquence, high-mindedness, and equation of ethics and esthetics made Victorian Gothic a frequent choice for institutions of art and education. The classical rotunda proposed by Ramée for Union College in Schenectady, New York, at the beginning of the century became, in Edward T. Potter's hands, an Italianate baptistery, serving as the Nott Memorial Library, now Alumni Hall (1872–75). Behind its polychromed stone arcading there is a partial iron skeleton (176). In the year in which it was begun his brother, William A. Potter, designed in a less declamatory manner the Chancellor Green Library at Princeton, which was an octagon with flanking Palladian-type appendages. Much simpler than either of these was Russell Sturgis's Farnam Hall at Yale (1869), whose expanses of plain brick wall would not have interested Ruskin but would have given pleasure to the eye of William Morris.

Ruskinian Gothic found little favor among the Anglicans, although they had previously been submissive to English church fashion. In 1848 Leopold Eidlitz, schooled under the Anglican Upjohn, settled on German Romanesque for St. George's, New York, where he provided a straightforward auditorium for its evangelical rector. Later, in 1873, he designed the Ruskinian Church of the Holy Trinity, also in New York City, for the rector's son (177). Here again he emphasized the function of the church as an auditorium with a curious elliptical interior contained within a rectangle, which, incidentally, provided Eidlitz an opportunity to apply his structural ingenuity with roof trusses. The striking appearance of Holy Trinity, with walls and roofs alike covered with diagonal patterns that are

*177
Church of the Holy Trin-
ity, New York City. Leo-
pold Eidlitz, 1873.
Exterior.*

178
Memorial Hall, Harvard
University, Cambridge,
Massachusetts. Ware and
Van Brunt, 1870–78.
Exterior.

more assertive than tasteful, provoked its nickname, "Church of the Homely Oilcloth." Throughout his long career, during which he designed more than thirty churches, Eidlitz was faithful to medievalism; for him structure was the generator of architecture even if he was unable to curb the restless eclecticism of his designs.

Memorial Hall at Harvard University (1870–78) has a strongly ecclesiastical look, although its architects claimed that its cathedral form was accidental and resulted directly from the requirements of the 1865 competition for a theater and a dining hall, the theater forming a "choir," the dining hall a "nave," and their shared circulation area a "transept" (178). Henry Van Brunt and William R. Ware, partners from 1863 to 1888, were never disciples of Ruskin. Yet Memorial Hall, designed by Van Brunt, was praised for this very connection. "It speaks of sacrifice and example," wrote Henry James, underlining the moral and esthetic unity of the Victorian Gothic Style.[3] Curiously enough in the introduction to his translation of Viollet-le-Duc's *Entretiens*, Van Brunt took exception to Ruskin as "dictator on questions of art," criticizing Victorian Gothic as "based in literary exposition [rather than] practical knowledge."

Frank Furness

Far more of value came from Ruskin's writings than Van Brunt gave credit for. It was Ruskin, more than anyone, who created that larger view of architecture as a "real" experience, who set the value of immediacy on the sight and feel of actual stones, bricks, and marble, preferring the rough to the smooth and demanding that materials be "true," not painted imitations. Rejecting the "prejudices of taste" and disdaining the book-learning and the perfunctory teaching of the academies, he conceived of architecture as, first and last, a participatory pleasure of the senses.

No architect was more Ruskinian than Frank Furness, who lived most of his life and did most of his building in Philadelphia. The independent and subjective eye of Furness gave "character" to all his designs; "wild" and "fearless" were the adjectives used of them by his contemporaries. The individuality of his work makes it difficult to place; the closest parallel is found in the New York buildings of Mould and Eidlitz, which were surely known to him during his apprentice years with Richard Morris Hunt immediately before and after the Civil War. Hunt's influence appears in the Néo-Grec that is reflected in the architectonic patterning and fluted details of the facade of the Pennsylvania Academy of the Fine Arts in Philadelphia (1871–76), designed in partnership with George W. Hewitt (179). The academy is a major work of Furness's early maturity. Its orderly facade comprises three mansarded pavilions, each with its pointed-

179
Pennsylvania Academy of the Fine Arts, Philadelphia, Pennsylvania. Frank Furness, 1871–76. Exterior.

arch window, changing gradually from simple to ornate as the building rises. Furness's unhesitant translation of Ruskin's "constructional coloration" and his irreverent mixing of stylistic motifs are visual shock treatment. Materials are given maximum definition: rusticated purplish brownstone, smooth pale sandstone, cylinders of polished granite, and sharp-edged panels of red brick sometimes set with black brick patterns, are ruthlessly juxtaposed. The architect's minister father gave utterance to the contemporary view: "The monotony of [Quaker] streets is disappearing [as] the spirit of beauty is beginning to brood over our city . . . ."

Furness's several banks express none of the traditional conservatism of those institutions. The Provident Life and Trust Company (1879) was the most daring (180). Here Furness defied the limits of a narrow facade with overscaled granite stones framing shadowed openings and a cantilevered mass over the entrance, as precariously stacked as a child's building blocks. The facade was tense and threatening; harmony and grace were scorned. While trying to adjust to its calculated rudeness, one could not escape its undeniable force. Inside, the walls of a high, simple hall were sheathed in patterned green and white tiles and the roof had skylights like those of the Pennsylvania Academy supported by visible, polychromed girders.

180
Provident Life and Trust Company, Philadelphia, Pennsylvania. Frank Furness, 1879. Exterior.

The Taste for the Exotic

Nineteenth-century scholarship provided architects and their clients with an ever-increasing choice of styles. In the uninhibited postwar years, the urge to mix them was indulged to the full. Governed only by subjective taste, the result was a synthetic eclecticism beyond all rules and precedent. "Let us glory in all styles, character is the thing," exclaimed an English lecturer. Among those available, thanks to Owen Jones's book on the Alhambra, was the Saracenic or Moorish Style. For his Hudson River retreat the American painter Frederic E. Church, assisted by Calvert Vaux, created Olana (1874), a picturesque and personal combination of Moorish themes. Like other styles Moorish was used indiscriminately for disparate building types; in New York alone, it was used for the Temple Emanu-El synagogue by Eidlitz (1866–68), a cast-iron store front, the Tweedy and Co. Building by Hunt (1871–74), and a billiard room in the W. K. Vanderbilt House, also by Hunt (1879–81). Reaction from the tensions of war and a certain recklessness and spirit of speculation found in society at large conditioned architecture far more than associations for the advancement of truth in art.

Henry Hobson Richardson

There are few hints in the mediocre work of Richardson's early years of what was to come in his maturity, when, beginning with his competition-winning design of 1870 for the Brattle Square Church in Boston, he adopted the Romanesque. As we have seen, the Romanesque Revival in America was initiated with Upjohn's churches of a quarter of a century earlier. Their Lombard and Germanic prototypes were not what inspired Richardson; his inspiration came rather from certain Parisian churches of the sixties, from sketches of early medieval churches in English and French magazines, and also from the early Christian churches of Syria, which had recently received archaeological study. Never pedantic in his use of historical styles, he organized his designs, in silhouette, materials, and stylistic details, with the greatest freedom. His dependence on the Romanesque in the early seventies soon gave way to a firmness of plan and massing that is more Richardsonian than Romanesque; the architect came to dominate the style and not the style the architect.

In 1872 Richardson won the commission for Trinity Church in Boston, the culminating work of his early career. Larger and more imaginatively Romanesque than his Brattle Square Church, it shares the open Greek cross plan, the breadth of which is better suited to preaching than liturgy (181). The short nave and stubby transepts of Trinity Church—all three provided with balconies—abut a crossing bay that is nearly fifty feet square, which has an equally wide combined chancel and apse that is deeper than the nave. The aisles

181
*Trinity Church. Boston,
Massachusetts. H. H.
Richardson, 1873–77.
Interior.*

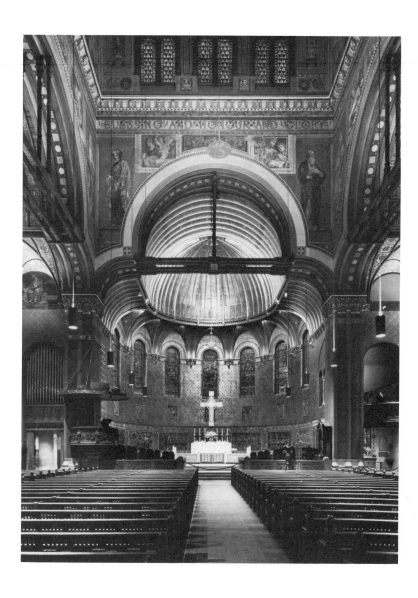

182
*Trinity Church, Boston,
Massachusetts. Exterior.*

are negligible, and the interior effect is that of a single great room. The space does not recall any Romanesque church ever built, nor does it convey visually the structural strength associated with medieval churches. Its roof is of timber trusses, it is not vaulted in stone—no nineteenth-century church ever was. All interior surfaces are furred out, plastered over, or otherwise sheathed in wood. This intentional concealment of the granite walls allowed applied decoration to achieve the "color church" Richardson wanted. Stirring yet not garish, the colors, primarily terra-cotta red, blue-green, and gold, remind us that we are still in the age of Ruskin. Even the four piers supporting the central tower were to have been sheathed in mosaic. John La Farge, assisted by the young Augustus Saint-Gaudens, was responsible for the murals and much of the stained glass.

The greater glory of Trinity Church is its exterior, notably the splendid massing of forms leading to the apex of the tower, freely observed on its isolated site facing Copley Square (182). With good reason it has always been admired. The competition design has been lost, but we know that Charles Follen McKim, who was in Richardson's office for two years, had a hand in the executed design. An early revision drawn by McKim shows a taller and more slender octagonal tower on a square base, somewhat Victorian Gothic in character. The present one was designed by Stanford White, McKim's replacement in the office. White followed Richardson's suggestion that the tower should be modelled on that of the Salamanca cathedral, using a photograph recently sent by La Farge from

Spain. White's tower may be a bit overdressed with detail for the more severe body of the church, but it is nonetheless a decided success. The entrance porch and the capping of the western towers of the facade were added by Richardson's successors, Shepley, Rutan and Coolidge; both features were intended by the architect, who spoke of his Trinity design as "a free rendering of the French Romanesque" (in particular that of ancient Aquitaine) and thought its central tower might be reminiscent "of the domes of Venice and Constantinople." The portal came from St. Gilles in southern France. This mixing of stylistic references to Spain, France, and the Byzantine world was a kind of eclecticism that Richardson later disavowed; however, in the eighties and beyond it became the accepted method of McKim, Mead and White and others, who relied more on intelligence than on intuition.

Although Trinity Church fixed his fame and caused congregations to seek duplicates, Richardson's forte was in secular rather than ecclesiastical work. He built only two churches after the completion of Trinity in 1877. He preferred monumental buildings, yet he accepted smaller commissions—houses, suburban railway stations, even two bridges for Boston's park system, which was laid out by his Brookline neighbor, Frederick Law Olmsted. "The things I want most to design" he once said, "are a grain elevator and the interior of a great river-steamboat."

Of Richardson's five libraries, all similar in plan, the Crane Memorial Library in Quincy, Massachusetts (1880–83), is the best (183, 184). It represents the culmination of the process of simplification seen in his work of the seventies. A picturesque silhouette is replaced by an unbroken roof-ridge, capping a rectangular plan as simple as that of a seventeenth-century colonial house. Richardson's concentration on the relation of solid to void, of wall to window, becomes the basis for a harmonious abstraction with scarcely a reference to any past style. The magnificent horizontal series of windows placed above the high-breasted wall and below the simple roof is one of Richardson's most lyrical passages. Like his English contemporary, Philip Webb, Richardson was reacting to the disordered eclecticism of the Victorian era. For both Webb and Richardson, walls, roofs, and chimneys were sacred. In the Quincy Library the random ashlar of gray granite is relieved by strips of brown granite trim. Sensuous details were shaped in this hardest of stones; for example, the sculptured lips of the corner waterspouts, which equal the best of Art Nouveau design yet to come. In all successful masonry the skill of the builder is paramount and the Norcross Brothers, Richardson's

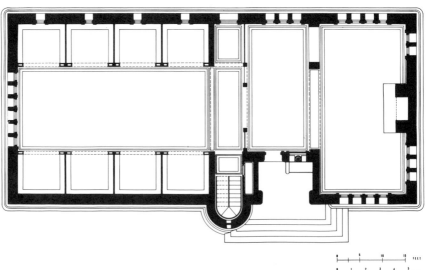

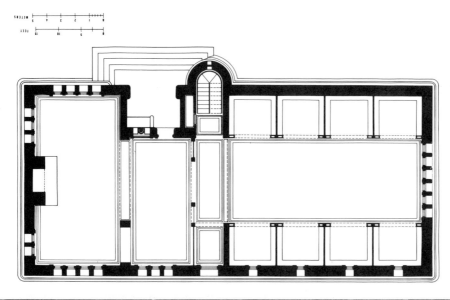

183
*Crane Memorial Library,
Quincy, Massachusetts.
H. H. Richardson, 1880–
83. Exterior.*

184
*Crane Memorial Library,
Quincy, Massachusetts.
Plan.*

185
*Sever Hall, Harvard
University, Cambridge,
Massachusetts. H. H.
Richardson, 1878–80.
Exterior.*

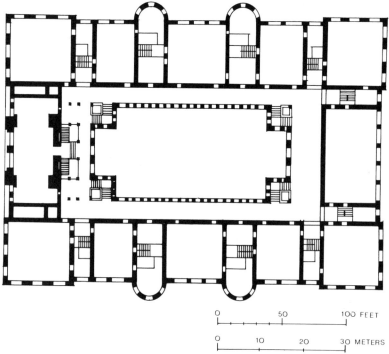

favorite contractors, were wonderfully skillful in realizing the effects their architect sought. Tactile experiences were not the least part of Richardson's "reality."

The commission to design Sever Hall in Harvard Yard, which came to him in 1878, may have hastened Richardson on his course toward simplicity (185). Nearby stood the utilitarian, red brick Massachusetts Hall of the early eighteenth century and Bulfinch's restrained, pale granite University Hall. Richardson followed their rectangular plans and simple roofs and played variations on the theme of their straightforward, symmetrical fenestration in the richer but disciplined grouping of his classroom windows. He achieved a design that was "neither monotonous nor restless" by relieving the red brick plainness of the walls with molded and cut brick panels and string-courses, handsome details whose assorted historical origins make Sever Hall Richardson's most hybrid work. Particularly notable are his wholly original fluted brick chimneys at the ridge of the low-hipped roof. In her biography of the architect, Mrs. Schuyler Van Rensselaer characterized Sever Hall as "so striking yet so serious, sensible, uneccentric, and appropriate." Her words might apply to all of Richardson's late work.

Richardson did not live to see the completion of his two favorite designs: the Allegheny County Courthouse and Jail in Pittsburgh (1884–88) and the Marshall Field Wholesale Store in Chicago (1885–87). One must not be misled by the quarry-faced gray granite walls and lofty tower of the Pittsburgh building and fail to observe that its logical plan and monumentality are qualities advocated by the Ecole des Beaux-Arts, where Richardson had studied after his years as a Harvard undergraduate (186, 187). Even the strong emphasis on corner pavilions suggests a French *hôtel de ville* scheme. The court-yard elevations, composed of unadorned masonry arcades in the tradition of ancient Roman aqueducts, are the part of the building one might regard as characteristically Richardsonian. But the intricate fantasy of the stairhall, the equal of any eighteenth-century northern Italian or Bavarian Baroque example, and as fine in its different way, is also Richardson's.

In the utilitarian commission of the Marshall Field Wholesale Store we recognize Richardson's true destiny: to compose cubic forms in rugged masonry, uninhibited by picturesque conventions of his time (188). The motif of layered arcades with graduated openings in his earlier commercial buildings, the Cheney in Hartford (1875–76) and the Ames in Boston (1882–83), is expanded and simplified and given an intensity and vigor unmatched in Richardson's previous work. First conceived for brick, the design was carried out in stone,

186
Allegheny County Court House, Pittsburgh, Pennsylvania. H. H. Richardson, 1884–88. Exterior.

187
Allegheny County Court House, Pittsburgh, Pennsylvania. Plan.

red granite for the two-story base and red sandstone above. Inside, timber framing carried plank floors, the typical construction of New England mills. Only on the first three floors were cast-iron columns used, and they were jacketed in terra-cotta, as was the practice in Chicago after the disastrous fire of 1871. Richardson was never particularly interested in new materials.

What form Richardson might have given to skyscraper construction, which was being proposed by Chicago architects in his last years of life, can only be suggested by the work of Sullivan, the architect who best understood Richardson's mind. The strength of Richardson's designs made most architects pause to reconsider the "wobbling mockeries" of their own. But when they heeded Richardson, it was less the severity of his Marshall Field Store that they regarded than the pictorial manner, which he had long since abandoned. Richardsonian Romanesque was perhaps too personal a style, too much of its own time to endure for long. Within a few years of his death, it vanished with scarcely a trace, except for what survived in the no less personal style of Sullivan.

188
Marshall Field Wholesale
Store, Chicago, Illinois.
H. H. Richardson, 1885–
87. Exterior drawing.

Richardson's Followers

The Richardsonian interlude is well represented in the Midwest, particularly in Chicago, St. Paul, and Minneapolis. These prosperous and ambitious "Western" cities, as they were then regarded, saw in Richardsonian Romanesque a congenial means of expression for their civic, cultural, and domestic virtues. To extend the Romanesque style to the commercial skyscraper, as Burnham and Root did in the Woman's Temple in Chicago (1892), for example, proved to be a mistake. The steel frame contradicts the structural message of the masonry-bearing wall. The architects were on better ground in their moderate-size Art Institute in Chicago (1886–87), in whose elevations logic and pictorial values are nicely balanced. The designer was John Root, whose talent almost matched his partner's ambition. Better trained than either Burnham or Root was Henry Ives Cobb, who had studied at Harvard and MIT. Although his design ability was less than Root's, his Chicago Historical Society (1892) comes closer to the essence of Richardson than the Art Institute. It is more emphatic in basic form and wall treatment, although hardly as felicitous as the work that inspired it.

The quality of Richardsonian Romanesque imitations was not necessarily commensurate with their proximity to the Brookline source. In Minneapolis an imposing replica of the Allegheny County building was built by Long and Kees, who were the devoted Richardsonians of that city. Their City Hall and Hennepin County Courthouse (1888–1905) is at once both more utilitarian and more picturesque than its prototype. The addition of numerous turrets to corner pavilions makes for a more animated roofline, but the arrangement of windows, greater in number but smaller in size, is better suited to office use. The solid shaft of Richardson's tower was here opened up with windows, unfortunately weakening the visual effect.

Another Richardson enthusiast was Leroy S. Buffington. His Pillsbury Hall (1887–89) on the University of Minnesota campus is evidence that architectural picture-making continued strong in the profession. Harvey Ellis, an itinerant draftsman employed by Buffington, was the actual designer. In designing, Ellis never paid any attention to construction, but his considerable talent in delineation—never Richardson's forte—led him to concentrate on details rather than on the simplification of plan and profile, which Richardson, however blunt and crude his sketches, never failed to do.

Within months of Richardson's death in 1886, a major commission came to his successors, Shepley, Rutan and Coolidge, who all were his young assistants. They were asked to design the new Stanford University in Palo Alto, California (189). The donor made it a troublesome assignment. The campus plan is a formal one based on two

189
Stanford University, Palo Alto, California. Shepley, Rutan and Coolidge, 1887–1902. North face of outer quad.

concentric rectangles formed by low buildings executed in rough yellow stone with tile roofs. Extensive arcades link the classrooms and provide them shade but also obscure their form. The arcaded courtyards suggest Spanish missions; whether intentional or not, this was something of which Leland Stanford approved. The short axis of the central quadrangle is marked by a memorial church in the manner of Boston's Trinity and, opposite the church, by a triumphal arch for which the economical architects rescued Richardson's 1875 proposal for a Civil War monument. The arch was toppled in the 1906 earthquake and was never rebuilt.

Richard Morris Hunt

Although Richardson looms larger in the perspective of history, it was Richard Morris Hunt who, after the retirement of Upjohn and Walter, was acknowledged by his contemporaries as the dean of American architecture. For forty years, from his return from the Ecole des Beaux-Arts, where he was the first American pupil, in 1855, to his death in 1895, Hunt was a prominent figure in the architectural scene despite the fact that he contributed little to the major stylistic trends of his time. The Second Empire Style as practiced in America was too coarse for his educated taste; the morality-laden Victorian Gothic could not interest a Francophile; Romanesque was alien to his temperament. A disciplined Romantic, Hunt is most often remembered for his brilliant adaptations of Loire Valley châteaux in grand houses, located mostly in New York and Newport.

Always a busy practitioner, Hunt was also active in the profession. He assisted in the founding of the American Institute of Architects in 1857. At a time when there were no architectural schools, he established a Parisian type *atelier* within his office that included such pupil-assistants as Post, Ware, Van Brunt, and Furness.[4] Once the young Sullivan sought his advice. In 1893 he became the first Amer-

ican to be awarded the Gold Medal of the Royal Institute of British Architects.

Hunt's early work does not flaunt Parisian Second Empire fashion; instead it restates the sober Néo-Grec of Henri Labrouste, the leading practitioner of this inappropriately named reforming style. Néo-Grec was a rationalized classicism that emerged in Paris in the 1840s and was soon eclipsed by the exuberant expressions of Napoleon III's reign. Hunt's simpler versions of Néo-Grec in New York are the Tenth Street Studio Building (1857) and the Stuyvesant Apartments (1869), both typically astylar with emphasis on flat surfaces. Hunt's best Néo-Grec building is the Lenox Library (1870–75), also in New York City (190). The rational composition of its plan and the way it is expressed in the elevations are clearly derived from the lessons of J.-N.-L. Durand.[5] Its monochromatic limestone and restrained ornament were departures from contemporary American taste. Though admired, the Lenox Library was not imitated, not even by Hunt; a later generation of architects, however, acknowledged its discipline.

In his last fifteen years Hunt found his *métier* in commissions for the Vanderbilt family and others of their kind. The first of his works in the château style that had a special appeal for them, and his masterpiece, was the William K. Vanderbilt House in New York (1879–81). Hunt skirted the free eclecticism of his time and followed a more scholarly path, pointing the way for the connoisseur's architecture of McKim and others. The facades of the Vanderbilt mansion were extremely flat, of finely tooled limestone, itself a contrast to the prevailing brownstone. Small-scaled decorative carvings were discreetly placed and sensitively executed (191). Hunt's assurance with manorial late French Gothic was shown in other town houses: the William Borden House in Chicago (1884), more severe than the

Vanderbilt mansion but with the same corbelled tourelle; the El-
bridge T. Gerry House in New York (1891), in which he used the
brick and limestone combination of Blois; and the double house for
the Astors, Mrs. William B. and John Jacob IV, also in New York
(1891), which aspires to the early Renaissance of Chambord.

At Newport, Rhode Island, Hunt helped to transform a modest
summer colony into a display of seasonal palaces and manor houses
for America's new aristocracy. The Breakers (1892–95) for Cornelius
Vanderbilt is his most successful Newport work. Here with great
flair he adapted an Italian Renaissance villa and arranged stately
rooms in a disciplined cruciform plan around a central two-storied
hall, suggesting a *cortile*, which served as a ballroom. From still
another Vanderbilt, George W., Hunt received his most regal commission, Biltmore (1890–95), near Asheville, North Carolina. It gave
him the opportunity to design, with the assistance of Olmsted, on
a regional scale, combining nature and art. The expansive landscaping
gives the house an appropriate detachment denied to those in Newport. Drawing heavily on the château of Blois, Biltmore stands as
the grandest house in America (192).

Hunt was at heart a knowledgeable eclectic rather than a rigorous
theorist. For him the value of an idea was less important than an
experienced eye. His polished works and cosmopolitan spirit were a
contrast to provincial practice in times when, as Van Brunt put it,
"sentiment was keenly aroused but discipline was silent."

192
Biltmore, Asheville,
North Carolina. Richard
Morris Hunt, 1890–95.
Exterior.

A New Skyline

In 1904 Henry James returned to America after more than twenty years' absence. As he approached New York by water, the skyline he saw astonished and displeased him. "Monsters of greed" were beginning to transform Manhattan into "a huge, jagged city." In his absence the skyscraper had been born.[1]

The two cities responsible were New York and Chicago. The skeletal metal frame, essential for the construction of tall buildings, appeared first in New York in the cast-iron structures of James Bogardus and Daniel Badger in the 1840s and 1850s. The crucial refinements that turned it into "Chicago construction" were assembled by William LeBaron Jenney in his Home Insurance Company Building of the early eighties in that city. If there has to be a "first" skyscraper, it was Jenney's "unlovely" building. By 1890 the perfected metal skeleton had been adopted by New York architects and the focus shifted back to the East, where the tallest examples were to be built, culminating in Cass Gilbert's Woolworth Building (1910–13), which stands nearly 800 feet high and was for twenty years the world's tallest office building.

The post-Civil War period marked the beginning of intense commercial growth. The convenience of doing business within a small number of blocks drastically increased the value of land in lower Manhattan and the Chicago Loop. Land values and technology were interrelated: as multiple floors became technically feasible, land values rose with increased heights. When the elevator broke the height limit of approximately sixty feet, changes were immediate. Greed and the elevator produced a serrated skyline in contrast to the relatively level one produced by five-story buildings. Certainly the primary motive was profit; yet in a competitive environment the tall office building was, on occasion, designed to be a mark of prestige. An example is "Publishers' Row" overlooking Manhattan's City Hall Park, consisting of the Tribune, the New York Times, and the New York World buildings, each with its own distinctive architectural treatment. But the bottom line of profit remained the most exacting: if the office building did not pay, it did not succeed. Never before in history had the demand for profit been so explicitly related to architecture.

Early Elevator Buildings

The first elevator building (to use the term current for high office buildings in the seventies) was the Equitable Life Insurance Company in New York (1868–70) by Arthur Gilman and Edward Kendall. It had seven stories of offices for rent, a modest increase over the usual

five but an increase that was only made viable by the elevator. Its
masonry exterior was Second Empire, with stories grouped in pairs
to belie its true height of 130 feet. The interior structure, partly of
iron, was the work of the consulting architect George B. Post, who
later, when more active on his own, was once introduced by Daniel
Burnham as the father of the New York skyscraper.

When one recalls that the elevator was used for the first time
commercially in the Haughwout Store, the appearance of the first
elevator office building a decade later seems remarkably tardy. However, the profitable Equitable Building soon provoked more lofty
rivals: Post's Western Union Building, 230 feet high, and Richard
Morris Hunt's Tribune Building, 260 feet high, both built in 1873–
75 (193, 194). Their dramatic heights made them skyscrapers in a
sense in which the Equitable was not. Yet, like it, they were structurally conservative, relying on masonry walls and partitions supporting iron beams, a type of structure that required walls four feet
thick at their base. Obviously this mass of masonry limited the
usefulness of the ground floor for shops, and the deep reveals of the
office windows impeded the admission of daylight. Visually the
Western Union and the Tribune buildings were clumsy; both were
horizontally banded with cornices and weighed down with enlarged
mansard roofs to contain the upper floors, a weak disguise of their
full heights. The esthetic of the Picturesque persists in a curious way
in the clock towers that rise well above their rooflines. Such Victorian
towers can be traced to the Gothic Revival work of A. W. N. Pugin
at Scarisbrick Hall and the Houses of Parliament in London; their
more distant ancestors were the towers of the late medieval town
halls, guild houses, and trade halls of Italy and northern Europe,
which symbolized the prosperity of the merchant class and its ascendancy over the nobility and independence of the Church. With
iconographic consistency the tower motif reappeared in many nineteenth-century commercial buildings and satisfied the Victorian taste
for a broken skyline.

The closest New York ever came to true skyscraper construction
in the eighties was in George B. Post's New York Produce Exchange,
built in 1881–84 (195). Perhaps it was the necessity of providing
a large banking room that led to the use of a complete metal skeleton,
with cast-iron columns supporting wrought-iron beams and joists.
The exterior loads were carried by the peripheral metal columns and,
to a lesser degree, by the brick piers of the facade; thus it was not
quite a true skeleton-support structure. The impressive banking

193
Western Union Building,
New York City. George
B. Post, 1873–75.
Exterior.

five but an increase that was only made viable by the elevator. Its masonry exterior was Second Empire, with stories grouped in pairs to belie its true height of 130 feet. The interior structure, partly of iron, was the work of the consulting architect George B. Post, who later, when more active on his own, was once introduced by Daniel Burnham as the father of the New York skyscraper.

When one recalls that the elevator was used for the first time commercially in the Haughwout Store, the appearance of the first elevator office building a decade later seems remarkably tardy. However, the profitable Equitable Building soon provoked more lofty rivals: Post's Western Union Building, 230 feet high, and Richard Morris Hunt's Tribune Building, 260 feet high, both built in 1873–75 (193, 194). Their dramatic heights made them skyscrapers in a sense in which the Equitable was not. Yet, like it, they were structurally conservative, relying on masonry walls and partitions supporting iron beams, a type of structure that required walls four feet thick at their base. Obviously this mass of masonry limited the usefulness of the ground floor for shops, and the deep reveals of the office windows impeded the admission of daylight. Visually the Western Union and the Tribune buildings were clumsy; both were horizontally banded with cornices and weighed down with enlarged mansard roofs to contain the upper floors, a weak disguise of their full heights. The esthetic of the Picturesque persists in a curious way in the clock towers that rise well above their rooflines. Such Victorian towers can be traced to the Gothic Revival work of A. W. N. Pugin at Scarisbrick Hall and the Houses of Parliament in London; their more distant ancestors were the towers of the late medieval town halls, guild houses, and trade halls of Italy and northern Europe, which symbolized the prosperity of the merchant class and its ascendancy over the nobility and independence of the Church. With iconographic consistency the tower motif reappeared in many nineteenth-century commercial buildings and satisfied the Victorian taste for a broken skyline.

The closest New York ever came to true skyscraper construction in the eighties was in George B. Post's New York Produce Exchange, built in 1881–84 (195). Perhaps it was the necessity of providing a large banking room that led to the use of a complete metal skeleton, with cast-iron columns supporting wrought-iron beams and joists. The exterior loads were carried by the peripheral metal columns and, to a lesser degree, by the brick piers of the facade; thus it was not quite a true skeleton-support structure. The impressive banking

193
*Western Union Building,
New York City. George
B. Post, 1873–75.
Exterior.*

194
Tribune Building, New
York City. Richard Morris
Hunt, 1873–75. Exterior.

195
New York Produce Exchange, New York City.
George B. Post, 1881–84.
Exterior.

room, lofty and skylighted, was identified by the four-story arcading of the Renaissance Style facade. The Produce Exchange was one of Post's most satisfying compositions. His reputation for progressive work, however, seems less well founded when we view his later World-Pulitzer Building in New York (1890), with twelve-story masonry walls carrying a vast French Baroque dome.

Jenney and Skyscraper Construction

In these New York buildings no substantial or consistent method of fireproofing the metal was employed. Builders of the 1870s were understandably cautious about metal structures; their vulnerability was dramatized in the collapsed heaps after the great fires of 1871 in Chicago and 1872 in Boston. The solution to an urgent problem came from Chicago with John Van Osdel's Kendall Building of 1873. At the suggestion of George H. Johnston, a New York employee of Daniel Badger, who had viewed the Chicago ruins, Van Osdel used light, specially molded, hollow terra-cotta tiles to replace the brick floor arches spanning metal joists; these hollow tiles weighed only a quarter of the brick counterparts. Soon molded terra-cotta integument over all metal supports came to be standard practice. Thus with a fireproofing solution at hand, a constantly improved elevator mechanism, and the understanding of the metal skeleton, the first true skyscraper was imminent. The epoch-making step was taken, perhaps fortuitously rather than intentionally, by Jenney in Chicago.

The term "Chicago School" is now commonly used to designate the commercial architects of Chicago in the 1880s and 1890s. However, the term was not always so used. Its first appearance in 1908 referred to Frank Lloyd Wright and contemporaries of his who were, for the most part, doing domestic work. Later, historians of the skyscraper, notably Hitchcock and Giedion, applied the term to the skyscraper designers of earlier decades and this usage now prevails.

The 1880s were a momentous decade for Chicago. There was a frenzy of activity by architects of talent: Jenney, Burnham and Root, Adler and Sullivan, Beman, Holabird and Roche. The eldest of these was William LeBaron Jenney, a practical man who had studied engineering at the Ecole Centrale des Arts et Manufactures in Paris and who had been a major in the Army Corps of Engineers during the Civil War and a professor of architecture at Michigan. Chicago's demand for commercial loft space often led to stringent designs, one of which was Jenney's first Leiter Building (1879). Originally of five stories, its interior framing was of cast-iron columns and girders with timber beams and joists. What was remarkable was that its peripheral loads as well as its interior loads were carried by cast-iron columns placed immediately behind brick piers of the facade. Carrying only their own weight, these slender piers allowed very large windows, which gave the facade an amplitude of scale prophetic of the boldness of Chicago skyscrapers to come (196). Technically the building was just short of skyscraper construction, but a step ahead of Post's New York Produce Exchange.

Jenney gained immortality with his Home Insurance Company Building, built in 1883–85 (197). This was the first true skyscraper, notwithstanding certain changes made during construction and the masonry party walls required by the city. Its historical eminence was corroborated by inspection during demolition in 1931. The first two stories were of granite load-bearing masonry, from the top of the second story to the sixth floor cast-iron columns and wrought-iron girders were used as a full frame except for the party walls; from the sixth floor up the newly available Bessemer steel beams were substituted for wrought-iron ones. Banded about its exterior at every second floor were cast-iron shelf angles bolted to the structure and carrying eighty-two percent of the masonry facing. True, this curtain wall was excessively thick, while its classical pilasters and cornices were inappropriate and diminished its apparent height. Likewise, the arched windows of the top story expressed a masonry esthetic un-

196
First Leiter Building, Chicago, Illinois. William LeBaron Jenney, 1879. Exterior.

197
Home Insurance Company Building, Chicago, Illinois. William LeBaron Jenney, 1883–85. Exterior.

related to the steel frame. Henceforth the skyscraper was no longer a technical problem but an esthetic one, one that caught architects unprepared. The prevailing nineteenth-century practice of eclecticism had conditioned them to think only in terms of historical models. How to design a building whose proportions had no historical precedent was a question that was finally answered in the 1920s by a German architect whose first skyscraper was not built—in Chicago—until 1950.

Other Chicago Pioneers

Among Chicago firms making history in the 1880s was that of Burnham and Root. Daniel H. Burnham and John Wellborn Root met as draftsmen in the Chicago office of Peter B. Wight in 1872 and formed their celebrated partnership in the following year. Their talents were perfectly complementary; Burnham was primarily the office manager and client-relations man, Root the sensitive and imaginative designer. They established their office in a building of their own design, the Rookery of 1885–86 (198). This was a hybrid example of the tall office building, with interior framing entirely of metal and richly ornamented street facades of bearing masonry. On the alley sides the architects proved more courageous, for the lower two floors were of stark metal skeleton construction carrying masonry walls above. Inside, a generous lightwell extended down to the second floor skylight over an enchanting two-story lobby, later to be remodelled by Frank Lloyd Wright (199). Root's richly inventive motifs on the two street facades range from Romanesque through classical to Hindoo. In his day Root's reputation as a facile designer rivalled that of Sullivan. His early death in January of 1891 aborted a career that promised much, including participation in the World's Columbian Exposition.[2]

Root's favorite building was the one he called Jumbo, the Monadnock Block (1889–91). With its sixteen stories of plain dark brick, it was the last of the great masonry load-bearing skyscrapers in Chicago (200, 201). Its construction was originally planned for 1885 but delayed by the shrewd Boston investor-client. In extended preliminaries Burnham and Root proposed using the new metal skeleton, but the client ruled it out, citing "risk and uncertainty in regard to its lasting strength"; the durability of iron against eventual rust was widely suspect at the time. As built, the Monadnock has an interior metal frame combined with two masonry crosswalls as wind bracing. The foundation problems presented by the spongy, compressible Chicago soil were sometimes solved with wood piles and sometimes, as in the Home Insurance Building, with massive subterranean py-

198
The Rookery, Chicago, Illinois. Burnham and Root, 1885–86. Exterior.

199
The Rookery, Chicago, Illinois. Interior court as originally built.

200
Monadnock Building,
Chicago, Illinois. Burn-
ham and Root, 1889–91.
Exterior detail.

201
Monadnock Building,
Chicago, Illinois. Ground
floor plan.

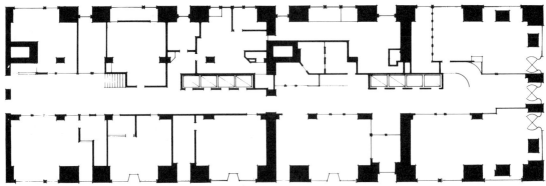

ramidal piers of layered masonry. In the Monadnock a concrete raft reinforced with a grillage of iron rails was used, extending well beyond the building line. Thus the weighty building was floated on the unstable soil.[3]

The Monadnock's most memorable aspect is its severe exterior, with slightly battered walls, delicately chamfered corners, and a subtly flaring cornice reminiscent of an Egyptian pylon. Vertical breaks occur with projecting tiers of bay windows, starting with the third floor and stopping short at the fifteenth. Had Root had his way, the simple drama of the building would have been enhanced by colored bricks, shading from yellow at the top to a dark brown below. But the client objected on the grounds that the effect would merely suggest dirt washed down. It was at his request that the Monadnock design was carried out without ornament or a dissenting line. The Monadnock Block shows how in the conflict between art and utility a decision mandated by a speculator in favor of the latter may result, paradoxically, in a handsome building.

The economy and regard for utility demanded by Chicago investors are reflected most consistently in the designs that came from the firm of Holabird and Roche. The objective clarity of their solutions drastically reduced pier and spandrel, allowing for vast areas of window. In their use of a large center pane of glass flanked by a narrower, operating sash, they originated what became known as the Chicago window. It is seen in their McClurg (now Crown) Building (1899–1900), which is as declarative of its metal skeleton as any of Mies van der Rohe's designs half a century later. Holabird and Roche's Tacoma Building (1887–89), once thought to be the first completely skeletal skyscraper, was faceted with multiple bay windows across its two facades (202). It was a precursor of an architecture to come, not of masonry with its shades and shadows but of reflecting glass walls around a skeleton frame. Tiered bay windows were cantilevered over the property line to obtain more office area—"stolen space," as Wright said—a practice now forbidden by municipal code, yet these bay windows also caught the breeze in canyoned streets and gave more light to offices within.

Similar to the Tacoma in appearance is the Reliance Building (1890–95) by Burnham and Root, the last design in their free experimental manner of the 1880s. After Root's death in 1891 the work of the firm reflected, more and more, the ideals of the Ecole des Beaux-Arts. The Reliance design was begun by Root and completed by Charles B. Atwood, who replaced him as Burnham's chief designer. The exact share of each is unclear; in any case, the result

202
*Tacoma Building, Chicago, Illinois. Holabird
and Roche, 1887–89.
Exterior.*

203
Reliance Building, Chicago, Illinois. D. H. Burnham and Co., 1894– 95. Exterior.

is a striking finale to the Chicago School and equal to any of Sullivan's skyscrapers (203). The exterior of the Reliance Building is largely of glass, and its minimal opaque portions are sheathed in white terra-cotta embossed with Gothic detailing.[4] As in the Tacoma, vertical tiers of bay windows are cantilevered out over the property line. Originally a flat roof plane also extended itself to this outer line, forming a most effective termination, but it was later removed in obedience to municipal safety regulations. A contemporary critic, Montgomery Schuyler, saw the Reliance Building as a statement rather than a solution of the skyscraper problem. "If this is the most and best that can be done with the sky-scraper, the sky-scraper is architecturally intractable. . . ." Schuyler was uneasy with the problems of skeletal design and preferred the Monadnock to the Reliance.

Minneapolis in the 1880s

That Chicago had no monopoly in inventive solutions is seen in Minneapolis. There in 1888–90 the Milwaukee architect E. Townsend Mix built the memorable Guaranty Loan (later the New York Metropolitan Life) Building (204). Its twelve-story masonry-wall exterior was a rather conventional example of Richardsonian Romanesque. But inside the architect's imagination took flight, and a metal skeleton formed a skylighted interior court running the full height of the building. Its thrilling effect was heightened by ambulatory balconies, which served as accesses to the ring of office suites. These so-called corridors were cantilevered out into space, and their lightness was accentuated by floors of translucent glass, one-inch thick, set in wrought-iron frames. This spatial experience was animated by a ride in one of its open-cage elevators, an experience similar to that received today in John Portman's hotels with their atrium courts.[5]

Another Minneapolis episode relevant to our story is the claim of the local architect Leroy Buffington, who might well be called the Jules Verne of the skyscraper. He claimed to have invented the metal frame skyscraper in 1882, but he delayed his application for a patent until 1888. His scheme proposed a continuous skeleton of laminated iron plates, structurally rather inefficient, to which shelf angles were attached to carry the collars of masonry walls around each story— essentially curtain-wall construction. His specific proposal was for a twenty-eight story building, but he envisioned buildings of fifty and even one hundred stories in which his principle could be used (205). He cited Viollet-le-Duc, the rebel historian who saw in Gothic cathedrals a language of structural rationalism whose translation into iron was imperative if a modern architecture was to emerge. Buffington's case was no doubt well founded; his mistake was to wait six years to patent his idea.

204
Guaranty Loan Building
(New York Metropolitan
Life Building), Minneapo-
lis, Minnesota. E. Tow-
send Mix, 1888–90.
Interior court.

205
Proposal for a twenty-
eight-story building.
Leroy Buffington, 1888.

Adler and Sullivan

It was Louis Sullivan who recognized and seized on the expressive possibilities of the skyscraper. "It must be tall," he wrote, "every inch of it tall. The force and power of altitude must be in it, the glory and pride of exhaltation must be in it. It must be every inch a proud and soaring thing, rising in sheer exhaltation that from bottom to top it is a unit without a single dissenting line . . ."

The fifteen years Sullivan spent with his partner Dankmar Adler were flourishing ones. After proving his talent as draftsman, Sullivan was invited to form the Adler and Sullivan partnership in 1881, when he was not yet twenty-five. As with Burnham and Root, complementary talents underlay their success. Adler, who took charge of clients and the office management, had a fine sense of structural matters, so that Sullivan was left to employ his imagination in the visual aspects of architecture. It is above all Sullivan's love of ornament and his originality in designing it that give a subjective stamp to all his designs. His genius escaped the bondage and anonymity of eclecticism, which he deplored. He applied Ruskin's theory of an architecture of encrustation to his own system of brilliant ornament. His earliest designs betray traces of the Gothic Revival and Frank Furness, once briefly his employer. Around 1900, in the Carson Pirie Scott & Co. store and the Gage Building, Sullivan's ornament became the most intricate and seductive in the whole history of architecture. Geometrical interlocking shapes are combined simultaneously with fanciful, curvilinear plant forms not unlike, though not derived from, the European Art Nouveau.

Adler and Sullivan's ability to execute large and complex commissions was put to the test in the Chicago Auditorium Theater and Hotel Building, built in 1887–89 (206). Adler showed his engineering skill in coping with foundation problems and devising a variable-size auditorium fitted with a remarkable acoustic shell. The entire building is of masonry-wall construction with iron framing within. For Sullivan the auditorium project recorded a swift passage from indecision to design maturity. (His earliest scheme was adorned with châteauesque turrets.) It was Richardson's newly completed Marshall Field Wholesale Store in Chicago that guided him toward a resolution. His final scheme incorporates Richardson's bold arcading and blocklike massing. The tower, which rises another seven stories above the ten-story building, is prescient of Sullivan's skyscraper designs. Both the tower and the motif of the lower block are articulated and graceful with slender arcading and recessed spandrels, giving a foretaste of Sullivan's characteristic handling of multistory elevations.[6]

Two office buildings stand out as Sullivan's finest skyscrapers: the Wainwright Building in St. Louis (1890–91) and the Guaranty (now

206
*Auditorium Theater and
Hotel Building, Chicago,
Illinois. Adler and Sulli-
van, 1887–89. Exterior.*

Prudential) Building in Buffalo (1895). In them are embodied Sullivan's whole theory of skyscraper design, which, starting in 1896, he set forth in published articles. In neither structure nor planning did they present any advance beyond current practice. What was new was the esthetic expression of the multistory repetitive bays of the steel frame. "Every problem contains and suggests its own solution," Sullivan wrote. In the Wainwright and Guaranty buildings Sullivan accented the essential verticality of the skyscraper instead of denying it or compromising it with incongruous historical styling (207, 208, 209). In recognition of the shops and entries at street level and the large suites on the second floor, reached by stairs, the first two floors are treated as a base. Above this Sullivan acknowledged the repetition of identical office floors by deliberate uniformity throughout the height and breadth of the composition, but chose to accent the vertical rather than the theoretically equally important horizontal. The topmost story, which functioned as a service floor for elevator machinery and toilets and such, was an opportunity for creating a friezelike termination to the whole composition, the final touch being a slab projection representing the roof plane. The logic of the design is plausible until one notices that extra nonstructural piers have been inserted between the structural ones, without any differentiation in form or ornament. The esthetic intent of these gratuitous piers is obvious: to multiply the vertical rhythms and to quicken the upward movement. In the Wainwright Building the verticals end with decorative capitals and are capped by the horizontal frieze of the tenth floor, which is interrupted only by small round windows; the piers are of wine-red brick and the recessed spandrels of decorative terra-cotta. In the Guaranty-Prudential Building the entire surface is animated by low-relief designs in reddish terra-cotta, and the piers are joined together at the top by arches occurring within the sixteenth-floor frieze. At street level the building is supported by stout, rounded piers with extensive glass between, so as to dramatize the openness of the ground level and give it a visual continuity with the street scene, a feature unhappily altered by remodelling.

The Wainwright and Guaranty-Prudential buildings meet the Aristotelian requirement that a work of art should have a beginning, a middle, and an end, like the classical column with its base, shaft, and capital. The so-called columnar theory of skyscraper composition, a theory not incompatible with the conventions of Beaux-Arts teaching, was widely discussed independently of Sullivan's application of it—which he would instantly deny, given his antagonism toward orthodoxy. Yet Sullivan's own education had included a year at MIT's Rogers Hall in Boston, where he admired its Beaux-Arts–

207
Wainwright Building, St.
Louis, Missouri. Adler
and Sullivan, 1890–91.
Exterior

208
Wainwright Building, St. Louis, Missouri. Plan of a typical floor.

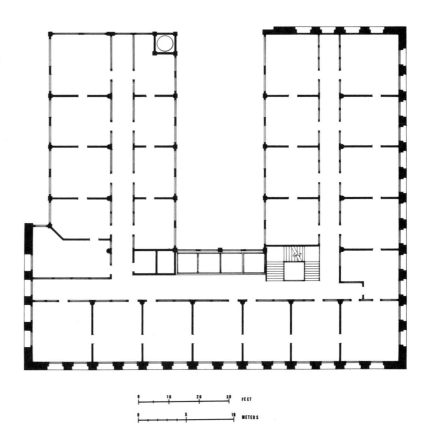

209
*Guaranty Building (Pru-
dential Building), Buffalo,
New York. Adler and Sul-
livan, 1895. Exterior.*

trained professor Eugène Letang, and an inconclusive year at the Ecole itself. Conservative compositional principles underlie Sullivan's designs although he detested the tyranny of the Ecole des Beaux-Arts and its pervasive influence in the official world of architecture. For him eclecticism was futile; a renewal of the creative process was imperative for salvation. Sullivan was given to philosophizing on these matters, sometimes abstrusely, always emotionally. "Form must ever follow Function," he demanded, but he himself understood that without the subjective element there can be no great architecture. Later modernists reared on such slogans equated functionalism with bald, utilitarian design. Nothing was further from Sullivan's intent.

Variety and richness characterize Sullivan's long series of multistory designs. His Gage Building in Chicago (1899) is an intimately scaled building, graced with two fluted, stalklike piers and an excrescence of crisp, stylized foliage breaking out at the top (210). Sullivan never designed a building that did not bear the stamp of his personality. The adjacent two structures to the south, also part of the Gage group, were designed by Holabird and Roche and contrast with Sullivan's in their leaner lines; they exemplify the more objective and programmatic approach that dominated the Chicago School.[7]

The Carson Pirie Scott & Co. store (originally Schlesinger and Mayer), built in 1899–1904, was a commission intended for the Adler and Sullivan firm but executed by Sullivan alone, with the assistance of George Grant Elmslie after the partnership with Adler had been dissolved. Here the facade is markedly horizontal and at first glance reminiscent of the European International Style of the 1920s (211). The banded rhythms of the horizontal windows are the expression of a department store's need for continuous, loftlike spaces. The treatment of the lower floors is rich in contrast with the simplicity above. Serving as a frame for merchandise in show windows, these wall surfaces are sheathed in decorative cast-iron ornament, energetic and fluid in character. This reaches a crescendo at the rounded corner entrance. Originally the top story was recessed as a shadowed loggia under a flat roof plane.

Sullivan's most dramatic skyscraper design, the Fraternity Temple (1891), intended for Chicago, was never executed (212). A signal departure from prevailing block forms, its composition was based on the setback principle, resulting in a pyramidal clustering with a central tower rising to thirty-five stories. The tower rather than the block became the characteristic form of later skyscrapers, especially in New York, where a fondness for towers was apparent early. Chicago faded as a center of interesting work when, in the last years

210
Buildings of the Gage
Group, Chicago, Illinois.
Holabird and Roche (left),
Louis Sullivan (right),
1898–99. Exterior.

211
Carson Pirie Scott & Co.,
Chicago, Illinois. Louis
Sullivan, 1899–1904.
Exterior detail.

212
Project for Fraternity
Temple, Chicago, Illinois.
Adler and Sullivan, 1891.

of the nineteenth century and the first of the twentieth, New York became the focus of skyscraper building. Adopting Chicago construction but not Chicago esthetics, New York architects created a commercial eclecticism based on book-learning rather than on imagination.[8] Sullivan's message was ignored.

New York Skyscrapers

The designing of skyscrapers in New York in the 1890s was accompanied by much talk concerning their proper form. Most architects held to the column analogy. This was convenient and popular because it allowed the bewildered architect to compose in a traditional manner at the bottom and top of his elevations, although at a dislocated scale, and released him from the obligation to be inventive in the middle. Bruce Price's proposal for the Sun Building (1890) was a "prototypical demonstration of the Beaux-Arts justification of the 'column analogy' for the composition of tall buildings." It was a picturesque version of the campanile in the Piazza San Marco in Venice; the middle portion, between the three-story decorated base and the pyramidal termination that began at the seventeenth floor, was treated with absolute uniformity. Price's American Surety Building of 1895 (now Bank of Tokyo), the most discussed and most influential skyscraper of the decade, was even more columnar; Price himself called it a "rusticated pillar." (213). Of white granite and handsomely finished off on all four sides, the American Surety Building rose conspicuously twenty-one stories without a setback, surpassing the 284-foot spire of Upjohn's Trinity Church across the street. The visual displacement of religion by commerce had begun; no longer would Manhattan's skyline be dominated by spires.

The wonder of skyscrapers may have impressed country cousins and European visitors, but concentrations of them caused serious urban problems. Antiskyscraper sentiments began to be heard when twenty-storied giants became common. Demands were made for regulating the skyscraper, even for outright abolition. Clustered skyscrapers vied for light and air, caused street congestion, and created a fire hazard—three disadvantages exacerbated in lower Manhattan with its narrow streets inherited from the Dutch-English village of the seventeenth century. In 1908 the architect Ernest Flagg proposed that street facades should be limited to 100 feet and towers should be permitted to rise to an unlimited height above them so long as they occupied no more than twenty-five percent of the site, a provision that was eventually adopted by the city code. Flagg wanted to "Parisianize" New York with even cornice lines yet allow for a "diadem of towers"; his own Singer Building (1908) shows what he meant.

213
*American Surety Build-
ing, New York City.
Bruce Price, 1895.
Exterior.*

214
Woolworth Building, New York City. Cass Gilbert, 1910–13. Exterior.

Similar experiences with overcrowding in other cities led to controls long before New York enacted its 1916 regulation providing for height limitations and setbacks.[9] Meanwhile New York went its anarchical way with skyscraper building, made more intense by the threat of impending legislation. The worst offender was perhaps the Second Equitable Building of 1915 by Ernest R. Graham; at the winter solstice its thirty-seven stories rising without a setback cast a shadow of seven and a half acres.

The unruly skyscraper may have been curbed by municipal laws but no consensus as to its proper esthetic was ever reached. In the great majority of cases architects resorted to historical eclecticism, however incongruous the result. (The Mausoleum of Halicarnassos was a particular favorite as an apex.) Flagg's Singer Building was richly clothed in a modified French Second Empire Style. In the glazed terra-cotta crest of the Woolworth Building, Cass Gilbert mixed French and English Gothic (214). The client, Frank W. Woolworth, was aware of the fame of the Singer tower and deliberately went out for a building that would be even more striking and thus advertise the Woolworth five-and-ten-cent stores all over the world. Preliminary schemes were for a smaller site and smaller building, but the Gothic theme was fixed from the beginning, when Woolworth had shown Gilbert a photograph of the Victoria Tower of the Houses of Parliament. Gilbert had already proved his skill in adapting Gothic in the nearby West Street Building (1905); his first design for this building included a fanciful clock tower above the ridge of a steeply pitched roof. In its colored terra-cotta and other details the West Street Building was a preparation for the Woolworth commission. When completed the Woolworth Building was called "The Cathedral of Commerce." The general opinion was that it would be New York's true fane, despite St. John the Divine, then slowly rising in northern Manhattan, and that Gilbert had not only given commerce its most notable monument but had removed forever the slur on skyscrapers.

Ecole des Beaux-Arts

In the 1880s the two preceding decades, with their strongly held convictions about decoration, structure, and morality, came to be regarded as an age of architectural darkness. What emerged in this decade, for all its Renaissance leanings and emphasis on scholarship, was not merely an academic reaction, as it has been called, but rather a return to discipline and an interest in form, unity, and sobriety in reaction to the vagaries, picturesqueness, and willful exhibitionism of the High Victorian period.

The basics of discipline, as well as its niceties, could be best learned in Paris. The famous architectural school there, the history of which went back to Colbert's founding of the Royal Academy of Architecture in 1671, had been reorganized in 1819 as the Ecole des Beaux-Arts. This governmental school had always favored reason and correctness and discouraged eccentricity. Its logic of planning composition was one of the lasting lessons impressed upon its pupils, among whom were foreigners drawn by the acknowledged artistic supremacy of France.

It could be said that Jefferson was the first Paris-trained American architect; the first American to enroll in the Ecole des Beaux-Arts was Richard Morris Hunt, in 1846. His compatriots who followed him there much later did surprisingly well in competition with their French classmates, perhaps because they were usually older, often graduates of an American school, and sometimes had office experience; as foreigners, though, they could not compete for the coveted Grand Prix de Rome. Back home, their allegiance to French principles was clearly demonstrated in many monumental public and private buildings between 1885 and the First World War. These were the years when American attendance at the Ecole was at its peak. Even the student who could not travel to Paris learned at home in one of the newly founded schools of architecture from a French Ecole graduate, without whom no faculty could be considered complete.

The Ecole des Beaux-Arts stressed the working plan of a building. The student was taught—or, more properly, learned by experience through competition—quickly to analyze the essential parts of a plan and distribute them logically along a circulation spine, aided by crossing points and turnings. The facade was developed as a corollary of a successful plan. An appropriate setting contributed much to the final effect of the lavish, colored presentation drawings that were in themselves minor works of art. The Ecole was indifferent to structural theories and paid little attention to transitory fashions in decoration. "Her atmosphere," reported a recent alumnus, Ernest Flagg, in 1894, "is not congenial to the growth of sentimentality; one hears little about the picturesque . . . ."

**McKim, Mead and
White**

More than twelve years lapsed between the completion of the Beaux-Arts training of the architect who became the leader in the renewal of classicism in America and his assumption of that historic role. On his return to New York from Paris in mid-1870, Charles Follen McKim joined the firm of Gambrill and Richardson. He withdrew in 1872, leaving unfinished drawings for Boston's Trinity Church for the new draftsman, Stanford White, who seven years later became his partner. McKim worked independently until 1878, when he formed a partnership with William R. Mead and William B. Bigelow. The latter resigned in 1879 and was replaced in the firm by Stanford White. All four shared a curiosity about Colonial architecture, then wholly neglected, and together, in 1877, went on a walking tour through the coastal towns north of Boston. Mead thought that the partiality of the office toward classical forms dated from this trip. Indeed, their memories prompted the two earliest essays in Colonial Revivalism: a house fot the Misses Appleton at Lenox, Massachusetts (1883–85), and one for H. A. C. Taylor in Newport, Rhode Island (1885–86). But the classical idiom with which McKim, Mead and

215
Villard Houses, New York City. McKim, Mead and White, 1883–85. Exterior.

White made their great reputation, that of the Italian Renaissance, was crystallized by an office draftsman named Joseph Morrill Wells.[1]

The firm's first work in Italian Renaissance was a group of six residences in New York City, built in 1883–85 and commissioned by Henry Villard, a friend of the McKim family and former Civil War correspondent and president of the Northern Pacific Railroad (215). The preliminary design for the U-shaped block was done by Stanford White; the exterior detailing was the work of Wells. However much the Villard group may recall Notman's Philadelphia Athenaeum of forty years earlier, Wells's inspiration was the Cancelleria palace in Rome, then thought to be by Bramante. Wells's passionate concern for finish and craftsmanship complemented the high design standards of the firm. The Renaissance ideal suggests a cultivated society, one of patronage and understanding of the arts; this was implied when the metropolitan leaders of financial and social life embraced it as patrons of architecture. It was a case of clients accommodating the taste of their architects.

McKim, Mead and White's conclusive statement in the language of the Renaissance was made with the Boston Public Library, built in 1887–95 (216). The high-minded patience and artistic conviction of Charles McKim over many years gave America one of its finest buildings, admired even by those doubtful of the validity of the revival of a dead language. The library's subdued white granite facade above a severe base—in the manner of Alberti, said McKim—contrasting with Richardson's Romanesque across Copley Square, proclaimed that a literate humanism best expressed America's culture. It put McKim, Mead and White indisputably at the head of the profession. Their Italian translation of Beaux-Arts French was soon imitated. Young men eagerly gained experience in their office and established competitive practices on their own.

In general form the Boston Public Library follows the hollow square of the Italian palace. A monumental staircase, a feature never found in Renaissance models but often in Baroque, is given a central position to reinforce the triple-portal entrance, preventing a direct view of the *cortile* beyond. The staircase leads to a high, barrel-vaulted reading room that stretches across the length of the facade. Book stacks on several levels are neatly compacted in the rear half of the overall square plan. The criticism sometimes levelled at the work of McKim, Mead and White, that content is suppressed in favor of external effect, with fitness giving place to show, may have some justification here. Yet the facade is superlative; it bears comparison with Richardson's Marshall Field Store and closely resembles Henri Labrouste's Néo-Grec Bibliothèque Sainte-Geneviève of

216
Boston Public Library,
Boston, Massachusetts.
McKim, Mead and White,
1887–95. Exterior.

1844–50 in overall arrangement and in detail, but it has its own special kind of civic dignity and patrician assurance. Furthermore, by its very reticence, it complemented the diverse structures facing the square, which then included the Ruskinian Museum of Fine Arts. It thus showed a sensitivity to ensemble, cultivated by the Beaux-Arts training, that is rarely in evidence today.

Praiseworthy too was the involvement of painters and sculptors. In the Boston Library are murals by Puvis de Chavannes, John Singer Sargent, and Edwin Austin Abbey, and sculpture by Augustus Saint-Gaudens and Daniel Chester French; Whistler was to have decorated the reading room. McKim's personal contribution was a naked bacchante by Frederick MacMonnies for the courtyard fountain. Prim Boston would have none of her, and she was banished.

The assured Renaissance manner of the Boston Public Library reflected the personality of its architect; in life as in art McKim avoided extremes. Outwardly deferential, he was as persistent in coaxing his clients to overspend as he was in seeking quality and refinement in his buildings, which never came cheap. J. Pierpont Morgan's request for a small private library to contain his collection of rare books and manuscripts proved to be a fortunate commission, although the client was a testy one (217). Built adjacent to Morgan's New York town house, the library was completed in 1906, inspired by a segment of Ammanati's Nymphaeum of the Villa Giulia in Rome. Like the stones of the Parthenon, its marble blocks were carefully honed to be laid without a mortar bed; thin strips of lead

217
*Morgan Library, New
York City. McKim, Mead
and White, 1906.
Exterior.*

separate their vertical joints. The understated exterior conceals three diverse, lavishly decorated spaces: the lofty, galleried library, Morgan's red-damasked study, and a central marbled entrance hall, interiors that express a "covert love of picturesque variety persisting beneath the decorous austerity of academicism."

The unexpected opulence of period-decorated rooms that often occurs in McKim, Mead and White's buildings reveals the hand of Stanford White. White, who had considered becoming a painter before he decided on architecture, had a versatility and flair that greatly appealed to certain clients. Most of the exceptions to the Italian Renaissance mode, which had become an office habit by the early 1890s, were his, as were many of the charming interiors in the firm's numerous shingled summer houses of the eighties. White's personal version of the Romanesque is seen in a family town house in New York, designed in 1882 for Charles L. Tiffany, founder of the famous silver and jewelry store. For this he introduced a special brick, elongated in shape, tawny in color, and slightly glazed. Tiffany brick, set with bands of molded ornament, was repeated for the Judson Memorial Baptist Church in Washington Square (1891–92) with brilliant effect. Here White adopted an early Italian Romanesque style with a tiered campanile. A polychromed portal White had designed in 1902 for St. Bartholomew's Church in New York was so admired by its congregation that they reused it in their new church designed by Bertram Goodhue in 1919. Paying a tactful compliment to Hunt, in 1905 White designed a town house for W. K. Vanderbilt, Jr., in a château style similar to that of his father's next door.

New York was liberally embellished by McKim, Mead and White. With each new gentlemen's club in midtown came another *palazzo*. The University Club (1897–99), in stern Florentine *quattrocento*, shows McKim's predisposition to severity, a trait he finally succumbed to by adopting a Roman Neo-Classicism. The contrast of artistic temperaments in the firm is made clear by comparing it with Stanford White's Century Association (1889–91), an ingratiating variation on the *cinquecento*, with a recessed Palladian loggia and ornamental terra-cotta combined with brick. One of White's most lavish designs, possibly suggested by the firm's restoration of Jefferson's library at the University of Virginia after the fire of 1895, was Madison Square Presbyterian Church, also a domed rotunda. Jefferson, however, would not have condoned White's polychromed Pantheon: its walls were of yellow brick, its columns of polished green marble, its dome of glazed green tile. Completed in 1906—the year White was shot to death in his own Madison Square Garden nearby—the church survived only to 1919, to be replaced by a skyscraper.

World's Columbian Exposition

The return to classical discipline was initially an East Coast phenomenon. Chicago and the Midwest were strongholds of Richardsonian architecture, but they soon surrendered after what has been variously regarded as a salutary or pernicious event, the 1893 World's Columbian Exposition held in Chicago. The grandiloquent scenery of its aligned facades projected classicism and the fair's principal adviser, Daniel H. Burnham, onto the national scene.

Despite congressional approval of Chicago over rival cities, participation in this provincial event did not immediately appeal to the Eastern establishment, which had been invited by Burnham in December of 1890 to design its central buildings. Hunt, McKim, Mead and White, Post, and Peabody and Stearns had to be persuaded; Van Brunt and Howe of Kansas City accepted immediately. Because Chicago was paying for the fair, five local firms, Adler and Sullivan among them, were chosen to balance the five outsiders. The participating architects were presented with a planning decision made by Burnham and Frederick Law Olmsted for an architectural court around a water basin, with additional waterways throughout the site to be reclaimed from the marshy edge of Lake Michigan. Beaux-Arts principles of axis and cross-axis dominated the site planning, relieved by a picturesque wooded island, where only the Japanese government pavilion was allowed.

The splendor of the completed ensemble, with its sculptured fountains, its electrically lighted buildings reflected in lagoons, was a novel visual experience for the admiring crowds. Harmony was particularly evident in the Court of Honor portion, where it was agreed to design in a classical style, conform to a sixty-five foot cornice line, and paint all the plaster facades white (218). Five of the six Court of Honor buildings were assigned to the visiting team. Because those done by Chicago architects were scattered and more individual in style (especially Adler and Sullivan's Transportation Building and Henry Ives Cobb's Fisheries Building), they made a less emphatic statement. The iconoclastic Sullivan painted his in vivid colors. Much irritated by the invasion of Eastern taste, he regarded the fair as a setback of the progressive ideals of the Midwest.

The architecture of the Columbian Exposition dramatized the swift esthetic change of recent years toward classical order. As the spectacle of the "White City" was to be temporary, its designers felt free to indulge in pomp and architectural license. Surprisingly, Hunt's domed Administration Building at the end of the Court of Honor was a notably audacious combination of forms and details from different sources. The most disciplined classical design was the Fine Arts Building, intended to be the only permanent structure (219). (It was rebuilt in 1932.) This was designed by Charles B. Atwood, who had recently joined Burnham's office. An 1867 winning Prix de Rome project for a palace of fine arts for an exhibition by Emile Bénard conveniently provided Atwood with his inspiration.[2]

The City Beautiful

With the aftermath of the Chicago exposition came the impulse for urban planning in the United States, the "City Beautiful Movement," as it was called. Now more planner than architect, Burnham was called upon to serve on the McMillan Park Commission to rehabilitate L'Enfant's violated and neglected city plan for Washington. An enlargement of L'Enfant's original scheme proposed by Cass Gilbert in 1900 antedated the similar plan by McKim and Burnham that was accepted in 1901. The most dramatic accomplishment was the clearing of L'Enfant's Mall of all encroachments—no small matter because these included the station and train tracks of a line controlled by the Pennsylvania Railroad. The marshes of the Potomac were reclaimed, as those by Lake Michigan had been, and mirrored images of classical temples appeared. The main axis of the Mall was extended westward with a reflecting pool and the Lincoln Memorial (220) by Henry Bacon (1922), and an extended axis to the south terminated in the Jefferson Memorial by John Russell Pope (1943).

218
*Court of Honor, World's
Columbian Exposition,
Chicago, Illinois. Daniel
H. Burnham and Freder-
ick Law Olmsted, 1893.*

219
*Palace of Fine Arts,
World's Columbian Expo-
sition, Chicago, Illinois.
Charles B. Atwood, 1893.
Exterior.*

220
Lincoln Monument, The Mall, Washington, District of Columbia. Henry Bacon, 1922. Exterior.

After further experience as consultant for Cleveland, San Francisco, and Manila, Burnham turned his planning experience to his own city. In 1909 he and Edward H. Bennett presented their comprehensive and grandiose scheme for Chicago and the suburbs. "Make no little plans, they have no magic to stir men's blood. . . ." Burnham's advice was an echo of a Beaux-Arts professor's to the students in his *atelier*.

Such comprehensive master plans achieved unity and monumentality at the risk of the loss of vitality in individual buildings. Two examples are McKim's 1894 plan for Columbia University in New York and Cass Gilbert's for the University of Minnesota in Minneapolis. McKim's plan of 1894 had as its central focus a domed library flanked by symmetrical groupings of separate classroom buildings. The grassy mall included in the campus extension of 1903 made its symmetry more monumental. This wish for outward-ordered uniformity was shared by Cass Gilbert. His University of Minnesota plan of 1908 followed Jefferson's University of Virginia, but without its intimate scale and variety in buildings. Like McKim's Columbia buildings, Gilbert's are competent rather than memorable; yet his plan included both practical suggestion and heroic measure. Major automobile traffic through the campus was to be subterranean, and a terraced amphitheater was to carry the main axis down the bluffs to the Mississippi below. Later generations were too timid to follow Gilbert's suggestions.

The Pennsylvania and Grand Central stations in New York were of an unprecedented boldness, whether considered as architecture or as engineering. Their architects, Charles McKim and Whitney Warren, respectively, realized in them ideals and dreams of their Beaux-Arts training: clarity of circulation and spatial grandeur. The urbanistic scale and complexity of these railway terminals made them megastructures long before the word was coined.

The muted Roman classicism of the Pennsylvania Station was a natural choice for McKim with his austere and correct taste. The president of the railroad, Alexander J. Cassatt—who earlier had magnanimously relinquished his claim on the Washington Mall—wanted a Manhattan terminal to eliminate the train shed in Jersey City and the ferry ride across the Hudson and to link the Pennsylvania Railroad with his newly purchased Long Island Railroad. The train tunnel was completed in 1906 and the station in 1910. The ancient Romans would surely have appreciated the ingenuity and heroic scale of this undertaking. Pennsylvania Station was McKim, Mead and White's largest work and the last project in which McKim participated before he died in 1909. The *parti* is simple but grand: a rectangle with an 800-foot axis transversed by two minor ones, which form the major axes of the waiting room and the train concourse (221). Six pedestrian entrances are located at the ends of these axes. Uniform screen facades of granite columns and pilasters recall Bernini's restrained colonnades before St. Peter's. Taxicabs swerve between Doric columns, down flanking ramps, to exit on side streets. Above the level attic story rise the eight lunette windows of the vast waiting room, McKim's translation of the tepidarium of the Baths of Caracalla, but exceeding the length of the original. The interior was of travertine, the first use of that "Roman marble" in America. From giant Corinthian columns, camouflaging steel supports, rose coffered groin vaults to a height of 150 feet. The spatial extravagance of this room (foretold by Hunt's pendentive-domed great hall at the Metropolitan Museum) was justified by the monumental character befitting a gateway to the metropolis (222).

Leading from the imitative Roman classicism of the waiting room toward the subterranean train tracks was the impressive concourse, as spacious as the waiting room (223). Built of unsheathed steel and glass, it was altogether modern in its transparency and lightness, even though these qualities were achieved in the traditional forms of groin and barrel vaulting. The destruction of the Pennsylvania Station in 1964 was an irreparable loss.

The ambitious circulation pattern of Grand Central is more complex, more compact, and more successful in a fully urban sense than

221
Pennsylvania Station,
New York City. McKim,
Mead and White, 1910.
Plan.

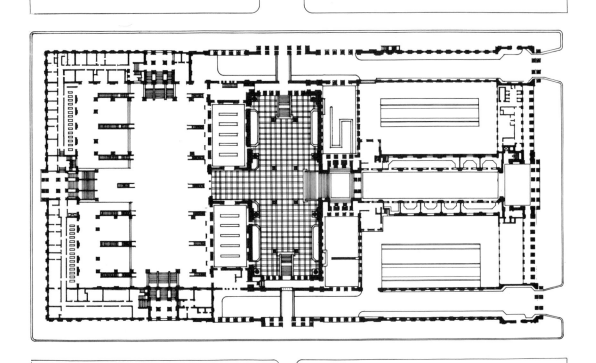

222
*Pennsylvania Station,
New York City. Waiting
room.*

223
*Pennsylvania Station,
New York City.
Concourse.*

224
*Grand Central Terminal,
New York City. Reed and
Stem; Warren and Wet-
more, 1907–13. Exterior.*

Pennsylvania Station. In the movement of people and machines, its designers attempted far more than what had been seen in any imaginary Beaux-Arts project, and they succeeded. There had always been a Grand Central Station straddling Park Avenue; its tracks originally lay in an open tunnel to the north. The third and present station, built 1907–13, was first planned in 1903 by Reed and Stem of St. Paul, Minnesota, specialists in railroad station design. In 1904 Warren and Wetmore were brought in as associate architects. It is fair to say that the planning concepts were Charles Reed's and the architectural expression Whitney Warren's. Credit should also be given to William J. Wilgus, chief engineer of the New York Central and Hudson River Railroad, for the initial suggestion of a multilevel terminal, using electric trains to eliminate smoke. By lowering the whole train yard and leasing air rights above, blocks of Manhattan were reclaimed for real estate. Pedestrian ramps and labyrinthine passages to adjacent buildings and city subway trains were part of Reed's initial plan; he also proposed the elevated roadway divided around the station to connect lower Park Avenue with the newly created northern extension. The reunited avenue exits through a pair of arches in the base of the thirty-four-storied New York Central (now Helmsley) Building, designed by Warren and built in 1929. (In 1963 the Pan American Building, fifty-nine stories tall, by Emery Roth and Sons, with Gropius and Belluschi as consultants, was built between it and the station to the south.)

The main concourse of Grand Central Terminal is comparable to McKim's tepidarium but of broader, lower proportions. Whitney Warren did not follow any specific historical model. The elliptical barrel vault, which appears to rest on simple, giant piers, is actually suspended from steel trusses; the lesser areas are vaulted in Guas-tavino tile.[3] Compared to the facades, which are derived from eigh-teenth-century France, these interiors are unexpectedly spare in detail (224).

Pennsylvania and Grand Central stations were the prodigies of the genre, but other stations in which Beaux-Arts ideals were realized on a more modest scale were no less effective: Union Station in Washington, D.C., (1908) by Daniel H. Burnham; Broad Street Station in Richmond, Virginia, (1919) by John Russell Pope; and Union Station in Chicago (1925) by Graham, Anderson, Probst and White, successors to Burnham's practice. All were in the restrained Roman manner initiated by McKim.

Civic Architecture

The Beaux-Arts decades, so to call them, were a time of much public building activity. Between 1886 and 1936 no less than twenty-four state capitols were built. The centers of American cities were defined by Beaux-Arts "palaces," which still serve as libraries, museums, city halls, and courthouses. Architects and laymen alike believed that some variation of the formal, classical facade expressed civic virtue, but this in no way circumscribed the actual results. The choice had widened. To the Italian model the French Renaissance was added. The plaster architecture of various expositions—St. Louis in 1904 and San Francisco in 1915 among them—encouraged a kind of ba-roque classicism: lavish decoration applied to an orderly arrangement of forms. Eventually a revival of the Georgian Style, again initiated by McKim, became an alternative, although one less often embraced in civic buildings than in schools, hospitals, and residences.

The City Beautiful Movement favored major buildings related to civic squares, public parks, or tree-lined boulevards. In Philadelphia the new Benjamin Franklin Parkway (1917–19) overlaid its baroque diagonal on William Penn's gridiron plan, terminating in Fairmount Park and the raised site of the Philadelphia Museum of Art. Horace Trumbauer's museum (1919–28) presented an acropolis grouping that centered on a temple front intended to be viewed from afar. (In his Hellenistic Widener Memorial Library of 1915, however, Trum-bauer completely ignored the scale of its setting in Harvard Yard.) San Francisco's rebuilding after the earthquake included a civic center based on the French eighteenth century, in particular the work of Gabriel. The ensemble includes the Civic Auditorium (1913) by John Galen Howard and the Public Library (1916) by George W. Kelham. Its centerpiece is the domed City Hall (1916) by Bakewell and Brown, whose competition design of 1912 initiated this development (225).

225
City Hall, San Francisco,
California. Bakewell and
Brown, 1916. Interior.

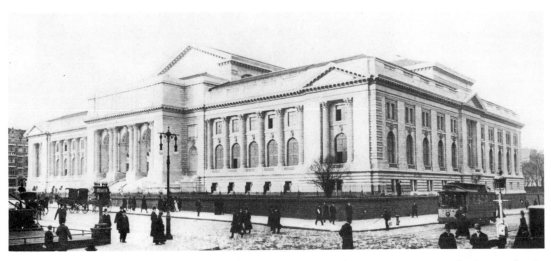

226
*New York Public Library,
Carrère and Hastings,
1897–1911. Exterior.*

Bakewell and Brown were not alone in expressing admiration for St. Peter's dome; Cass Gilbert copied it too in his Minnesota State Capitol in St. Paul (1893–1904).

A specifically French character was favored by the younger generation of Beaux-Arts–trained architects, such as Carrère and Hastings, whose former employers, McKim, Mead and White, were never partial to French styles. Carrère and Hastings's preference is expressed in their masterpiece, the New York Public Library, a commission won in open competition in 1897 that took fourteen years to complete (226). Here all ceremonial approaches, axes, and turnings eventually lead to the grand reading rooms at the top. One of Horace Trumbauer's twin buildings on Franklin Parkway serving as the Philadelphia Free Library (1927) is also French, but is wholly plagiarized from Gabriel's facades in the Place de la Concorde. This was a departure from the principles of the Ecole, where direct copying was never approved.

Residential Architecture

A demand for houses of comparable academic character led some architects, including a number whose training at the Ecole des Beaux-Arts could hardly be considered appropriate preparation for it, to specialize in domestic work. Mansions, perhaps less grand than the Newport palaces but ample by any standard, appeared in the countryside and suburbs of major cities, such as Long Island, Chicago's North Shore, and Philadelphia's Main Line. An interest in authenticity, particularly in interior decoration, was stimulated and nurtured by Stanford White, who imported mantels and other architectural accessories—even panelling and ceilings of whole rooms—for his clients. Most popular was eighteenth-century Colo-

227
Castle Hill, Crane Estate,
Ipswich, Massachusetts.
David Adler, 1927.
Exterior.

228
Vizcaya, Deering Estate,
Miami, Florida. F. Burrall
Hoffmann, Jr., 1914–19.
Exterior.

nial, from Georgian to Adamesque, a taste that grew out of an awareness of the national heritage and advancing architectural scholarship and was epitomized in the Rockefeller restoration of Williamsburg, begun in 1927.

Prominent architects of domestic buildings in the East were William Adams Delano, his partner Chester Holmes Aldrich, Aymar Embury II, and Charles A. Platt. Their large houses, characteristically symmetrical in massing, were complemented by symmetrical settings. Platt is credited with the introduction of the formal Italian garden, which was sometimes attached incongruously to Georgian Style houses. His gardens were furnished with pergolas and balustrades as well as terraces whenever the site permitted. In Chicago distinguished work was done by David Adler, whose practice was solely residential. Most of his houses are on Lake Michigan's North Shore, but his largest is on the Atlantic coast, namely Castle Hill at Ipswich, Massachusetts (1927), built for Richard T. Crane, Jr. (227). Adler imitated the manner of Christopher Wren, using a pink Holland brick with limestone quoins; the roof balustrade and cupola formed a Baroque "widow's walk." In Atlanta, Georgia, Adler had a counterpart in Philip Trammell Shutze, whose Swan House for Edward Inman (1926–28) was English Georgian in design, though its placement on a terraced hill enlivened with cascades but bare of flowers recalled Italy rather than England. More idiosyncratic was the Norman farmhouse style of Mellor, Meigs and Howe of Philadelphia. Spanish models were usually restricted to Florida and California. Carrère and Hastings had much earlier, in 1887, introduced a free interpretation of the Spanish Renaissance to Florida in their Ponce de Leon Hotel in St. Augustine for Henry Flagler, the developer of Florida as a winter resort. Palm Beach became America's Riviera when the First World War prevented the very rich from travelling abroad. Addison Mizner was its leading architect. Of the many Florida houses of this period, Vizcaya, the Deering estate in Miami (1914–16), designed by F. Burrell Hoffmann, Jr., to take full advantage of its watery setting, is one of the more imaginative (228).

Cram and the Late
Gothic Revival

To the dismay of committed classicists, who constituted the great majority of the profession, the winning entry of the 1902 competition for the Military Academy at West Point was a Gothic design. The award brought national fame to its Boston architects, Cram, Goodhue and Ferguson, and initiated a popular modern Gothic style, which had a discipline of its own and proved a hardy rival of the prevailing classicism. Ralph Adams Cram was its leading practitioner.

From the beginning of his practice, Cram consciously chose to specialize in Gothic. His philosophy, embodied in his books as well as in his buildings, had little to do with the romanticism or the rationalism of the earlier Gothic Revival but much to do with ritual and a personal belief that art and religion were inseparable. Converted to Anglo-Catholicism at the age of twenty-three, Cram absorbed the liturgical and architectural teachings of the Oxford Movement; another influence was the architect Henry Vaughan, an English disciple of George F. Bodley, who was dispatched to Boston in 1882 on a High Church assignment.[4] Cram believed that the Reformation had destroyed art and that his duty was to return to the point reached in Tudor England in the early 1500s and continue the development by working creatively in the Gothic style. He aimed for re-creation, not archaeological imitation—in this like McKim, although the esthetic sympathies of the two were poles apart.

With All Saints', Ashmont (1891), Cram demonstrated his theory of creative development from an English Gothic base (229). A resolute, four-square entrance tower merges with the broad nave of this Boston church, which is built of uncoursed brown granite; the window tracery and a carved reredos supply the only relief from the general austerity.

The stubbiness of the Ashmont tower reappears in the stern silhouette of the firm's various West Point buildings, including the Cadet Chapel (1910) (230). The buttressed gray granite walls of the Post Headquarters (1904), rising from the ramparts of the Hudson, show the same respect for topography as Mont-Saint-Michel. The architectural heritage of West Point—Gothic buildings from the mid-nineteenth century, designed by one of its superintendents, Colonel Delafield—made Cram, Goodhue and Ferguson's choice of Gothic a reasonable one; McKim, Mead and White, in their Cullum Memorial Hall of 1899, a white, colonnaded form perched on the outer edge of the acropolis, had ignored such considerations.

Bertram Grosvenor Goodhue's association with Cram, which began in 1891 and lasted nearly a quarter of a century, is not unlike White's with McKim. Once a draftsman with Renwick, Goodhue

229
All Saints' Church, Ash-
mont, Boston, Massachu-
setts. Ralph Adams
Cram, 1891. Exterior.

230
Cadet Chapel, United
States Military Academy,
West Point, New York.
Cram, Goodhue and Fer-
guson, 1910. Exterior.

231
*St. Thomas's Church,
New York City. Cram,
Goodhue and Ferguson,
1906–13. Exterior.*

brought to the partnership a talent for rich architectural detail that complemented Cram's interest in plan and composition. St. Thomas's in New York City (1906–13), which replaced an Upjohn church destroyed by fire, points up their respective abilities (231). A freely conceived design, it mixes French and English sources and nicely balances simplicity and richness. The architects well understood that fine craftsmanship and embellishments of sculpture and stained glass were essential to the success of their modern Gothic. The reredos of St. Thomas's, designed by Goodhue and carved by Lee Lawrie, extends the full height and breadth of the chancel wall with dramatic effect, fulfilling the expectation set by the church's fine exterior. St. Thomas's is certainly Cram and Goodhue's joint masterpiece.

Cram's proclaimed disdain of copybook Gothic and pretensions to progressive developments are contradicted by his late work. Listless elegance replaced the vigor of the Ashmont church. His refectory for the Graduate College at Princeton, completed in 1913, while spatially magnificent, merely reproduces at a larger scale the dining halls of Oxford and Cambridge.[5] His University Chapel at Princeton (1925–28) likewise revives rather than revivifies Gothic.

The ultimate commission for a medievalist, a major cathedral, came to Cram in 1911 when he was asked to redesign the unfinished St. John the Divine Episcopal Cathedral in New York City. The choir had recently been completed according to Heins and La Farge's Romanesque scheme of 1889. But the Romanesque Revival had long since passed, and the trustees suggested a change of style; they now wanted Gothic, the current ecclesiastical fashion for which Cram was largely responsible. Cram obliged with a Gothic nave whose aisles are vaulted at the same height, approximately 124 feet, creating the spaciousness of a hall church and recalling the cathedral of Palma de Mallorca, an island where Cram had vacationed. Before his death in 1942, Cram was privileged, as no medieval master mason was, to walk the full length of his completed cathedral nave.

The momentum of the medievalism originated by Cram in Boston carried it nationwide. Cram's own firm accepted commissions in Houston and Los Angeles, and his example provoked architectural reassessment within American Roman Catholicism. Distinguished churches by Maginnis and Walsh can be counted among the results: St. John's in Cambridge, Massachusetts (1906), and St. Catherine's in nearby Somerville (1904–20), which was in an erudite Italian Romanesque (232).[6] Collegiate Gothic was built everywhere. Its most famous and costly example is James Gamble Rogers's Harkness Memorial Tower at Yale (1917–21), in French Gothic rather than the

232
*St. Catherine's Church,
Somerville, Massachu-
setts. Maginnis and
Walsh, 1904–20. Exterior.*

English Gothic usually favored by universities. Yale's adjacent dormitory quadrangle recalls the ambitious master plan, with four linked
quadrangles, for Trinity College in Hartford, Connecticut, which
was submitted by the English architect, William Burges, in 1874,
but of which little was ever executed.

Goodhue and Cret

In 1913 Bertram Goodhue expressed his growing dissatisfaction with
modern medievalism by his amicable departure from the Cram partnership. The final period of his career began with a shifting interest
in other architectures—ancient Egyptian, Persian, Byzantine, and
Spanish Baroque—some of which were expressed directly in his
work, such as the 1915 Panama-California Exposition in San Diego
with its Spanish theme. Goodhue ended his years with an inconclusive search for a modern style independent of historical precedents.
Oddly enough, Beaux-Arts classicism, with its system of sequential
spaces and the symmetrical resolution of ordered masses, captured
this once devoted medievalist. Its influence is unmistakable in Goodhue's last works, completed after his death in 1924: the Nebraska
State Capitol in Lincoln (1916–28) and the Los Angeles Public Library

(1922–26) (233, 234). What Goodhue thought was a move toward modernism was in reality a move towards classicism. His use of axis and cross-axis, his flat wall surfaces and simplified massing, the smoothly vaulted forms, are no more than the dry bones of Beaux-Arts classicism.

Perhaps because he risked less, Paul Philippe Cret of Philadelphia achieved a more successful modernism with a Beaux-Arts base. A French graduate of the Ecole, he was invited to teach at the University of Pennsylvania in 1903. Without struggle, yet without abandoning principles, Cret simplified the classical language of form, reducing the number and smoothing the profiles of mouldings and turning columns into rectangular piers. Outwardly his public buildings are stiffly heroic, marked by flat surfaces and set off by thin lines or edges of shadow, which create simultaneously massive and dainty effects. Inside, they are enduring examples of the straightforward, functional planning advocated by the Ecole. Cret's Indianapolis Public Library (1914) in its stripped classicism is a case in point (235).

For some architects the 1920s were a decade of lessened confidence and self-questioning, as they had been for Goodhue; others, Cret among them, believed that the times called for a move toward greater abstraction to be made without relinquishing the satisfactions of classicism. Cret's Folger Shakespeare Library in Washington (1930–32) shows the result of such thinking; here the engaged Doric colonnade of his Indianapolis Library becomes a wall of abstracted fluted piers. Cret's evolution toward modernism had its earlier parallels in Europe in Auguste Perret's and Joseph Hoffman's; unlike theirs, Cret's failed to provoke radical change. Yet liberal and individualistic spirits, not to be contained within an academic discipline of design, medieval or classic, were astir. Revolutionary rather than evolutionary changes lay ahead.

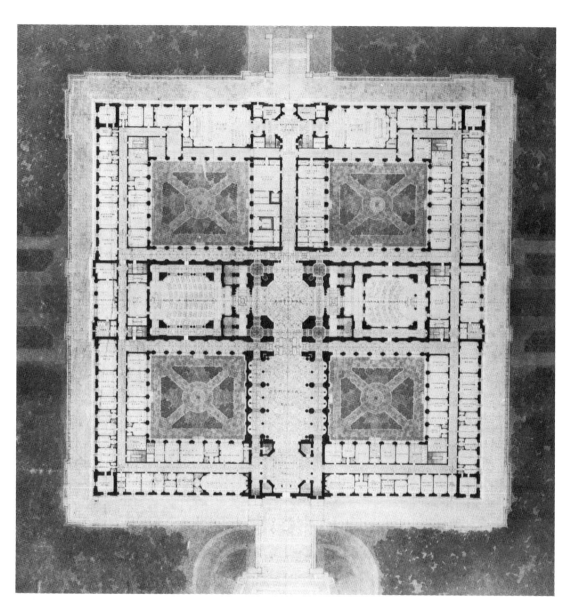

233
Competition Drawing:
Nebraska State Capitol.
Bertram Grosvenor
Goodhue.

234
Nebraska State Capitol, Lincoln, Nebraska. Bertram Grosvenor Goodhue, 1916–24. Exterior.

235
Indianapolis Public Library, Indianapolis, Indiana. Paul Cret, 1914. Exterior.

The 1876 Centennial Exposition in Philadelphia gave a new direction to the development of the American house. It was in the pavilion erected by Japan that Americans saw Oriental architecture for the first time. The entire pavilion was authentically Japanese; its cedar timbers, black roofing tiles, and other materials were imported from Japan and assembled by native workmen, "as nicely put together as a piece of cabinet work," remarked a contemporary observer. Although it was two stories, the building was emphatically horizontal, with continuous latticework below, sliding wood panels above, and a low-hipped roof.

The Japanese pavilion in Philadelphia helped to stimulate a popular craze for things Japanese. At a deeper level its influence soon appeared in the American house in a predilection for the open plan, latticework, extended eaves, a craftsmanlike assembly of parts, and the integration of the building with its landscaped setting. In 1886 Edward S. Morse's comprehensive illustrated book, *Japanese Houses and Their Surroundings*, appeared in Boston. Then in 1893 the Columbian Exposition in Chicago produced a second pavilion erected by the Japanese government. Called the Ho-O-Den, it also was imported and assembled by Japanese workmen. In the following year in San Francisco a Japanese village was erected for the Midwinter International Exposition. These recurring oriental stimuli influenced American design well into the early years of the twentieth century.

America was predisposed to accept the constructivist esthetic of Japanese building. Beginning in 1840, aided by pattern books and the popularity of Andrew Jackson Downing's views, a skeletal Stick Style emerged, far more declaratory of wood structure than the board-and-batten-clad mode of Davis and Upjohn. Its most conspicuous feature was trim in the form of diagonal and cross bracing, whose patterns enlivened the sides of suburban villas. The Griswold House at Newport of 1863, designed by Hunt, is a well-developed example; another is the Cram House at nearby Middletown, designed in 1871 by Dudley Newton. And at the Centennial several of the state pavilions, enlargements of domestic prototypes, proclaimed the cresting of the Stick Style.

It was also at the Philadelphia exposition that the American public had its first glimpse of the so-called "Queen Anne" Style, in two houses built by the English government for its officials and staff. Both buildings (in reality modest versions of Elizabethan-style manor houses made popular by Richard Norman Shaw in the late sixties in England) were two-storied, half-timbered, stucco panelled, and surmounted by steep roofs with cross gables and prominent chimneys. They presented a seductive image for American domestic architecture, justifiable on practical grounds and serving as mythic symbols of shelter and ancestry. Professional critics were enthusiastic on both counts about these "specimens of modern cottage architecture in England" and urged immediate adoption. The informality of the Queen Anne Style suggested the wholesome countryside rather than the wicked city, which Americans have always shunned, and the style was soon assimilated into the stream of American development.

One particular feature of Shaw's Queen Anne was the combination of a central hall with a stairway and a fireplace, a feature that was freely adapted in American practice in the simplified shingled houses which soon replaced the Shavian model. Commonly the largest room in the house, this stair-and-living hall was joined to adjacent rooms by large openings made possible, in part, by frame construction and, in part, by the advantages of central heating in winter and the need for breezes in summer. Thus began the development of the open plan, which culminated in the houses of Frank Lloyd Wright in which his aim was, as he expressed it, "to eliminate the room as a box and the house as another by making all walls enclosing screens— the ceiling and floors and enclosing screens to flow into each other as one large enclosure of space . . . ."

Queen Anne to Shingle Style

All the early Queen Anne characteristics appeared a year before the Centennial in Richardson's Watts Sherman House at Newport, the first example of the style in America (236). Its assorted textures of materials and picturesque roof lines were set out to please and may well have been the work of his assistant Stanford White. (The later interior embellishments are definitely White's). The living hall, extending the full depth of the plan, predicted the openness to follow. Although terraces partially encircle the house, it is without the covered porches which soon became standard and, when provided with French doors, continued the flow of interior space into the garden. Another imminent modification, first seen in a house at Mount Desert, Maine, designed in 1879 by William Ralph Emerson, was the use of shingles to cover the walls as well as the roof. Shedding its overt historical detail and becoming uniform in surface and more open in plan, the Queen Anne was transformed into the Shingle Style.

Wholly different in character from the firm's later work but equal to it in quality are the Shingle Style buildings done by McKim, Mead and White at Newport in the 1880s. Their Isaac Bell House of 1883, an informal house with a bell-roofed turret and a corner bay window, is a fine example of the simplifications and pleasantries that connote this style (237, 238). Its plan is particularly successful. The

236
Watts Sherman House, Newport, Rhode Island. H. H. Richardson, 1874– 75. Exterior. (Service wing addition by Dudley Newton.)

extended fireplace alcove of the hall with a lowered ceiling and the elaborately carved and screened stairway next to it subdivide and furnish the room architecturally. All openings to adjacent rooms are generous, and the largest is provided with a pair of sliding doors in the manner of a Japanese house. The Orient is also suggested by the frequent use of latticed or spindled screens to modulate space. The Casino at Newport (1879–81), one of the firm's most original buildings, combines a row of Queen Anne shops along the street and a private tennis club behind, also with a bell-roofed turret. Its extensive porches (piazzas as they were then called) are screened by a haremlike fantasy of wooden grillwork just short of frivolous.

A measure of the unorthodoxy of the Shingle Style is the frequent casually angular treatment of plan, including irregularly shaped porches. The Casino at Narragansett Pier, Rhode Island (1881–84), by McKim, Mead and White, follows an extended Z-shaped plan. Linear arrangements were favored by Wilson Eyre in his suburban Philadelphia houses, such as the Richard Ashurst House at Overbrook (ca. 1885), with its meandering sequence of connected spaces that were one-room deep, affording cross-ventilation and light (239). Eyre complemented the contour of the ridge into which his stone-based house is set by the extended length and lowness of the structure and by a linear porch across the rear. Indeed, the asymmetrical massing of such designs are as much a part of their potent charm as the varied textures and ornamental profiles. Symmetry was rare.

237
*Isaac Bell House, New-
port, Rhode Island.
McKim, Mead and White,
1883. Exterior.*

238
*Isaac Bell House, New-
port, Rhode Island. Plan.*

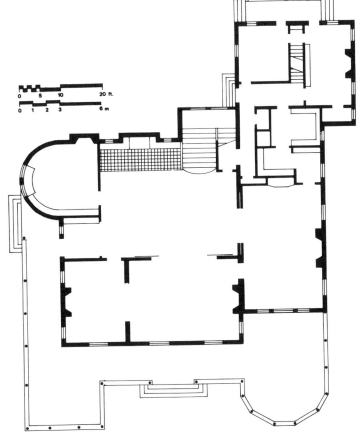

239
Richard Ashurst House,
Overbook, Pennsylvania.
Wilson Eyre, circa 1885.
Exterior.

240
William Kent House,
Tuxedo Park, New York.
Bruce Price, 1885.
Exterior.

241
Mrs. F. M. Stoughton House, Cambridge, Massachusetts. H. H. Richardson, 1882–83. Exterior.

Several houses by Bruce Price at Tuxedo Park, New York, such as the one for William Kent of 1885, are exceptions; their cruciform plans hint at Wright's later development of this idea (240).

The Shingle Style was the spiritual heir of the seventeenth-century New England house, and it was in New England, from Maine to Rhode Island, that its purest examples were raised. Several seaside houses by John Calvin Stevens in Maine revive the gambrel roof, a feature never seen in the Queen Anne. The sharp edges of these colonial houses were carried over into the Shingle Style to give a similar emphasis on volumetric enclosure, a quality that Vincent Scully has observed to be germane to twentieth-century modernism. The dominance of the roof in vernacular medieval building (which is what American building of the 1600s was) was strikingly translated by McKim, Mead and White in the William Low House of 1887 at Bristol, Rhode Island, where a single, unbroken gabled roof encompasses the entire house, including its porches. Richardson, too, simplified his designs; in the few years that separate the Sherman House and the Stoughton House in Cambridge, Massachusetts (1882–83), one observes the change to a lower, simpler massing and the uniformity of the shingle skin for wall and roof (241).

The 1880s witnessed a revived interest in the American past. Some architects, Robert Peabody of Boston for one, regarded current trends as a legitimate development of colonial architecture, and this view found support in the designs of Arthur Little and in some of those of McKim, who as early as 1872 had done a "Colonial" interior for an eighteenth-century Newport house. But the results of these antiquarian tendencies were quite free from pedantry; at most a classicized wooden support might faintly resemble a column or a spindle a Georgian baluster. This later Queen Anne, widely popular across America—as the Shingle Style was not—was deplored by the critic Montgomery Schuyler, who viewed its "emancipation from all restraints" as corrupting. The most audacious specimens, mixing mansarded and Victorian Gothic strains with "free classic," were the work of the prolific Newsom brothers, Samuel and Joseph, in California. Their wholly original detailing—"bizzare" was Charles Locke Eastlake's word for the style named after (and disavowed by) him—is epitomized in the Carson House at Eureka (1884–86). In southern California the Reid brothers, James and Merritt, concocted, with only slightly less exuberance, a giant Queen Anne gazebo for the Hotel del Coronado (1886–88) across the bay from San Diego.

Wright and the Prairie House

In the spring of 1887 a youth of nineteen left Madison, Wisconsin, for Chicago, determined to become an architect; his name was Frank Lloyd Wright.[1] His first job was as apprentice draftsman to Joseph Lyman Silsbee, who had recently arrived from Syracuse, bringing the Shingle Style to the Midwest with him. Before the year's end Wright had left Silsbee for Adler and Sullivan, a momentous move because the following years were to give him the only architectural education he ever had, with Louis Sullivan acting as his informal teacher.[2] Then in 1893 Wright was dismissed by Sullivan for doing outside work, his "bootlegged" houses as he called them.

Two of Wright's early houses, his own house in Oak Park, Illinois (1889), and the W. H. Winslow House in River Forest (1893), illustrate the influence of Silsbee and Sullivan, respectively. His own house, with its open plan and inglenook, its steeply gabled roof and row of casements, recalls the Eastern Shingle Style. Wright added a studio in 1895, a remarkable design wholly different from the house to which it is attached. One sees Wright forging a personal style, favoring a lower profile, deeply shadowed elements, and blocky geometry, a contrast to the taut and angular house that rises above it.

In the Winslow House there is much that came from Sullivan. Its facade is a symmetrical boxlike enclosure of orange glazed brick. The effect is monumental and massive and utterly unlike the asymmetrical domesticity of the Shingle Style (242). Above the brick runs a deeply molded dark brown terra-cotta frieze, setting the height of the second-story windows. The low-hipped roof is capped by the horizontal mass of the chimney, reinforcing the multiple horizontals that begin with the water-table base. The white limestone panel framing the doorway and adjacent windows is bordered with an

242
*W. H. Winslow House,
River Forest, Illinois.
Frank Lloyd Wright,
1893. Exterior.*

intaglio band repeating the motif (perhaps designed by Wright him-self) of Sullivan's 1892 Wainwright tomb in St. Louis.

The entrance hall of the Winslow House continues the symmetry of the facade with a formal fireplace and inglenook, screened from the passage by a Sullivanesque arcade in wood. Though reminiscent of earlier stair-living halls, the effect is far more ceremonial, and Wright has hidden the stair from view, attaching it to one side of the chimney mass. The central chimney acts as a pivot for the encircling elements of the plan in much the same way as the chimney of the seventeenth-century New England house did. In the rear the boxlike form is broken open by the dining room bay that projects boldly beyond it, a screened service porch that juts from one corner, and a side terrace that is subtracted from the implied rectangular form; adding to these disruptions, which suggest an unfolding from within and an incipient dynamism in Wright's approach, is a polygonal stair-tower.

In 1900 Wright produced four designs that established the prin-ciples of the Prairie house, which gave its name to Wright's first mature period. Two of the designs, never executed, were commis-sioned by the *Ladies' Home Journal* and published the following year; the first was entitled "A Home in a Prairie Town." The Bradley and the Hickox houses are in Kankakee, Illinois. All four are deci-sively cruciform in plan, and major first-floor rooms are intercon-nected spatially but not in the loose manner of Shingle Style houses. The house for Warren Hickox exemplifies the principles of the Prairie house (243). The short axis is fixed by the masonry core of the fireplace and extends outside to an ample terrace as wide as the

243
*Warren Hickox House,
Kankakee, Illinois. Frank
Lloyd Wright, 1900.
Exterior.*

length of the living room. A long axis is formed by the polygonal alcoves for a dining room and a library, which project from the short ends of the living room. The alcoves are separated from the living room by spur walls, embryonic piers that were to become basic to Wright's structural rhythms. Both the dining room and library are banded with a continuous row of leaded casement windows, which act as "light screens" and reinforce the horizontal motifs of the exterior. The combination of dark wood trim with light-colored stucco suggests the Japanese post-and-panel module, although it may be seen as a variant of Queen Anne half-timbering or even a residual feature of the Stick Style. The gabled roofs likewise suggest Japanese, medieval, or American prototypes. Whatever his sources (and he usually denied all and any), Wright established his own esthetic. More significantly, he introduced a dual theme of continuous space and integrated structure, to be developed further in the following years.

With his engaging manner and articulate convictions, Wright found it easy to secure clients for his radical houses, most of them of modest scale but having a compactness and deceptive simplicity that affords a sense of generous space in a limited area. Clarity and consistency are ensured by Wright's innate sense of order. Exteriors are reduced essentially to one material, and ornament—with the exception of the decorative leading of the windows, which takes the place of curtains—is rare. Simple banding is often used inside and out. Wright extolled the beauty of machine-made materials, and his use of them recalls the Japanese "severe simplicity of form and beautiful materials left clean for their own sake." Notwithstanding his admitted admiration for Japanese domestic architecture, Wright

cautioned C. R. Ashbee, whom he had asked to write the introduction
to an edition of his work, that it would be wrong to say that he had
adopted Japanese forms.[3] This volume, published by the German
Wasmuth Press in 1911, had been preceded the year before by
another Wasmuth publication of Wright's work, a sumptuous folio
of one hundred plates of drawings. These two publications accorded
Wright his first formal recognition. They also influenced a generation
of European architects.

The evaluation of Wright's position in the history of architecture
was not left by him entirely to others; Wright participated to the
full in this self-satisfying task. He saw Richardson, Root, and Sullivan as his predecessors in the search for an "organic architecture."
This concept, first presented in 1908, was defined in a later essay of
1914 as "an architecture that *develops* from within outward in harmony with the conditions of its being as distinguished from one that
is *applied* from without." Relations of form and function, which
Wright saw as one, were to be learned from Nature's pertinent object
lessons, the basis for design. This method did not ensure a beautiful
building, Wright admitted, but it did have an integrity that the
architecture of taste and erudition, namely that of the Renaissance
and Baroque, wholly lacked. Thus he conceived his Prairie houses as
metaphors for moral goodness and honesty—precisely those ethical
qualities sought by Pugin and Morris.

The Prairie houses show no consistent development as a series. A
late example, the J. K. Ingalls House in Oak Park of 1909, is as
resolutely symmetrical as the facade of the Winslow House of 1893.
Wright interchanged three roof types in the Prairie houses: the
gabled roof was used in the Kankakee houses; the low-pitched, hipped
roof, presenting an even ridge against the sky or assembled in pyramidal group, was used in the Winslow stable; and the flat roof was
proposed in his third design for the *Ladies' Home Journal* in 1906
and used in the Mrs. Thomas Gale House in Oak Park (1909), the
most cubistic of all his early designs.

The compact, elementary cruciform plan of the Hickox House was
succeeded in 1901 by the extended cruciform of the Ward Willits
House in Highland Park (244, 245). Here the forward, two-story
pavilion for the living room (with its own high-waisted terrace) on
the first story and the master bedroom on the second is flanked by
the movement and tension of the cross-axis, whose comparatively
open wings of one story stretch out for more than a hundred feet.
The plan is an enlargement of Wright's second *Ladies' Home Journal*
design. Especially effective is the pinwheel motif of the rotated fire-
places with their space-modulating screens.

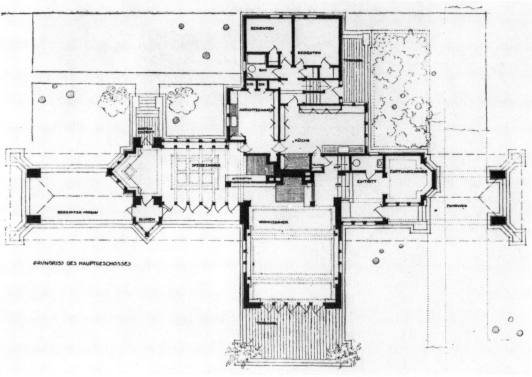

GRUNDRISS DES HAUPTGESCHOSSES

244
Ward Willits House,
Highland Park, Illinois.
Frank Lloyd Wright,
1901. Exterior.

245
Ward Willits House,
Highland Park, Illinois.
Plan.

246
Darwin D. Martin House,
Buffalo, New York. Frank
Lloyd Wright, 1904. Plan.

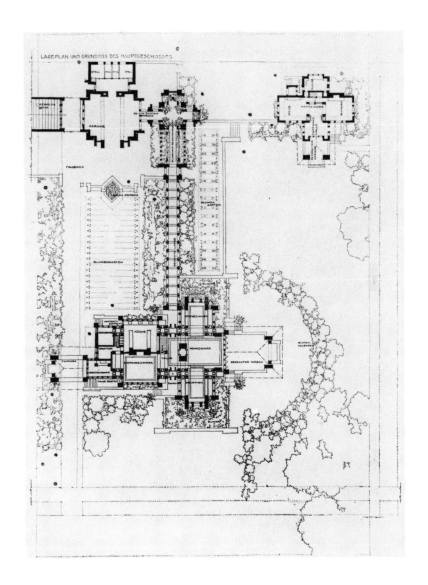

The Darwin D. Martin House in Buffalo of 1904 is similarly open and expansive (246). It is also the most ceremonial and the most radical of all Wright's houses: here there are no walls, only piers. Wright arranged them on the flat site to define spatial boundaries and the several axes of the composition, in a way reminiscent of Stonehenge. Space became fluid, and yet the design reveals restraint and geometry as well. Wright captured that "fragrance of rhythm" which eluded Sullivan, who had a relatively inert conception of the pier. Even the heating system is incorporated into the sets of quadruple piers that also serve to frame the bookcases. Form, space, function, and structure have merged into one.

The Chicago suburb of Riverside, laid out by Olmsted in 1869, contains the most extensive of Wright's Prairie houses and, in his opinion, the most successful: the Avery Coonley House of 1908 (247). Its plan is an elaboration of the centrifugal design for the Hillside School of 1902 at Spring Green, Wisconsin. All major rooms are on a second level above grade to provide a balconylike perspective of the surrounding gardens and a river beyond. The house and its setting became one. Jens Jensen, whose insistence on using native plants of the prairie complemented Wright's thoughts about the self-sufficiency of the Midwest, was responsible for the landscaping. To experience the grandeur of this villa by encircling its fretted periphery may suggest that Wright consciously sought picturesque effects. But the impression is false; rather he conceived the Coonley design as an intense, sculptured order of volumes whose various axes project strongly outward, relating to the flat site. A service road skirting the major block of the house passes underneath two projecting wings. This conscious threading of the warp and woof of the plan is restated in the rectilinear stucco decoration of the upper story, which is enlivened with insets of colored square tile.[4]

Equal to the Coonley House but of completely different character—blunt rather than gracious—is the house built for Frederick C. Robie in Chicago in 1909 (248). Perhaps the intensity of the city and the marginal site conspired to shape its aggressive, overscaled forms. Wright, curbed from developing a cruciform scheme, arranged two parallel but dislocated masses, one for living and dining, the other for kitchen and servant quarters. He emphasized the primary axis by stressing horizontal layers in the elevation: the parapets of red brick with their stone copings, the extended series of windows, and the dramatic cantilevers of the low-hipped roof, which reach far beyond the central chimney mass from which they seemingly originate. In its fortresslike security, the Robie House is a miniature

247
*Avery Coonley House,
Riverside, Illinois. Frank
Lloyd Wright, 1908.
Exterior.*

248
*Frederick C. Robie House,
Chicago, Illinois. Frank
Lloyd Wright, 1909.
Exterior.*

Mycenae, to be breached only by discovering the hidden, shadowed entrance located at the rear. The circuitous path with triple turns leads across the entrance hall and up a folded stair to the living room hearth in the very center of the house. Living room and dining room are brought into one flowing space by a continuous ceiling passing through the separate fireplace flues and by a dozen French windows arrayed like an extended Japanese screen across the entire front of the house.

Both poet and pragmatist shaped the interiors of the Robie House. Wright's concern for practicality is apparent. Heating is provided by recessed radiators under every window and hot water pipes set into the floor beneath the row of window-doorways leading to the south balcony. Electric lights, controlled by dimmers, are concealed behind oak grilles and frosted glass in the ceiling strips. Fresh air is brought through the eaves to ventilate the low attic and then exhausted through an adjacent chimney. And the provision of the first attached garage, here an ample three-car one, makes the Robie House a landmark in the history of the American house.

Not the least of Wright's concerns was the furnishing of his houses. Disdainful of miscellaneous possessions and crude, mission-style furniture, he was pleased when clients allowed him to design appropriate furniture, which was almost always severe and angular with few concessions to comfort. Wright was at his best in dining rooms, where the ceremony of the family meal and the opportunity for a built-in sideboard could reinforce his architectonic scheme. The Robie House dining room is a prime example: Six high-backed chairs are placed around a thick slab of oak supported by four miniature plinths, each topped by a fragile lantern shading an electric light (249).

Wright's concepts of space and structure were applied to buildings other than houses with equal success; for example, the Larkin Company Administration Building in Buffalo (1903) and Unity Temple in Oak Park (1906) (250, 251). These differ significantly from the Prairie houses because they are rigidly symmetrical in plan and largely opaque in exterior form; consequently interior spaces are more static. Yet, despite that, they are no less open. The dissimilar problems of an office building and a church have been solved in similar ways: both have introverted, skylit interiors with peripheral balconies served by enclosed stairs within opaque pylons at the outer corners of the composition. The result is an intense focus within to the exclusion of the outside world, a sense of concentration and mysterious power. The Larkin Building is as much a sanctuary for work as Unity Temple is for worship.

249
Frederick C. Robie House,
Chicago, Illinois. Dining
room.

250
*Larkin Building, Buffalo,
New York. Frank Lloyd
Wright, 1903. Interior.*

251
*Unity Temple, Oak Park,
Illinois. Frank Lloyd
Wright, 1906. Exterior.*

Wright's Followers   Among the assistants in Wright's studio who subsequently became
independent architects were Walter Burley Griffin, Marion Mahony
(later Griffin's wife), and William E. Drummond. All three copied
their master's manner with personal variations instead of developing
their own formal language from his principles as he would have
wished. Other Midwest architects who were never Wright's employees but shared the progressive ambience of Chicago, such as George
Maher, William Gray Purcell, and George Grant Elmslie, drew heavily on Wrightian models as well as on those of Sullivan, who had
been on his own since the end of his partnership with Adler in 1895.
Sullivan continued to practice, but at a drastically lessened pace. His
work also contributed to what Wright labelled in 1908 a "New School
of the Middle West." Sullivan's few house designs are overshadowed
by several elegant, highly decorative banks in small Midwestern
towns. Wright, however, remained the fountainhead of the Prairie
School. After 1909, when Wright closed his Oak Park studio and left
for Europe, the Prairie School group, released from his dominating
presence, had its most flourishing years.[5] Then it went down before
the demand for revivalism. Ironically, the change of taste was abetted
by those very women's magazines that had earlier supported the
Arts and Crafts Movement and the Prairie house.

Bay Area Architects   The years 1890 through 1915 saw a similar burst of creative activity
in domestic architecture on the West Coast. In Northern California
this was the result of the arrival of four architects in the Bay Area:
Ernest Coxhead, Bernard Maybeck, Willis Polk, and John Galen
Howard. These men were not amateurs. Maybeck and Howard had
attended the Ecole des Beaux-Arts, and Howard had experience in
the offices of Richardson and McKim, Mead and White. Coxhead,
an Englishman, had been well trained in London. Polk had worked
for Van Brunt and Howe in Kansas City and for A. Page Brown in
New York; he came to San Francisco with Brown, who moved his
office there in 1889.

The informality of California and its climate combined with an
aspiring but undogmatic clientele to produce a distinctive Bay Area
tradition, with strains of the imported Queen Anne and Shingle
styles modified by local materials and craftsmanship. The engaging
work of the Bay Area, however, was neither centered on any intellectual position nor articulated by any single spokesman.[6]

The work of Coxhead, although overshadowed by Maybeck's reputation, is of substantial interest. His commissions were divided
between Anglican churches and residences, and in both he used his
favorite siding material, shingles. The rounded shapes of St. John's

252
Porter House and Waybur House, San Francisco, California. Ernest Coxhead, 1904 and 1902. Exterior.

Episcopal Church in Monterey (1891) suggest an Expressionist design, in contrast to his residential work, which commonly exhibits knowledge of English manor houses and historical detail. In San Francisco the Waybur House of 1902 and the adjacent Porter House of 1904 suggest Norman Shaw's London town houses on the Chelsea embankment and his turn toward Neo-Georgian (252).

Simplicity and sophistication, juxtaposed in Coxhead's designs, are more likely to be found separately in Maybeck's. His capability in the grand manner is evident in his Neo-Baroque Palace of Fine Arts for the Panama-Pacific International Exposition held in San Francisco in 1915, which contrasts with his numerous informal redwood houses in Berkeley across the bay. In the construction of Maybeck's houses, corbels, struts, and trusses common in medieval timberwork are reduced to domestic scale and are poised on posts evenly distributed on a modular plan. The effect is at times astonishingly Japanese. The early Laura Hall House in Berkeley (1896), Alpine Gothic in its exterior silhouette with a sensitively constructed and exposed redwood frame inside, is a good example of his work. Other houses of similar size and construction are the Boke (1902), the Flagg-Ransome (1912), and the Mathewson (1915), all in Berkeley (253). Alcoves and window bays and sometimes sliding doors assist in dividing a basically open plan into one of diverse spatial character, often augmented by enclosed gardens and pergola-covered terraces.

253
George H. Boke House,
Berkeley, California. Ber-
nard Maybeck, 1902.
Exterior.

254
First Church of Christ,
Scientist, Berkeley, Cali-
fornia. Bernard Maybeck,
1910. Exterior.

Maybeck's architecture was at ease in the suburban hills of Berkeley, but less so in San Francisco. Whether to assert itself in a competitive urban setting or to indulge a wealthy client, the Leon Roos town house (1909, additions 1926) is aggressively stylistic; it displays Maybeck's romantic medievalism almost to excess. Tudor motifs, notably the bold half-timbered effect of dark painted wood and light stucco panels, are heightened by the heavily scaled, vaguely Gothic carving of the balustrade and roof brackets. Maybeck's personalized historicism, not to say eccentricity, is more fully expressed in what many consider his masterpiece, the First Church of Christ, Scientist, in Berkeley (1910, enlarged 1928). Here his uninhibited use of exposed concrete, asbestos siding, and factory windows, his free mixture of Oriental, classical, Romanesque, and Gothic motifs all combine to produce one of the most unusual monuments in America (254). That it defies the historian's classification would delight the mischievous Maybeck.

Willis Polk's sympathies were attuned more to cosmopolitan life than to suburbia and the moral values of the simple house. An early example of his work is the Batten House in San Francisco (1891), a mixture of Queen Anne and Colonial Revival with charming irregularities of plan and facade. His Bourn mansion in the same city (1894) is handsomely Georgian but hardly academic. Polk's urbanity was continued in suburban Belvedere in the Rey House (1893), which states his version of the Monterey Peninsula Style with arched stucco walls, cantilevered wooden balconies, and red-tiled roof. Polk was versatile, stylish, and unpredictable—a verdict he would readily endorse. As further proof of his unpredictability there is that remarkable forerunner of the glass curtain wall, the Hallidie Building in San Francisco (1917).

The opportunity to design buildings for the University of California brought John Galen Howard to Berkeley. The Hearst Mines Building of 1907 illustrates his eclectic approach; it was imaginatively Mediterranean Renaissance with a metal-framed interior court with skylight domes. One of Howard's employees—and Maybeck's too—was Julia Morgan, an engineering graduate of the university who went on to Paris to study at the Ecole, the first woman to do so. Like Howard, her loyalties were divided between the local tradition in wood, as seen in her residentially scaled St. John's Presbyterian Church in Berkeley (1910), and a free eclecticism, as seen in W. R. Hearst's San Simeon (begun in 1919), her most well-known (if not her best) work.

The Bungalows of
Greene and Greene

The term bungalow, a corruption of a Hindustani word meaning "of Bengal," came to be applied in the early twentieth century to almost any kind of single-story house with a low sloping roof, which, more often than not, extended to form a porch or veranda. According to a popular book on the subject, however, a house of more than one story could not be a true bungalow but might be "built along bungalow lines." The bungalow was valued for its suitability in a warm climate and also for its creative possibilities. Divisions between inside and out could be minimized, rooms could open freely into one another, generous eaves would protect against the sun, and natural materials and colors would blend into the landscape—advantages not so very different from those possessed by the shingled houses of New England or the cottages advocated by Andrew Jackson Downing. Although they were built from coast to coast, bungalows were identified particularly with southern California. Some Los Angeles firms offered sets of working drawings for as little as five dollars, but at the other end of the scale were the bungalows of the brothers Charles Sumner and Henry Mather Greene. Their most famous bungalow in its day—it has been much altered—was the Bandini bungalow of 1903 at Pasadena. Built around a court, it was the first of the so-called patio bungalows.

All the houses of the Greene brothers are "built along bungalow lines." As open in plan as any, they are remarkable for their gentleness and elegance and extraordinary craftsmanship and sensitive use of materials—in the cobblestones and native plants of their settings no less than the wood of their structures. Two Pasadena houses, those for Robert C. Blacker (1907) and David B. Gamble (1909), and one at Ojai for Charles M. Pratt (1909), with their ample budgets and sites, stand out as *chefs-d'oeuvres* (255, 256). More modest commissions, however, such as the Crow House at Pasadena of 1909, are equally successful; perhaps their scale and modesty are more in keeping with the craftsman esthetic.

Without question, the monuments of the Arts and Crafts Movement in the United States were built by Greene and Greene. They conceived their houses as pieces of cabinetwork, extensions of the furniture they often designed. C. R. Ashbee, that most cosmopolitan follower of William Morris, recognized their genius; on one of his American visits he expressed greater sympathy for the Greenes' work than for Wright's. Like Wright, they came under the spell of Japan, most obviously in the Adelaide Tichenor House of 1904 in Long Beach. Japan was the land where carpentry was transformed into art. The articulated trellises and porches that embellish Greene and Greene houses can be seen as transformations of temple architecture.

255
*David B. Gamble House,
Pasadena, California.
Greene and Greene, 1909.
Exterior from garden.*

256
*David B. Gamble House,
Pasadena, California.
Plan.*

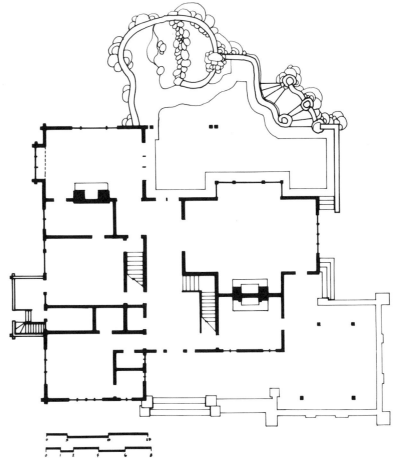

Comparison with Maybeck is inevitable. The Greenes' work, although perhaps intrinsically finer, is more limited in its range of
expression and lacks the provocative quality of Maybeck's. But no
greater serenity can be found in any other houses in the Western
world.

Irving Gill

The houses of Irving Gill are very different in appearance from those
of Greene and Greene and his Bay Area contemporaries. Abstractions
of the California missions, their blocklike massing suggests the even
earlier pueblos of the Southwest Indians, such as those at Taos,
which he had visited and admired. Purity of shape and the reduction
of every detail to its least obtrusive form make Gill America's first
minimalist architect. This is somewhat unexpected. His limited ap-
prenticeships prior to his arrival in San Diego in 1893 included a
year or so with Adler and Sullivan in Chicago. His early work gave
little hint of the novel simplicity that surfaced in 1907 in two works,
the Homer Laughlin House in Los Angeles and the Melville Klauber
House in San Diego. This abrupt change in style came with his use
of a structural system of concrete and hollow tile and appropriately
simple details both outside and in, the latter from a conscious desire
for a sanitary, labor-saving house. Gill's wide range of practical
devices—built-in storage walls, skylighted bathrooms, a central vac-
uum-cleaning system, even an automatic car-washing device in the
garage—would appeal to the American consumer today. By comparison Le Corbusier's house as a machine-for-living-in is a tardy concept. Gill's concern for structural economy and functional efficiency,
his interest in low-cost housing, and his belief in the social respon-
sibility of the architect make him akin to the German avant-garde
of the 1920s. Even more striking is the similarity of his stark facades
to Adolf Loos's Steiner House of 1910 in Vienna. It was Loos who,
in a famous pamphlet written in 1908, proclaimed that ''the evolution
of culture marches with the elimination of ornament from useful
objects.'' Although he was not given to declamatory statement, Gill's
work was no less prophetic.

The Walter L. Dodge House in Los Angeles (1914–16) was Gill's
masterpiece (257). Its extended shape, related to its generous site by
balconies, terraces, and garden walks, suggests a parallel with
Wright's Coonley House, although Gill's interior spatial planning
was never as dynamic as Wright's. The basic rectangular form was
hollowed out on the southeast by a court open to the sky but walled
with arched openings as a room, foretelling the similar feature in Le
Corbusier's Villa Savoye of 1929. These ''green rooms,'' as Gill

257
*Walter L. Dodge House,
Los Angeles, California.
Irving Gill, 1914–16.
Garden facade.*

called them, often with pergolas supported by Tuscan columns, are frequent in his work. The garden facade of the Dodge House, with its seamless unity of creamy white walls yielding to an asymmetrical arrangement of frameless windows but betraying no sign of the hidden roof, conveyed a tranquil but not solemn classicism. Gill should have had more influence on twentieth-century architecture, but his productive years, like those of other progressive architects in California, and many in the Midwest as well, were ended by the First World War.

The conception of the skyscraper, wholly American bred, fascinated the avant-garde architects of Europe. To them it symbolized the modern world of the machine. Auguste Perret conceived a visionary city of towers linked by a ten-story-high roadway. The Italian Futurists, Antonio Sant'Elia and Mario Chiattone, sketched designs that suggested giant pieces of machinery. Equally dramatic are the designs of the Russian Constructivists, particularly Eliezer Lissitzky, whose daringly cantilevered skyscrapers still belong to future worlds. In his Expressionist phase Mies van der Rohe made two designs for all-glass skyscrapers with irregular plans but absolute uniformity in elevation. And the archpropagandist Le Corbusier shocked Parisians with his Plan Voisin of 1925, which replaced the venerable Marais quarter with a marching rhythm of sixty-storied towers openly spaced in a parklike landscape. Successive books by architects of the twenties, Eric Mendelsohn (1926), Richard Neutra (1927), and Bruno Taut (1929), gave a prominent place to the American skyscraper, its form and construction, and extolled it as an image of the future.

It is therefore not surprising that of the 260 designs submitted in the competition for a tall office building for the *Chicago Tribune* held in 1922 no less than 100 should have come from Europe. The entries from Germany and Holland were particularly numerous and, when compared with the American submissions, proved the advanced esthetics of these two countries, where tall buildings had never been built. But it was the half-modern entry of the Finn Eliel Saarinen, which placed second, that earned the greatest praise from American critics and architects, including Louis Sullivan, who wrote an article on it (258).[1] Eliel Saarinen's design influenced American skyscrapers of the twenties and thirties, and the generally more radical character found in other foreign architects' submissions had its belated impact in succeeding decades. It is not too much to say that it was Europe that supplied answers to the esthetic problem of the American skyscraper.

In contrast to the Neo-Gothic design (259) by Howells and Hood that took first prize and was executed as the Tribune Tower, Saarinen's proposal was not overtly based on any recognizable historical style. What made it immediately appealing were its fluent vertical lines, its rhythmic setbacks faintly suggestive of a medieval tower, and the softening effect of its ornament and sculpture. Both of the winning architects paid tribute to Saarinen's design by adapting it in later works: Raymond Hood in his American Radiator Building (1924) and John Mead Howells in his Panhellenic Hotel (1927–30), both in New York.

258
Competition Drawing,
Chicago Tribune Tower.
Eliel Saarinen, 1922.

*259
Tribune Tower, Chicago,
Illinois. Howells and
Hood, 1922. Exterior.*

260
*Christ Lutheran Church,
Minneapolis, Minnesota.
Eliel Saarinen, 1949–50.
Interior.*

261
*Crow Island School, Win-
netka, Illinois. Eliel Saarinen, 1939–40. Exterior.*

Saarinen's near-success in the *Chicago Tribune* competition led to his settlement in America. In 1924 he was appointed visiting professor of architecture at the University of Michigan, where one of his students was a son of George G. Booth, publisher of the *Detroit News*. The young Booth introduced him to his father, who commissioned Saarinen to design a series of educational buildings. The first was a boys' school in 1925, and the last was a museum and library in 1940 on the Booth estate, called Cranbrook, in Bloomfield Hills, Michigan. From 1932 until his death in 1950, Saarinen was president of the Cranbrook Academy of Art, for which the museum and library were built. Saarinen's philosophy of design was craft oriented—he admired the traditional materials of wood, brick, and stone and the craftsmanship they demand—and his Cranbrook buildings are eclectic in style, recalling the early twentieth-century work of such architects as Berlage, Olbrich, Hoffmann, and Behrens, as well as the Scandinavian cultural renaissance in which he himself participated during his earlier years in Finland.

Admittedly derivative, Saarinen's work is always sensitive. His Tabernacle Church in Columbus, Indiana (1940), and Christ Lutheran Church in Minneapolis, Minnesota (1949–50), are among the handsomest American churches of the century (260). However, the elementary school in Winnetka, Illinois, Crow Island School, which he designed in 1939, is his most significant work, even though it lacks his usual decorative details; its scale and the individualized learning spaces attest to his human approach to design (261). A very different commission was the Smithsonian Gallery of Art, to face the Mall in Washington, D.C. This unexecuted project of 1939, designed in collaboration with his son Eero, is monumental, as was required, yet still poetic. That its sculptural massing should recall Willem Dudok's buildings in Holland or Gropius's proposed Academy of Philosophy in Erlangen of 1924 shows how lasting was the effect that the Dutch de Stijl esthetic had on architecture.

Art Deco

The influence of Joseph Hoffmann and the Wiener Werkstätte, which he founded in 1903, was very potent in the twenties. The Wiener Werkstätte is the primary source of the so-called Art Deco Style. Other Viennese architects, Otto Wagner and Joseph Maria Olbrich, had prepared the way in their Secessionist Movement, a revolt against the Academy and a turning away from Art Nouveau as well. Hoffman's work marked an important step forward in twentieth-century art. He may have lamented the use of the machine, but his furniture and other designs produced by traditional handicraft methods were startlingly geometric in form; they combined simplicity

262
*New York Telephone
(Barclay-Vesey) Building,
New York City. Mc-
Kenzie, Voorhees and
Gmelin, 1923–26. Exte-
rior detail.*

with low-relief or linear ornament and were frankly decorative and modish as well as expensive. New Yorkers came to know the Wiener Werkstätte at firsthand when it opened a showroom there in 1919 under the management of Austrian-born Joseph Urban, who was later an architect of Art Deco buildings in Manhattan. The most telling instances of its wide influence were the decorative exhibits and pavilions of the Paris Exposition Internationale des Arts Décoratifs et Industriels Modernes of 1925, from which the popular style of the twenties took its name.

Paris, which initiated the department store in the nineteenth century, lent its new style to the 1928 Bullock's Wilshire Store in Los Angeles by John and Donald B. Parkinson. The exterior, sheathed in tan terra-cotta with decorative spandrels in copper, is marked by a distinguished tower intended to cap a ten-story block that was never completed. The store's elegant interiors, enhanced by the work of several muralists and designers, bear witness to the contribution of the artist and craftsman to Art Deco's success.

Curiously and not altogether appropriately, this style of surface ornament and rich materials, so effective in interior design and objects of luxury, was applied to the outside of giant skyscrapers. The small scale characteristic of Art Deco was hardly suited to the bulk and economic purpose of the skyscraper; yet Art Deco ornament satisfied a certain self-conscious urban taste for modernity, albeit much of it is lost to the distant eye. On close inspection decorative spandrels and other embellishments come into view. Two New York examples are the exotic animals and plants carved on the New York Telephone (Barclay-Vesey) Building (262) by McKenzie, Voorhees and Gmelin (1923–26) and a lively cubist pattern of red and black bricks on the spandrels of the Daily News Building by Raymond Hood (1929–30). Art Deco ornament was more appropriate in entrance portals and elevator lobbies, where the display of fancy metalwork, colored marbles, and contrasting wood veneers could be fully appreciated. Curvilinear patterns appear alongside zigzag motifs derived in part from the Expressionistic architecture of Holland and Germany and sometimes even from Mayan or Egyptian sources. Certainly the most exuberant Art Deco concoction is William Van Alen's crown for the Chrysler Building in New York (1928–30), which terminates in a needlelike spire rising from diminishing semicircles, each set with a radiating zigzag rhythm of triangular windows (263). Recognizing that it was the design of its apex that gave a skyscraper a distinctive identity, Van Alen seized an opportunity that was resolutely ignored by the architects of the flat-topped office buildings of the succeeding decades.

263
*Chrysler Building, New
York City. William Van
Alen, 1928–30. Exterior.*

264
Zoning Envelope Dia-
grams, Hugh Ferriss.

Figure 1.

Figure 2.

Figure 3.

Figure 4.

265
Daily News Building,
New York City. Raymond
Hood, 1929–30. Exterior.

266
Rockefeller Center, New
York City. Raymond
Hood and others, 1932–
40. Aerial view.

A far more important consideration in the design of the New York skyscraper than its decorative treatment was the necessity of conforming to the 1916 zoning regulations. Such a law need not have inhibited creativity. In a series of convincing renderings published in 1923, Hugh Ferriss showed how, starting with the overall zoning envelope, an evolving sequence of setbacks could result in a dramatic composition (264). A zigguratlike base and a lofty tower, as seen in the Barclay-Vesey Building and the Chrysler Building, became the usual formula.

In the Daily News Building, Raymond Hood chose a rectangular plan for the tower, giving it a slablike effect suggestive of Le Corbusier's skyscraper designs (265). A more emphatic slab is seen in the seventy-story RCA Building, which is the centerpiece of several skyscrapers constituting Rockefeller Center in New York City (266). This complex project (1928–34 and later) extending over three whole city blocks was fundamentally shaped by the city Zoning Resolution of 1916 and its amendments. With its generous provision of services and the amenities of urban life as well as light and air (and a high financial return), the RCA Building answered the vexing questions posed by the skyscraper at the beginning of the century. Perhaps a clue to its enduring success is to be found in the fact that lawyers and businessmen (including John D. Rockefeller, Jr.) sat with the architects and engineers on the design committee.

The essential form of the RCA Building was proposed by Raymond Hood. Its layered and staggered blanks reflect the interior plan and function; in particular, the terminations of certain elevator banks leave a constant usable floor area and standard distance from inner office wall to outside windows. Unfortunately the lithe vertical rhythms of Hood's Daily News Building were not carried over into the RCA Building, but the latter is far more dramatic in its chiseled, slender mass and also benefits from its calculated placement in relation to other buildings in the ensemble.

Streamline Moderne

Around 1930 the Art Deco was replaced by a simpler and more economical style, which has been named Streamline Moderne. In contrast to the exclusive Art Deco Style, which had relied on custom handicraft, Streamline Moderne was stripped of ornament and easily adapted to mass duplication. Furthermore, it was thought to be symbolic of the dynamic twentieth century, of speed and machines, fast motor cars, railway trains, and steamships. It penetrated deep into the vernacular of American building and appeared in small towns everywhere, in the modest WPA post office as well as the roadside diner. Its popularity was promoted by a new professional, the industrial designer, who eagerly gave streamlined shapes to every implausible object, from pencil sharpeners to fountain pens.[2]

Like Art Deco, Streamline Moderne had European origins. Two architects in particular had experimented with curved forms: the Belgian Henri van de Velde in a theater built for the 1914 Deutscher Werkbund Exhibition in Cologne, and the German Eric Mendelsohn in three department stores, in Stuttgart, Chemnitz, and Breslau, in the late twenties. In its American adaptation, sleek, mechanically perfect curves appeared everywhere—at the corners of buildings, in cylindrical helix stairs, circular windows, and spherical knobs. It became a largely autonomous style for commercial commissions, especially office buildings and movie theaters; Radio City Music Hall in Rockefeller Center is its most distinguished interior. Many of the sensitive designs were often private residences, notably those designed by Edward Durell Stone, George Fred Keck, and the Swiss-born William Lescaze. In its usual manifestations, Streamline Moderne shunned the color experiments and expensive materials of Art Deco and happily relied on synthetics—plastics, plywood, ivory-colored formica, black glass, and chrome strips.

An American architect who avowedly rejected all forms of modernism from Europe nonetheless produced a classic monument of Streamline Moderne while avoiding its clichés. In his Johnson Wax Company Administration Building in Racine, Wisconsin (1936–39), Frank Lloyd Wright used streamlined massing rather than material or color to convey the spirit of the thirties (267, 268). Like the Larkin Building and Unity Temple, Wright's Racine Building is internalized, sealed behind rhythmic curved bands of brick walls and glass-tube glazing that make an outside view from within impossible. To achieve this effect Wright used his favorite constructive principle, the cantilever. The focus of the plan is a lofty columnar hall for clerks and typists. Its fifty-four white concrete supports, reinforced with metal mesh, taper downward to a nine-inch-diameter base. The large concrete discs they carry form the roof, with the spaces between filled with more tubular glazing. The effect is as ceremonial and awesome as the hypostyle hall at Karnak or the mosque at Cordoba. Wright believed it to be "as inspiring a place to work as any cathedral was in which to worship" and immodestly proclaimed it "one of the world's most remarkable structures."

267
Johnson Wax Administra-
tion Building, Racine,
Wisconsin. Frank Lloyd
Wright, 1936–39.
Exterior.

268
Johnson Wax Administra-
tion Building, Racine,
Wisconsin. Interior.

Schindler and Neutra

In Europe, meanwhile, a new and fundamentally different architecture had established itself. Inspired by the precepts and practice of such pre-First World War pioneers as Auguste Perret of France, Peter Behrens of Germany, and Adolph Loos of Austria, its advocates insisted that viable architecture must employ the new materials and methods of construction introduced in the nineteenth century, welcome the contributions of the engineer, and satisfy the special functional needs of the day; only thus could it become (as Sullivan had demanded) a true expression of its age. They had no use at all for ornament, so much a part, and indeed sometimes the whole, of Art Deco.

Three of the leaders of the movement, Walter Gropius, Ludwig Mies van der Rohe, and Eric Mendelsohn, left Europe to settle in the United States in the late thirties and early forties. They were preceded by three younger men with a commitment to and first-hand knowledge of the new architecture: Rudolph Schindler as early as 1914, William Lescaze in 1920, and Richard Neutra in 1923. Each of the latter three arrived soon after completing his architectural studies, and their work in the twenties was comparable to the best in Europe.

Chicago was a magnet for European architects; it was where Schindler, like Neutra later, first worked in the United States. When America entered the war in 1917, Schindler, an enemy alien, became a grateful employee of Wright. Through the Aline Barnsdall (Hollyhock House) commission, which Schindler supervised while Wright was in Tokyo busy with the Imperial Hotel, he came to know Los Angeles, where he was to live and practice independently.

In 1921 Schindler began building his own house, a double one shared with the family of a contractor named Clyde Chase (269). His astonishing originality is immediately apparent in the cunningly arranged pinwheel plan, which provides a private patio garden for each unit of the design, and in the economical yet vigorous construction, with tilt-slab concrete walls, sandblasted redwood timbers, and canvas sliding doors, all on a four-foot module. Schindler's concrete technology was a distinct advance over that of Irving Gill's, whose Dodge House stood immediately across the street. Wright's influence may be detected in the plan and in the pervasive tactile quality, but everywhere Schindler's independence, as well as his special buoyant, primitive qualities, shines through. The sliding movement of planes—with walls of clipped shrubbery as well as actual walls—extends outward, defining spatial areas, with little distinction between indoors and out. (Mies van der Rohe's 1923 project for a brick country house proposes a similar if more abstract spatial conception.)

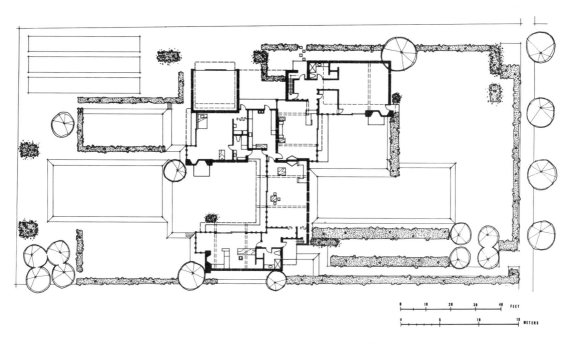

269
*Schindler-Chase House,
Los Angeles, California.
R. M. Schindler, 1921–
22. Plan.*

270
*Philip Lovell Beach
House, Newport Beach,
California. R. M. Schind-
ler, 1925–26. Exterior.*

271
Philip Lovell House, Los Angeles, California. Richard Neutra, 1928.

As early as 1912, while still in Vienna, Schindler's manifesto declared that "the architect has finally discovered the medium of his art: SPACE." His double house was little noticed when new; today one admires it as an experimental design wholly at ease in all its parts, doctrinaire perhaps, yet nevertheless gratifyingly habitable.

Even more astonishing is Schindler's design for Dr. Philip Lovell's Newport Beach house, conceived in 1922 and built in 1925–26 (270). It may be baffling for the historian who sees tantalizing parallels with Russian Constructivism and projects by Le Corbusier, yet nothing quite like the Lovell House was ever built again, even by Schindler. An assertive structural skeleton composed of five parallel open concrete frames, unmasked and evenly spaced, carries two upper floors, leaving the sandy ground free except for a garage. An open sleeping balcony juts beyond the line of supports, and within the house a gallery giving access to the bedrooms overlooks the two-story living room. The Wrightian patterns of the sash bars do not compromise the building's unique character as a powerful, open sculpture that receives and directs a flow of ambient space. Subsequently Schindler yielded to more conventional structural methods and in his later (mostly residential) work employed interlocking forms like those of the Dutch de Stijl artists.

Schindler and Neutra had much in common: both were born and educated in Vienna; both admired the progressive architecture of the Midwest and worked briefly for Wright; both did their most significant work in the twenties while struggling with lean Los Angeles practices. Jointly they submitted a scheme for the 1926 competition for the Geneva Palace of the League of Nations that was honored by being chosen for exhibition by the Deutscher Werkbund. And the same Dr. Lovell, a health faddist by profession, became Neutra's client for another memorable house, one in the Hollywood hills of Los Angeles designed in 1928 (271). Concrete walls were sprayed against reinforcing mesh, and standard steel casement windows were fitted into the modular rhythm of the skeleton. Neutra's details here are more impressive than his interior planning. Sharp edges and the thin planes of wall and window suggest enclosed volumes rather than mass: the house looks like a giant paper kite tethered for the moment to the hillside. The similarity of the second Lovell House to European work, its precision and its visual weightlessness—together with Neutra's writings and flair for publicity—brought the house wide recognition abroad, whereas Schindler's rugged experiments and spatially more active designs were ignored. Neutra's theoretical projects for Rush City Reformed (1923–30) show the range of his abilities. Limited in quantity though it was, the work of Schindler and Neutra in the Los Angeles area was the most progressive in America in the 1920s. It suggests an intriguing hypothesis: a modern architecture might have matured in the United States without the aid of the celebrated architect-immigrants who arrived in the late thirties.

Howe and Lescaze

While Neutra's Lovell House was under construction on the West Coast, an American-born East Coast architect, George Howe, who trained at Harvard and at the Ecole des Beaux-Arts, courageously abandoned a successful practice as an eclectic and enrolled full time in the modern movement. Commissioned to design a new office building for the Philadelphia Saving Fund Society (PSFS), Howe collaborated with William Lescaze, ten years his junior, who had studied in Zurich under Karl Moser. Lescaze's intuitive and visual approach to design complemented Howe's intellectual and rational convictions. What each partner actually contributed may be debated, but no one contests that the PSFS Building was the most advanced skyscraper of its time. Even more significant, it was as skillful and complete a summation of European modernism as could be found in Europe; it was comparable to Walter Gropius's Bauhaus at Dessau, even if without its seminal importance.[3]

The PSFS Building consists of a tower, T-shaped on plan, rising from a base containing shops at street level and a banking hall above, with elevators grouped at the rear (272). A canonical requirement of the new architecture was expression of the structural rhythms, here supplied by the continuous projected verticals of the flanks, which, incidentally, were insisted upon by the client, who vetoed the uniformly layered design proposed by the architects because he thought it looked like a warehouse. Banded horizontals with continuous win-

272
*PSFS Building, Philadel-
phia, Pennsylvania. Howe
and Lescaze, 1929–32.
Floor plans.*

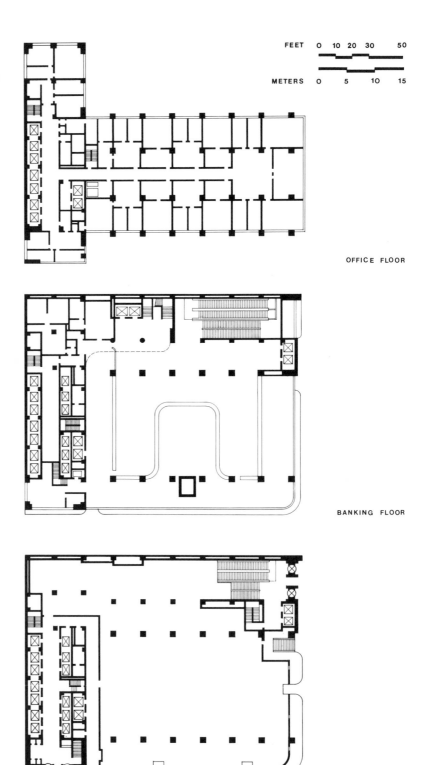

FEET   O 10 20 30   50

METERS   O   5   10   15

OFFICE FLOOR

BANKING FLOOR

GROUND FLOOR

273
*PSFS Building, Philadel-
phia, Pennsylvania.
Exterior.*

dows set flush and placed forward of the structural skeleton emphasize volumetric enclosure rather than mass—another canonical requirement (273). Mendelsohn and Le Corbusier had earlier exploited the ribbon window, which became a cliché, and Hood followed suit with mixed success in his sixty-story McGraw-Hill Building of 1931 in New York. The conflicting obligations to express structure and volume are nicely balanced in the PSFS Building by retaining the banded windows folded around the corners of the cantilevered face of the building. The PSFS was also obedient to the demand for purity of surface. By means of sharp and thin detailing, the masonry veneer of polished granite, limestone, and smooth brick is made to appear as a continuous skin; nowhere is there any applied ornament, a feature of the new style that was most difficult for the layman to accept.

The International Style

In 1932, the year in which the PSFS was completed, the architecture it represented was christened "The International Style" by Henry-Russell Hitchcock and Philip Johnson in a book with that title. The book was written on the occasion of a retrospective exhibition held by the Museum of Modern Art in New York, which they had organized. Although it was primarily European in coverage, the exhibition gave some recognition to American architects, namely Wright, Hood, Neutra, and Howe and Lescaze, on the insistence of the museum trustees; Schindler offered work, but it was rejected.[4] In the book, from which Wright was excluded, Hitchcock and Johnson adopted a critical and didactic tone; not content to summarize and draw objective conclusions, they wrote what is in effect a primer, giving explicit instructions about such matters as how to maximize the effect of volume, what materials to use, and how to arrange lettering on a building. With its first exhibition of architecture, the Museum of Modern Art made history. It soon became the tastemaker for design in the United States, which, for the next two decades, was dominated by the principles of the International Style as set forth by Hitchcock and Johnson.

Gropius, Breuer, and Aalto

Another event that helped establish the International Style in the United States was the arrival of Walter Gropius, in 1937, after two years in England. Heir to the lessons of Peter Behrens, for whom he had worked early in the century, and the principles of the Deutscher Werkbund, Gropius was exemplary of the tough-minded Germanic approach to the new architecture, but with his visionary yet analytical powers he was remarkably successful in presenting his ideas. From 1919 to 1928 he had been the director of the school of design

274
*Walter Gropius House,
Lincoln, Massachusetts.
Gropius and Breuer,
1937. Exterior.*

called the Bauhaus, which was virtually his own creation, first in Weimar and then in Dessau; in 1937 he became chairman of the Department of Architecture at Harvard. In this manner the United States was formally introduced to a radical German educational program, which, as it spread from school to school, overturned the doctrines and methods of the Ecole des Beaux-Arts. The Bauhaus curriculum, as rerun in the United States, was inevitably tempered by the passage of years. An academic edifice was built to house memories of its lively, polemical youth, and year after year young graduates, indoctrinated with the convictions of an older generation, went forth as zealous emmissaries to fight the battle of progress.[5] Modern architecture, particularly in the view of its German adherents, was not only to fulfill the functional needs of the new century but assume an ethical and social role and bring about a reformed and collective society.

Gropius's first American works were detached houses, mostly in New England, done in collaboration with Marcel Breuer, who had been a student at the Weimar Bauhaus, later an instructor in charge of woodworking, and who was Gropius's partner from 1938 to 1943. The houses they designed were quite unlike the work either had done in Germany or in England (where Breuer also had practiced briefly). Gropius's own house in Lincoln, Massachusetts (1937), illustrates an immediate and sympathetic response to the vernacular New England

275
Robinson House, Wil-
liamstown, Massachu-
setts. Marcel Breuer,
1947. Exterior.

276
Robinson House, Wil-
liamstown, Massachu-
setts. Plan.

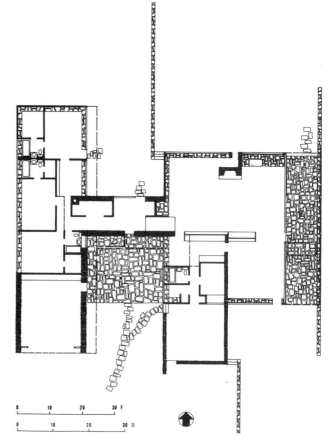

building tradition (274). Interest in joinery and tactile surfaces contrasts with the impersonality of Gropius's 1925–26 houses for the Bauhaus faculty at Dessau, including his own. The Lincoln house is constructed of a wood frame with vertical board siding, painted brick, steel Lally columns, glass block, paving and low walls of irregular stones, and a prefabricated cast-iron spiral stair—a mixture hardly intellectually or esthetically consistent, yet one which supports Gropius's belief in architecture as an ever-changing search. To have defined the movement as a "style," as Hitchcock and Johnson did, was in his opinion harmful and misleading.

The houses designed independently by Marcel Breuer were more agreeable and also more influential than the work he did as Gropius's partner. Bauhaus-trained though he was, Breuer was unafraid of frankly pictorial elements. His designs have substance and visual weight. He was partial to fieldstone walls and natural siding and, even when he sensibly adjusted his interior planning to the disciplines of timber framing, he never denied spatial richness. In the Geller House of 1945 in Lawrence, Long Island, he reintroduced the sloping roof and initiated a binuclear type of plan that separated active from passive functions, which he repeated in the Robinson House of 1947 in Williamstown, Massachusetts (275, 276). Breuer influenced many architects of the first Bauhaus-guided generation in America, among them Carl Koch and Hugh Stubbins.

Breuer's career became identified with a personal style, whereas Gropius, however prominent as spokesman, favored anonymity. Always a believer in teamwork, in 1946 Gropius and seven young architects established a group practice called The Architects Collaborative (TAC), which still exists today. An early commission in which he had a leading hand is the Harvard University Graduate Center, designed in 1949 (277). Elements of Gropius's pioneer work in mass housing, such as his Siemensstadt Siedlung in Berlin, reappear in the Harvard project, though treated with less rigidity. The site plan intentionally recalls Harvard Yard nearby with loose, courtyardlike spaces defined by separate dormitory units. An ambitious effort was made to integrate the arts, an old Bauhaus ideal, by commissioning works by Jean Arp, Joseph Albers, Richard Lippold, and others.

The Harvard Graduate Center is to be honored more for its intentions than for its achievement. Much more forward-looking, forecasting the experiments of the sixties, is another building for student housing by a European architect (though not an immigrant) in the same city, namely the Baker House dormitory at MIT, designed by Alvar Aalto in 1948 (278). Aalto dared to replace the smooth recti-

277
*Harvard Graduate Center,
Cambridge, Massachu-
setts. The Architects Col-
laborative, 1949–50.
Exterior.*

278
*Baker House, Massa-
chusetts Institute of Tech-
nology, Cambridge,
Massachusetts. Alvar
Aalto, 1948. Aerial view.*

linear slab of the International Style with a six-story serpentine one,
aggressively textured in red brick. The building curves along the
Charles River embankment in order to obtain views up and down
the river, and nestled in one of its bends is the angled square block
containing the student lounge and dining hall. The entrance elevation, completely different from the river front and far more complex,
is centered on a conspicuous pair of cantilevered stairways, originally
detailed for light metal. The building had no immediate influence on
American work; indeed its enigmatic character puzzled many who
were just learning the rules of the International Style.

**The Acceptance of
Modernism**

The lingering years of the Depression and the entry of the United
States into the war in 1941 were not propitious for the new architecture. The influence of Gropius and the other immigrants was
muted until after the war. Yet several federally sponsored low-cost
housing projects demonstrated, with modular framing, prefabrication, and simple, functional planning, the very qualities that modern
architecture espoused. Among them were Channel Heights in San
Pedro, California (1943), by Richard Neutra, and Aluminum City
Terrace housing at New Kensington, Pennsylvania (1941), by Gropius and Breuer; another project of the same class, the Agricultural
Workers' Community at Chandler, Arizona (1936), by Burton D.
Cairns and Vernon DeMars, was built of adobe. Stringent cost limits
proved beneficial in these spartan but distinguished examples of
bureaucratic architecture. Baldwin Hills in the Los Angeles area,

dating from 1942, is another excellent example of housing integrated with community facilities and shared open space.

The full tide of the new architecture came in the late 1940s with the accumulated needs of building in the postwar years and the rush of veteran enrollments in schools of architecture infiltrated by European modernism. Gropius at Harvard and Saarinen at Cranbrook were not the only European educator-architects. Laszlo Moholy-Nagy, a Dessau colleague of Gropius, had founded a new Bauhaus, the Institute of Design, in Chicago in 1937. A year later Mies van der Rohe had been invited to teach at Illinois Institute of Technology, then still the Armour Institute. In 1940 Alvar Aalto had become a part-time professor at MIT while retaining his practice in Helsinki. Eric Mendelsohn taught a graduate class at Berkeley starting in 1945. Konrad Wachsmann, a former associate of Gropius, gave courses on prefabricated structures at the University of Southern California. With one accord the educational establishment gave way to expatriate leadership, and in one school after another curricula based on Beaux-Arts theory and practice were dealt the coup de grâce.

Of all the proponents of European modernism of the 1940s only one pressed on to achieve a new synthesis: Ludwig Mies van der Rohe. In this country and abroad his reflected images are everywhere, so that we speak of Miesian architecture; only once before in history has an architect's name, that of Palladio, become synonymous with a unity of theory and style.

What identifies Mies van der Rohe's architecture is his singular concern with structure. He viewed architecture as an expression of the order and reason that are embodied in structure, which in turn is dependent on science and the technology of the time. In this he shows himself an intellectual heir of Eugène Emmanuel Viollet-le-Duc, who, in his *Entretiens sur l'architecture* (1863, 1872), cited structure as the cultural expression of an age. Viollet-le-Duc saw Gothic cathedrals not as symbols of Christianity but as logically constructed cages of cut stone wherein every part—pier, rib, and buttress—was necessary for the stability of the whole. For him medieval architecture was the quintessence of stone construction. He admonished his contemporaries: "All forms not dictated by structure should be suppressed." This principle of structural rationalism using the new material of iron, he was convinced, should be the basis for a monumental and significant architecture of the nineteenth century.

This recurrent French view of the interaction of architecture and technology, expressed earlier by Henri Labrouste and later by Auguste Perret, was central in Mies's philosophy. "Whenever technology reaches its true fulfillment, it transcends into architecture." Mies saw two driving and sustaining forces in the twentieth century: economics and technology. Only if architecture was fully responsive to such forces could it hope to give expression to an epoch. For Mies, this was architecture's ultimate goal.

Structure was inseparable from materials to Mies, who often spoke of the healthy beauty of timber and of well-laid masonry walls. In his veneration of materials, steel and concrete among them, he understood, more than any other modern architect, their distinctive characteristics, individual capacity, and the discipline of design appropriate to each. For Mies the lowliest brick had a no less hallowed place in building than a bronze mullion.

The arrival of Mies van der Rohe in Chicago in 1938 was an historically appropriate event in the city that half a century earlier had surprised the world with its first steel-framed skyscrapers. "The most important idea in modern architecture is the skeletal idea developed right here in Chicago," said Mies of his adopted city and spiritual home. His designs for tall buildings have been accepted as the most complete embodiment of that idea.

Mies did not come unprepared for the task fate had in store for him. In Germany, beginning in 1919, he had worked out various solutions for the skyscraper, none of which was ever built. Given the skeletal frame and the enclosing skin, future architecture would no longer be one of shades and shadows but of reflective glass surfaces. Accordingly, his proposals are for all-glass skyscrapers, crystalline and transparent. Mies disliked the interior light courts common in rectangular office buildings and suggested irregular, indented peripheries and later, starting in 1926, more disciplined, thin rectangular forms. Often he placed the glass curtain wall in front of the line of supports, which were revealed only at street level as a colonnade in front of a recessed entrance. We recognize these designs of the twenties as already mature prototypes for his American buildings.

Mies van der Rohe's first executed tall building was the Promontory Apartments in Chicago (1948–49).[1] Studies began in 1946 with two preliminary steel versions before the final version was built in reinforced concrete (279). At first glance it appears elementary, even prosaic, with the regular grid of its structural frame evident in all elevations. As the building rises, one notices subtle variations, such as the reduced beam depths on the flanks and the reduced cross section of the vertical supports across the front and back. Also, incised pouring joints are carefully considered. Such concern for details is typical of Mies's approach, even with the ordinary materials of this building, which uses exposed concrete, buff-colored common brick, and aluminum-framed windows. Mies's architecture does not depend on expensive, elegant materials, as is often supposed, although he was always willing to consider these when the budget allowed. In terms of Mies's precision and care, one can understand a bricklayer's son's definition of architecture as "one brick . . . laid upon another brick, *carefully*."

How to treat the enclosure of a skeletal building is a major theme in Mies's American work—a seemingly narrow problem, but for Mies a justifiable obsession. The classic example is the pair of apartment towers for 860–880 Lake Shore Drive in Chicago (1948–51). Mies's details for the identical elevations are as direct and expressive of their steel frames as the Promontory Apartments is of its reinforced concrete frame (280, 281). The fireproofed columns and edge beams are encased with black-painted steel plates. Each bay is subdivided into four window units by three wide-flange steel mullions needed for stiffening; a supplementary mullion is welded to the face

279
*Promontory Apartments,
Chicago, Illinois. Ludwig
Mies van der Rohe, 1948–
49. Exterior.*

280
860–880 Lake Shore Drive Apartments, Chicago, Illinois. Ludwig Mies van der Rohe, 1948–51. Lobby and exterior.

281
860–880 Lake Shore Drive Apartments, Chicago, Illinois. Plan.

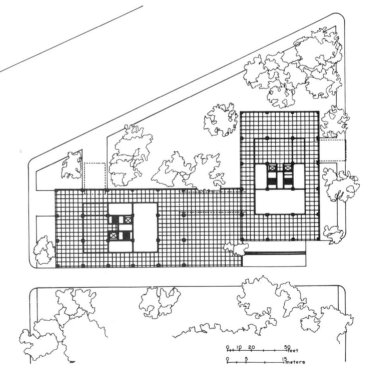

of each exterior column to sustain the rhythm set by the others. Placed within these divisions are aluminum-framed floor-to-ceiling windows with a lower transom whose horizontal bar acts as an enclosing rail. Each element has its place in a structural hierarchy. Later buildings by Mies have more uniform and more efficient curtain-wall treatments, but none more fully satisfies the eye and mind than that of 860–880 Lake Shore Drive.

The manner in which these twin towers are placed on the trapezoidal site is also effective. The open colonnade on ground level creates a ceremonial welcome, an unexpectedly expansive horizontal movement given the limited site, while continuous travertine paving, suggesting the stylobate of a classical temple, links the two buildings. A connecting canopy also links the buildings, and two additional canopies cantilevered over the separate entrances invite exploration of the space, besides providing psychological cover from street to lobby. Such deceptive simplicity, purged of dross, is the end result of exhaustive study and revision and is confirmation of the dictum, "Less is more" (attributed to Mies, though in fact it originated with his early employer, Peter Behrens).

In successive apartment buildings Mies developed a curtain wall placed in front of the structural frame to accommodate vertical heating and cooling ducts, resulting in an unbroken array of wide-flange mullions running the full height of the building. This solution, which appeared a decade earlier in a steel version for the Promontory Apartments, was followed for the Esplanade and Commonwealth Apartments in Chicago (both 1953–56), where tinted glass was introduced.

Because the technology and spatial requirements of an office building are similar to those of an apartment tower, Mies did not alter his factual approach in designing his first commercial building to be constructed, the Seagram Building, built in 1954–58 in New York (with Philip Johnson as associate architect) (282). He also satisfied the client's wish for a building of fine quality by the use of bronze and an indented plaza on Park Avenue. Dark, amber-tinted glass reinforces its warm and sensuous color, unifying a surface already made more dense by a greater number of bronze mullions per bay. The rich materials, however, do not lessen the somber mien of the building. The wide, granite-paved plaza is treated simply, a space relieved only by flanking pools and a discreet planting of trees. The effect is urbane, impersonal, and classical. Commerce assumes a noble presence usually reserved for religion and government.

282
Seagram Building, New York City. Ludwig Mies van der Rohe, 1954–58. Exterior.

Design of Low Buildings

The low buildings of Mies form a separate category and, though varied requirements make their solutions more varied, they are also governed by structure. But because fireproofing of the steel was not always necessary, structure is often expressed more directly and more eloquently.

It was on the campus of the Illinois Institute of Technology, for which he designed the master plan (1939–41) as well as the buildings, that Mies's distinctive structural language was first spoken (283). A 24-by-24-foot grid laid over the entire site determined the placement and shape of the buildings, and a 12-foot module controlled their height. Mies chose very simple materials: black-painted steel, buff-colored brick, and aluminum-framed windows. The product of these self-imposed restraints is a campus of great spatial diversity and buildings with surprisingly varied elevations. The austere rectangles delineated by dark frames suggest a Mondrian painting, although Mies said he was not influenced by de Stijl art. The welded assembly of wide-flange, channel, and angle sections in these steel-framed buildings and the nonstructural infilling of brick and glass received the same minute attention of Mies's exacting eye for detail. In particular it is the structurally descriptive corner detail that elucidates the steel skeleton. Mies made every architect corner-conscious; talent became equated with ability to turn a corner—a problem as ancient as the Greek Doric order.

The IIT project, together with Mies's curtain wall, became the origin of a generic style of the forties. However intrinsically aristocratic or demanding his approach, Mies's precedent provided a workable vernacular for modern American architecture for more than two decades. To adapt Mies was the best most architects could do.

Mies's series of clear-span structures, which began in 1945–46, are a dramatic demonstration of the passage of engineering into the realm of pure art. They also point up, even if they do not explain, the anomaly of discipline interlocked with spiritual content. The first two designs of the series were for all-glass buildings without interior support, the Cantor Drive-In Restaurant in Indianapolis and the Edith Farnsworth House at Plano, Illinois; only the latter was built, and not until 1950 (284). These designs share the concept of a single, universal space with free-standing partitions and a fixed service core. Historically they are progressive extensions of his 1929 Barcelona Pavilion, itself an extension of the "decellularization" of space that began with Wright's flowing Prairie house plans. Crown Hall (1950–56), which houses the department of architecture at IIT (and was Mies's favorite building), is similar to the Drive-In Restaurant: major spanning elements of structure are visible above a flat roof plane

283
Illinois Institute of Technology, Chicago, Illinois. Ludwig Mies van der Rohe, 1939–41 and later. View of campus.

284
Edith Farnsworth House, Plano, Illinois. Ludwig Mies van der Rohe, 1946–50. Exterior.

285
Crown Hall, Illinois Institute of Technology, Chicago, Illinois. Ludwig Mies van der Rohe, 1950-56. Exterior.

suspended from their underside (285). For the restaurant Mies used two open-work trusses placed longitudinally and supported on four columns; for Crown Hall he used four plate girders placed transversely on eight columns; in both, the roof plane is cantilevered outward, exploiting the tension, elasticity, and strength of steel.

The sensation of lift—almost the denial of gravity—is intensified in the final development of Mies's clear-span series: the two-way stressed roof structure. It first appeared in a design made in 1950–51 for a 50-foot square house. Here welded steel plates form a rigid egg-crate roof that is supported by a single exterior column at the center of each side. With enclosing walls entirely of glass, the double cantilever frees the corners, opening up the interior to the surrounding landscape. This project became the basis for the Bacardi Office Building in Cuba (1957), designed for reinforced concrete but never built, and the National Gallery in Berlin (1962–68), designed in steel and measuring 214 feet square. Completed thirty years after Mies left that city for Chicago and one year before his death, the Berlin Museum is the only executed example of his two-way structures.

Mies's achievement cannot be properly assessed without taking his unexecuted projects into account. One of these is an enduring challenge to the timidity of twentieth-century architecture as a whole. For the Chicago Convention Center (1953–54) Mies proposed a huge multipurpose hall seating fifty thousand persons within a 750-foot square clear-span structure (286). Its latticework steel roof was to be formed by 30-foot deep two-way trusses carried by 60-foot deep outer wall trusses that were to rest on six tapered concrete supports on each side. All unnecessary weight was to be removed. Gigantic scale and structural vigor were to be projected without ambiguity or

286
Project for Convention
Center, Chicago, Illinois.
Ludwig Mies van der
Rohe, 1953–54. Model.

disguise in the lively triangular pattern of its exterior. It would have been the largest uninterrupted enclosed space in the world.

In the context of the modern movement Mies van der Rohe is atypical in many respects: in his interest in traditional values, symmetry, structure, and craftsmanship, in his self-imposed restrictions, his distrust of propaganda and the role of architecture in social reform. He himself was temperate, fastidious, and philosophical. The future may well see his buildings as a tranquil and coherent episode in a century as stylistically diverse as the preceding one.

Followers of Mies

It was always Mies's intent that his approach and vocabulary be put to wider use. The most ambitious examples of Miesian architecture came from large firms staffed with devoted and knowledgeable designers, some of them former pupils from IIT, where he headed the architecture faculty from 1938 to 1958. Curiously, while a former generation of rebellious architects renounced authority and precedent, the postwar generation willingly accepted the preeminence of Mies. They put aside the pursuit of novelty and concentrated on clarifying formal relationships and perfecting details of construction, at times overlooking Mies's own caution that a mechanistic principle of order fails to satisfy our feelings.

The curtain-wall grid became the outward and visible sign of Miesian convictions and a popular expression of a technological culture. A remarkably early example appeared in Portland, Oregon, in 1948, the Equitable Savings and Loan Building by Pietro Belluschi. Even though it is a tall building, it draws upon the IIT project. A polished sheet aluminum skin covers its reinforced concrete frame, and darker, cast-aluminum spandrels and tinted glass are set within

an inch of their covering so that the effect is that of a single, smooth
reflective plane—more machinelike than any building by Mies.

The firm of Skidmore, Owings & Merrill, with major offices in
New York and Chicago, early identified itself with the Miesian esthetic and, in turn, with its prestige commissions for corporate business headquarters, made Miesian architecture a symbol of financial
probity. Its first such commission was Lever House in New York
(1952), designed by Gordon Bunshaft (287). Ironically this building,
with its elegant curtain wall of stainless steel, opaque blue glass, and
tinted windows, became more influential than any single building by
Mies; for instance, similar curtain-wall effects were soon made easy
by catalog components. Lever House was also praised for creating
pedestrian open space in the city—Rockefeller Center had more
successfully achieved this earlier—and for breaking the linear uniformity of Park Avenue with its vertical slab perpendicular to the
street—which some critics now regard as unfortunate.

For the Inland Steel Building in Chicago (1954) Walter A. Netsch,
also of Skidmore, Owings & Merrill, put aside the usual cellular
structural frame and adapted the Miesian concept of universal space
for commercial use. Each floor of the Inland Steel Building resembles
a Farnsworth House, a totally column-free space, with vertical supports confined to the outside flanks. The elevators and other services
are contained in an opaque tower attached to one side of the building.

Eero Saarinen's early works acknowledge the precedent of Mies
van der Rohe. Mies's IIT campus plan clearly provided the model for
Saarinen's General Motors Technical Center in Warren, Michigan
(1948–65), which serves as a research branch of the company (288).
Saarinen designed six major buildings around a huge artificial lake,
but they are so widely spaced that no interrelationship between them
is possible. The IIT campus concept, based on pedestrian scale, is
disconcerting when enlarged to that of the automobile. Saarinen was
more successful with his study of details; for example, his technical
advance in the curtain wall, adapting a rubber gasket seal similar to
that of an automobile windshield, and the introduction of color, red,
blue, or yellow, in panels of glazed brick, heightening the suggestion
of a Mondrian painting. Saarinen's role in developing Miesian architecture was that of an intermediary. With his special ability to
present a building as a visual package acceptable to American taste,
he filled his role as an interpreter extremely well.

Philip Johnson was a quite different interpreter of Mies. First, as
an architectural historian, he presented Mies in a fine monograph
appearing in 1947. Second, as an architect, he restated Mies's idea
of an all-glass house in his own residence in New Canaan, Connect-

287
Lever House, New York City. Skidmore, Owings & Merrill, 1952. Exterior.

288
General Motors Technical Center, Warren, Michigan. Saarinen and Saarinen Associates, 1948–65. General view.

289
*Johnson House, New Ca-
naan, Connecticut. Philip
Johnson, 1949. Interior.*

icut, built in 1949 (289). Like Lever House, Johnson's glass house became more famous than its prototype, the Farnsworth House (not yet built but known to Johnson from the plans). But for all its fame and refinement, the Johnson House as a bachelor's country retreat was of limited value as a model and was not directly emulated. Its similarity to the Farnsworth House lies in the visible steel framing and the open plan, where living and dining areas, bedroom, and kitchen are implied by partial partitions or the placement of furniture; only the bath is enclosed, in a brick cylinder that projects slightly above the roof. As historian turned architect, Johnson has said of his own house that far stronger influences than Mies are at work and he knew them all.[2] Certainly in the Johnson House, as the visitor experiences it, structure is the least insistent element, whereas in the Farnsworth House it is the dominant one. Mies's house is rigorous and demanding; Johnson's is sybaritic and subordinate to the landscape.

More valuable as models were Johnson's versions of those unbuilt atrium-house projects Mies designed in Germany between 1931–35. Johnson reinterpreted their simple brick planes and wide expanses of glass in a series of houses of intentionally formal character. The Davis House of 1954 in Wayzata, Minnesota, is an example: its flowing interiors, its exacting craftsmanship in brick, and its podium setting are unmistakably the result of lessons learned from Mies, lessons well learned and sensitively applied. (On the opposite coast, another disciple, Craig Ellwood, adapted light-weight steel framing for a number of elegant yet simple houses in Southern California.)

More often than not what passes for Miesian architecture is Miesian in outward appearance only, resulting in bland uniformity. Most of the exceptions are works by the small circle of architects who studied under Mies at ITT and remained loyal to his doctrine of structure. In the Civic Center (1963–68) by Jacques Brownson, a former pupil of Mies, Chicago honors Mies with its municipal offices and courts housed in skyscraper form, a building that is at once fellow to the commercial skyscrapers of the Loop and yet is quickly perceived as civic, not by any superficial pomp or symbol but by its visual weight and heroic measure of proportion. The eighty-seven-foot length of the bays, requiring Warren trusses, was unprecedented in high-rise construction at the time the Civic Center was built. Mies's fondness for the immediacy of construction—one of the things the nineteenth century called "reality"—is expressed with an alloy of steel called Cor-Ten, whose rusted surface is self-healing and darkens with age. As an unofficial memorial to Mies, leader of the

290
McCormick Place, Chicago, Illinois. C. F. Murphy Associates, 1968–71. Exterior.

so-called "Second Chicago School of Architecture," the Civic Center appropriately shares Dearborn Street with buildings by Jenney, Burnham and Root, Holabird and Roche, and the Federal Center (1956–65) by Mies himself.

Another reflection of Mies's late preoccupation with large scale—most obvious in his Convention Hall project—is a similar building, McCormick Place in Chicago (1968–71), designed by another pupil, Gene Summers, while he was working in the office of C. F. Murphy Associates (290). McCormick Place consists of an exhibition hall and an auditorium. Both are sheltered by the same lofty, flat roof composed of 15-foot-deep trusses, all exposed and painted black, spanning 150 feet in each direction and cantilevered half as much on all sides. As Mies would have conceded and Viollet-le-Duc might have approved, McCormick Place can claim a more distant antecedent than the nearby Crown Hall: the train sheds and exhibition halls of nineteenth-century Europe.

Wright's Second Career

In 1940 Mies van der Rohe recalled how thirty years earlier he and other young modernists in Europe had been stirred by the "clarity of language and disconcerting richness of form" in the work of Frank Lloyd Wright as revealed to them by the exhibition of his work in Berlin and the Wasmuth portfolio. "So after this first encounter," he wrote, "we followed the development of this rare man with wakeful hearts. We watched with astonishment the exuberant unfolding of [his] gifts. . . . In his undiminishing power he resembles a giant tree in a wide landscape, which year after year, attains a more noble crown."[3] What Mies could not have known was that the giant tree—one of the two giant trees in the wide landscape of

American twentieth-century architecture—still had nearly two decades in which to put out new growth.

The 1920s and the early 1930s were personally difficult and architecturally unproductive for Wright. In the midst of the Depression Wright despaired of ever seeing another project built and resigned himself to rural life at Taliesin, his ancestral farm near Spring Green, Wisconsin. In 1932 he established the Taliesin Fellowship for young people who wished to study architecture informally, to live and work as part of Wright's extended family. He saw his remaining years as a philosopher-architect inculcating his apprentices with his oblique wisdom and prejudices. His recovery and his second career began in 1934 with the unexpected but welcome commission for a modest house for the Malcolm Willeys of Minneapolis. Two years after the Willey House, even more unexpectedly, came two unique commissions within months of each other, the Kaufmann House called "Fallingwater" and the Johnson Wax Building. The year 1940 began two more decades sustained by continued opportunities and a bold display of his incomparable talent, fully justifying Mies van der Rohe's tribute.

Baroque Interlude

Between Wright's first mature period, ending with his departure for Europe in 1909, and his second career, beginning in the mid-1930s, is work of a wholly different character. Some have called it his Baroque phase, for it is characterized by very complex forms and florid decoration. Wright's new fascination with the triangle and the circle is also evident during these years. He subsequently withdrew from Baroque exuberance, but triangular and circular motifs became the basis for many of his late works.

Two examples illustrate Wright's Baroque interlude, one very large and one very small. Midway Gardens occupied a full city block in Chicago, comprising a restaurant and a large outdoor cafe with a bandstand (291). Built in 1914, its short life ended sadly with Prohibition. The extensive base was overwhelmed by patterned concrete block, cubist figure sculpture cast in concrete, and fanciful towers in which sculptural and architectural forms were interwoven.[4] This decorative treatment was appropriately festive and not wholly unexpected in view of Wright's earlier use of pattern, as in the stucco and tile panels of the Coonley House. But in the earlier work decoration is fully controlled by architectonic effects; in Midway Gardens it is the other way about. Wright's Imperial Hotel in Tokyo (1918–22) is even more flamboyant, with its decorative details in lava stone instead of concrete.

Pleased with his transformation of the lowly concrete block into
a decorative as well as structural material, Wright called it "textile
block" because he threaded its joints with strands of reinforcing steel.
He used this technique for a small house in Pasadena, California, for
Mrs. George Millard (1923), illustrating as well his continued interest in decoration. Restrained only in silhouette, the exterior is entirely of patterned concrete block, some of it pierced for a trellised
effect. The identical block appears inside, where its scale is perhaps
less appropriate. Yet in total effect "La Miniatura," as the Millard
House is called, enchants us with an almost Venetian sensuality,
veiled by eucalyptus and reflected in a pool in the hollow of its ravine
site. Wright continued to use decorative concrete block through the
twenties in a number of buildings, including several houses in Los
Angeles, none as satisfying as that in Pasadena.

Usonian Houses

During the idle years of the early thirties Wright created his imaginary Broadacre City, which illustrates "Usonia," Wright's 1927
coinage for an idealized America.[5] Beginning in 1936 he applied the
term to a series of small houses that realized the impossible: distinctive architecture and privacy at a modest price. The first Herbert
Jacobs House in Madison, Wisconsin (1937), is the complete Usonian
prototype, although many elements of Usonian planning were anticipated in the Willey design. Wright began with an advantageous

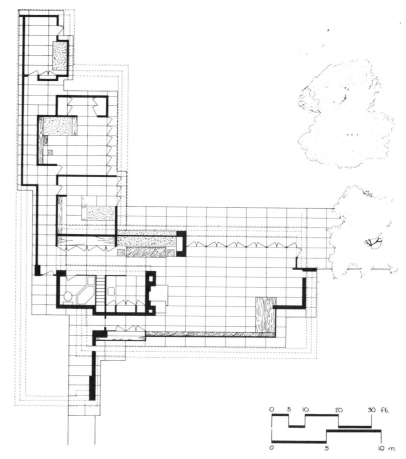

292
Herbert Jacobs House,
Madison, Wisconsin.
Frank Lloyd Wright,
1937. Plan.

293
Goetsch-Winkler House,
Okemos, Michigan. Frank
Lloyd Wright, 1939.
Exterior.

off-center placement of the house on its site; there is no useless front yard; a carport near the street supersedes the driveway; and all major rooms look out on a generous garden (292). Anticipating prefabrication, he simplified construction by replacing the conventional stud wall with a triple-layered board sandwich separated by insulating paper, standardizing construction details, and basing the whole plan on a modular grid, usually two feet by four. Heating is by the gravity system, with hot water or steam circulating in coils embedded in a concrete slab poured on grade. The kitchen, which Wright called the workspace, together with the bath, utility room, and often the fireplace, are located at a central point in these houses— at the elbow in L-shaped plans such as that of the Jacobs House. Spaciousness is achieved by combining the dining room with the living area and linking it to the nearby workspace, more an alcove than a separate kitchen. This openness differs from the bedroom wing, where the chambers are minimal and the corridor is often as narrow as that of a Pullman car. The cost of the Jacobs House, including the architect's fee, was only $5,500.

With his Usonian series Wright confirmed that he was by temperament primarily a designer of houses. The sensitivity and variety seen in it is remarkable. Even in conventional flat locations Wright's layered horizontal roofs, on occasion visually reinforced by banked earth berms, make a perfect marriage of house and site. The most lyrical of all Usonian examples is the Goetsch-Winkler House in Okemos, Michigan (1939), with its arrested movement of shifted planes both in plan and elevation (293). As we turn from the nearly thirty-foot sweep of windows and French doors to the seclusion of the fireplace alcove, we become fully aware of an interior integral with the exterior and the supporting role of built-in tables and seating. What is overwhelming is the poetry of space and structure that Wright shrugged off as "natural simplicity." To live in a Wright house, as owners have happily confessed, is to acquiesce in Wright's values and way of life.

Square, Triangle, and Circle

The idea of a weekend house set deep in the woods does not conjure up the high drama of "Fallingwater," one of the two or three most famous houses of the twentieth century (294). Here is not a timid act of deference to the wilderness but an exaltation of man-made geometry. However unprecedented in being poised over a rocky stream, Fallingwater is esthetically familiar: here is the same play of intersecting and projected planes in space that appears in the Prairie houses, most emphatically in the Mrs. Thomas Gale House of 1909. But in Fallingwater Wright assembled his supporting piers

294
*Fallingwater, Kaufmann
House, Bear Run, Penn-
sylvania. Frank Lloyd
Wright, 1936. Exterior.*

all to one side, on one bank of the stream. This cluster acts as a dislocated pivot for a triple tier of rooms with extended terracelike balconies in three directions. Fallingwater suggests spontaneity; in fact, those working with Wright at the time have said that the design was conceived almost instantaneously. Certainly its intensity is appropriate for intermittent rather than continuous occupancy. The Kaufmann weekend retreat remains the freshest monument of modern architecture.

In his long lifetime of triumphs and disappointments, Wright could never have forgotten the significance of the year 1936: the start of his Usonian cycle of houses, the Johnson Wax commission, and the popular success of Fallingwater. At the age of sixty-nine he surprised the world, if not himself, with his seemingly inexhaustible lode of talent. He continued to flout the architectural establishment and scorn the advancing modernism from Europe.[6] The work that followed was increasingly subjective, willfully assertive, daring, even improbable, such as his fantasy proposal for a mile-high skyscraper for Chicago (1956). Wright had no patience for the tabulation of requirements, budgets and bureaucracy, or design by committee. The diversity of his last works resists stylistic analysis. The individual artist simply yielded "to the fascination of creation."

To comprehend Wright's diversity it is perhaps useful to return to his theory of organic architecture. For example, the botanical analogy of a plant stem suggested the design of a wooden windmill called "Romeo and Juliet," which he built for his aunts at Spring Green in 1897. This organic concept of growth and the relatedness of parts was elaborated for several skyscraper designs using the cantilever principle, the structure analogous to the supporting trunk of a tree, its branches, and the outer enclosure of leaves. One of these was the St. Mark's Tower project of 1929 for New York City, abandoned on account of the Depression. Here Wright devised an ingenious pinwheel plan of four duplex apartments on each floor with an intermediate bedroom level rotated 30° so that it formed a balcony overlooking the living room; one bedroom was to have an outside balcony as well. The exterior form expresses every interior condition. Years later, in 1956, the design was executed in modified form as the H. C. Price Tower in Bartlesville, Oklahoma (295). Three of the quadrant tiers are standard office floors, but the fourth tier is retained as duplex apartments almost identical to those of the 1929 prototype. The Price Tower and the earlier Johnson Wax Research Tower (1950) at Racine are Wright's only executed tall buildings. Overlooking his own anti-urban prejudices—Wright could

295
Price Tower, Bartlesville,
Oklahoma. Frank Lloyd
Wright, 1953–56.
Exterior.

never live or work in a skyscraper—his proposals give us a personal view of an assignment that Mies saw as a generic one.

On numerous other occasions Wright recycled his unexecuted ideas in part or in whole. A recurrent motif is the prow-shaped terrace that first appeared in projects of the early twenties, among them the Doheny Ranch for the Sierra Madre mountains and summer cabins for Lake Tahoe. It is reused in the Willey House, Taliesin West, and the First Unitarian Church in Madison, Wisconsin. In the church, completed in 1950, Wright heightened the prow effect with a copper-sheathed, pointed roof above a triangular plan, a roof he likened to folded hands in prayer, even though the form appears earlier in the Lake Tahoe Summer Colony project and elsewhere. Symbolism aside, the Madison church is one of Wright's most disarmingly simple compositions with many subtleties of plan and siting. His most dramatic sloping roofs, however, were those that combined wall and roof, such as in his tentlike, steel-and-glass cathedral for a million people proposed for New York in 1926. Changing his cluster plan to a more simple tripartite one and substituting corrugated plastic for glass, Wright finally, in 1959, realized his interfaith cathedral design in the Philadelphia suburb of Elkins Park, the Beth Sholem Synagogue.

That the circle is far more difficult to adjust in plan than the square or triangle or that its corollary forms—arc, spiral, and dome—are difficult to construct was hardly a limitation for Wright. He understood the circle as a readily identifiable and satisfying form and used it in both large and small projects. His two most interesting houses based on the circle are the Ralph Jester House (1938) and the second Herbert Jacobs House (1948–49). In the Jester project, planned for a hillside at Palos Verdes, California, the rooms are separate circles loosely connected by a partially roofed rectangular terrace whose edge borders a huge, circular swimming pool.[7] The Jacobs House in Middleton, Wisconsin, is set at the edge of prairie farmland. In this 1943 design Wright used a hollow ring, part house, part earth berm, to enclose a circular, sunken garden, viewed through a crescent of tall windows.

The venerable shadow of the Pantheon, with its countless copies, conditions us to accept the circle and dome as appropriate to monumental buildings. Yet Wright was able to reinterpret these motifs as if he were using them for the first time in history. That is the thought when viewing his Annunciation Greek Orthodox Church in Wauwatosa, outside Milwaukee, Wisconsin (1956), or the Guggenheim Museum in New York (1956–59). Both illustrate the plastic shaping made possible with concrete. The form of the church

296
*Guggenheim Museum,
New York City. Frank
Lloyd Wright, 1956–59.
Interior.*

suggests two cupped saucers, separated by a decorative ring of windows, the whole cradled by four supports; it could possibly be an abstraction of a raised chalice. It is a spectacular image in ivory-colored concrete, accented by a dazzling blue dome and girdled with gold anodized aluminum—the same colors are used inside—an effect that to some may evoke the Arabian nights rather than the traditions of the Greek Orthodox Church.

The Guggenheim Museum project, begun in 1943, suffered many changes and delays (296). Over more than a decade before construction, Wright struggled with his concept of a circular, spiral-ramped interior, even at one time proposing a hexagonal version. A commission that came to him during this period, the V. C. Morris Store in San Francisco of 1948, gave Wright the chance to experiment with this concept in a limited way, remodelling an existing building into a miniature Guggenheim and giving it a handsome flat facade recalling both Richardson and Sullivan. An open spiral is an unorthodox solution for either a gift shop or a museum. It suggests an automobile ramp, which is exactly the function it had in Wright's Maryland planetarium project of 1925 and a Pittsburgh self-service garage scheme of 1947. For all that, the ramp concept affords a clear circulation path for museum visitors: one takes an elevator to the top level and then strolls downward past the exhibits, although

297
Taliesin West, Scottsdale,
Arizona. Frank Lloyd
Wright, begun in 1938.
Exterior.

everything is admittedly viewed on a slant. The dynamic interior of the Guggenheim is, for some, too competitive for the display of art, but no one disputes that it is one of the memorable spaces in all architecture.

The city was not Wright's milieu, as the anomalous character of the Guggenheim Museum in its New York setting proves. His own choice, in 1938, was the then lonely Arizona desert north of Phoenix as the site for a permanent encampment to serve as winter home for himself and his Fellowship. Wright's Taliesin West was a low, extended arrangement of primitive desert stone and poured concrete with a superstructure of spaced redwood frames fitted with taut, white canvas (now replaced with plastic) (297). This brooding, introspective monastery, modified by Wright over the years, is still inhabited by his disciples, who work under the name of Taliesin Associated Architects and the leadership of William Wesley Peters, the first Fellowship apprentice in 1932. After Wright's death they completed his largest commission, the Marin County Civic Center at San Rafael, California.

Under his enormous shade few of Wright's students were able to summon up the self-confidence necessary for independent, creative work. Among those who did are Alden Dow and John Lautner. Lloyd Wright (Frank Lloyd Wright, Jr.), one of two sons who became architects, was never formally his father's pupil, but he did supervise the building of Wright's Los Angeles houses in the twenties. It is instantly recognizable that Lloyd Wright's work was inspired by his father's, even if it is always more agitated. This is immediately apparent when one compares the redwood framing of Taliesin West with that of the Wayfarers' (Swedenborg Memorial) Chapel (298). Designed in 1946 and built in 1951 with later additions, this chapel at Palos Verdes, California, suggests prisms of glass, which are combined with triangles set with blue tile; both are held in a structural web that itself suggests the armature of vaulting. The chapel complements its dramatic setting amid redwoods on a promontory overlooking the Pacific where architectural reticence would have been inappropriate.

Among those who savored life in Wright's Oak Park studio at the turn of the century was Francis Barry Byrne; an assistant for seven years, he left in 1908. Byrne was always loyal to the progressive stance of Sullivan and Wright, but his curiosity and open-mindedness allowed him to absorb such divergent viewpoints as the abstractions of Irving Gill and (notably in the Church of St. Thomas the Apostle in Chicago built in 1922) the Expressionism of Hans Poelzig, both of whose works he knew firsthand. He was favored by the Roman Catholic hierarchy in the Midwest with several churches in the twenties that demonstrate a mature and original style. The sculptor of Midway Gardens, Alfonso Iannelli, assisted him on several projects. One of Byrne's later buildings, the Church of St. Francis Xavier (1949) in Kansas City, Missouri, with a fish-shaped plan and smoothly curved brick walls, is his best-known work.

Wright's precedent guided many young architects other than those who had worked under him. Bruce Goff is doubtless the most conpicuous, though not for his Wrightian forms. (As a curious boy, Goff wrote to Wright asking for information about his work and Wright replied by sending him gift copies of the Wasmuth volumes.) Goff made Wright's stand for individuality, respect for site, and use of materials points of departure for his own career and work. Starting at the age of twelve, Goff learned architecture in the Tulsa office of Rush, Endacott and Rush; by fifteen he had designed his first building, a creditable Prairie Style house near Los Angeles (1919). Sullivan influenced him in his Boston Avenue Methodist-Episcopal Church (1925–28) in Tulsa, Oklahoma, which he designed

298
*Wayfarers' Chapel, Palos
Verdes, California. Lloyd
Wright, 1951. Interior.*

299
Gene Bavinger House,
Norman, Oklahoma.
Bruce Goff, 1950–55.
Exterior.

while working for the same firm. Goff's first independent commission, the Unseth House in Park Ridge, Illinois (1934–41), began a series of radical and entertaining houses that have been the despair of critics and the joy of their owners. His architecture is literally inimitable, and only his pupil Herb Greene has worked in the same spirit. The Bavinger House near Norman, Oklahoma (1950–55), is based on a seashell curve in stone, which rises to support a mast from which tension cables descend to support "floating" bedrooms as well as a roof and stairs (299). Goff's maverick architecture is very different from Wright's, yet by reason of that difference the more impressive as testimony of the fructifying power of Wright's example.

The Bay Region Style

The doctrines of the International Style were not accepted everywhere. All through the 1940s and beyond the architects of the San Francisco Bay region and the Pacific Northwest resisted them, despite the presence of Mendelsohn at Berkeley. This resistance was rooted in the self-conscious regionalism that Maybeck and his circle had originated in the early years of the century. An architect who continued this trend in his residential work in the late twenties and thirties was William W. Wurster. Wurster respected tradition but did not regard it as sacrosanct. His houses were modest yet precisely built; one of the best (and earliest) is the Gregory farmhouse in Santa Cruz (1927), which follows the courtyard plan of Anglo-Spanish ranch houses. Although in the forties the geometrical clarity and modular rhythms of the International Style could be detected in Wurster's designs, his buildings remained unobtrusive, their scale small, and their material often wood; an example is the rural office building for the Schuckl Canning Company in Sunnyvale (1942).

Following Wurster's lead in the forties were John Funk, Gardner Dailey, Joseph Esherick, and Harwell Hamilton Harris. Further north, in Oregon, the domestic work of Pietro Belluschi is similarly sensitive and regional in feeling, unassuming yet personal. Belluschi's churches, for example the redwood Central Lutheran Church in Portland (1948), are reminiscent of the wooden churches of Richard Upjohn and they are equally fine.

In 1947 the critic Lewis Mumford, calling into question the deficiencies of the International Style in domestic architecture, praised the houses of Maybeck and Wurster for their "native and humane form of modernism."[1] "They took good care," he wrote, "that their houses did not resemble factories or museums." Thus the Bay Region Style, as the manner of the West Coast architects came to be called, was recognized as another modernism—and a native one—at a time when modernism from Europe in the form of the International Style was beginning to come under fire from former adherents as well as architects and critics who had never accepted its claim to be the style of the twentieth century.

Reevaluation of Modernism

By the mid-1950s the International Style was being attacked from all sides, the motivation of its assailants ranging from dissatisfaction with its narrow esthetic to disappointment with its diversion from lofty goals. Many were openly critical of the very premises of the twentieth-century modern movement, although their own objectives were diffuse, their vision clouded, and their criteria subjective. Some proposed an existentialist architecture to express the uncertainties of the age; others advocated a return to neglected symbols to increase communication in an architecture that had become too abstract; yet others, restless from the inhibiting limitations of the International Style, were for deserting the Phileban forms of solid geometry for freer shapes. Uniformity and dogma were replaced by diversity and experiment.

It must be acknowledged that the products of the International Style in the thirties and forties had their weaknesses; however, these were only the delayed effect of what occurred earlier when modern architecture withdrew from the rigorous structural, technological, and functional objectivity that it originally espoused to compromise with an easier, more painterly manipulation of visual forms and surfaces. For example, the early resolve to employ the industrial process and materials was followed up to a point only. Experiments with mass-produced, prefabricated houses were limited; never did a satisfactory solution sustain itself in the marketplace. It was Buckminster Fuller, more inventor than architect, who in 1927 designed the truly original Dymaxion House, with its hexagonal form suspended from a central mast anchored in the ground (300). Totally uninterested in conventional visual solutions, even of the modern sort, Fuller had as his goal maximum performance with maximum economy. His second version of the Dymaxion principle, a house built in Wichita, Kansas, in 1946, resembled a sheet-metal igloo. Fuller's challenge to live in a metal capsule was not taken up, and architects were reluctant to follow his lead for fear of abandoning their traditional role as visual designers. In 1949 Charles Eames designed a much admired semiprefabricated house for himself in Pacific Palisades, California (301). Assorted standard sections of factory glazing and opaque panels were fitted between a light steel skeleton. The two-story living room with bedroom balcony derives from LeCorbusier's series of artists' houses; its esthetic ancestor is the post-beam-panel Japanese teahouse. But much of the appeal of the house came from the juxtaposition of its terse form with the surrounding trees and the flair with which the designer furnished it. Although traditional by comparison with Fuller's inventions, the Eames House did not, despite its popularity, provoke much direct imitation.[2]

Nor was the ideal of reuniting engineering with architecture realized. The space-frame constructions of Konrad Wachsmann and the Geodesic domes of Fuller were employed only in limited ways. One exceptional structure was the State Fair Arena at Raleigh, North Carolina, completed in 1953, which the Polish-born Matthew Nowicki designed before his death in 1950. It was the first major suspension-roof structure. two giant arches are positioned to form

300
Dymaxion House. Buck-
minster Fuller, 1927.
Model.

301
Charles Eames House,
Pacific Palisades, Califor-
nia. Charles Eames, 1949.
Exterior.

a cradlelike structure from which suspension cables span a distance of 325 feet. Secondary cables placed at right angles to the primary cables form a net to support the roof.

Expressionism Revived

Even those who believed that the cycles of art history ensure a return to individualism after the impersonality of a classic period must have found it surprising that the change should first appear in the work of an architect who had been a tasteful interpreter of Mies. Eero Saarinen's later buildings, those designed between 1956 and 1961, revived the assertive forms of German Expressionism of the early 1920s, particularly those of Mendelsohn. The streamlined shapes used have analogies in automobile styling, which considers visual identity above all else. Saarinen was, without a doubt, also affected by the bold concrete structures of Nervi and Candela, but his interest was more visual than technical. The Kresge Auditorium at MIT built in 1955, is a concrete shell—one-eighth of a sphere resting on three points—with neither the inevitable logic nor the soaring grace of the engineer's art; it contains an inner acoustic shell of different profile, a spherical segment being exactly the shape to be avoided for the acoustics of an auditorium. Unsuitability aside, Saarinen created an image that is instantly recognizable though not really expressive of anything but its own geometry (302).

Saarinen's Expressionist period began in 1956 with the Ingalls Hockey Rink at Yale University, which was completed in 1958, and the Trans World Airline Terminal at Kennedy Airport in New York, completed in 1962 (303, 304). These buildings flaunt Saarinen's then unorthodox view of choosing "the style for the job"; he sought to express in them the excitement of ice hockey and air travel, creating a vessel for sport and a winged canopy for flight. The Yale rink is spanned lengthwise by a center parabolic supporting arch in reinforced concrete; tension cables are suspended from the arch and are anchored laterally in low concrete walls, which enclose the building and are of similar curvature on plan. At each end the arched spine is extended outward in a reverse curve to form a cantilevered beam supporting entrance canopies. Once a student of sculpture, Saarinen contrasted curves with countercurves, concave with convex.

The TWA Terminal, developed from a more complex program than the Yale rink, achieved a similar visual drama. That its arching roofs looked like a bird in flight was coincidental, according to the architect, though he had long felt that the "urge to soar great distances . . . to reach upward and outward [is] man's desire to conquer gravity." The building consists of a reinforced concrete roof

302
Kresge Auditorium, Massachusetts Institute of Technology, Cambridge, Massachusetts. Eero Saarinen & Associates, 1955. Exterior.

with four curved segments supported by four Y-shaped buttresses, all of which shelters a central waiting room. The thickness of the concrete shell varies from seven to forty inches. Pier Luigi Nervi said that it was too heavy and the design too elaborate for the problem it seeks to solve. But Saarinen was a sculptor-architect, not an engineer. Inside the terminal, one inhabits a piece of sculpture. A search for precedents uncovers a Naum Gabo project of 1931 for a double auditorium in Moscow, the twisted forms of sculpture by Gabo's brother Antoine Pevsner, and the cavelike spaces of Antonio Gaudi.[3]

For the Dulles International Airport (1958–62), which serves Washington, D.C., Saarinen reverted to a rectangular plan but maintained a sculptured effect (305). The mobile lounges that shuttle passengers between the terminal and the planes simplified the plan and made for compactness. Three terraced levels, serving as access ways for automobiles, provide a visual platform for a series of monumental concrete piers across the front. Between these and a lower row of piers across the back is hung a cable roof, infilled with precast panels where wood had been used at Yale. The piers lean dramatically outward to counteract the pull of the cables, and the projection of the roof resulting from this serves as a bold canopy for the 600-foot length of the structure. The building was designed to be easily extended at either end. In the Dulles Airport, his last Expressionist work, Saarinen balanced, in nearly equal measure, utility, structure, esthetics, and symbolism. At a time of widespread questioning about architectural directions, Saarinen's answer was that public architecture should express the nature of its special purpose in our lives.

Saarinen's work aside, most Neo-Expressionist buildings are churches. Three examples illustrate their range: the First Presbyterian Church in Stamford, Connecticut (1958), by Harrison and Abramovitz; the Chapel of the United States Air Force Academy at

303
*Ingalls Hockey Rink, Yale
University, New Haven,
Connecticut. Eero Saari-
nen & Associates, 1956–
58. Exterior.*

304
*Trans World Airlines Ter-
minal, New York City.
Eero Saarinen & Associ-
ates, 1956–62. Interior.*

305
*Dulles International Air-
port, Chantilly, Virginia.
Eero Saarinen & Associ-
ates, 1958–62. Exterior.*

306
*Chapel, United States Air
Force Academy, Colorado
Springs, Colorado. Skid-
more, Owings & Merrill,
1956–62. Exterior.*

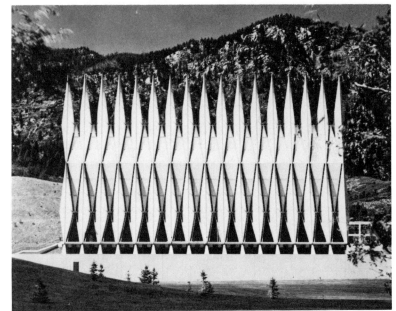

Colorado Springs (1956–62) by Walter Netsch of Skidmore, Owings & Merrill; and St. Mary's Cathedral in San Francisco (1971) by Pietro Belluschi and Pier Luigi Nervi. The radical appearance of the Stamford church is due in large part to its fish-shaped plan, employed for reasons of acoustics as well as symbolism. The structure is a jigsaw assembly of one hundred fifty-two precast-concrete panels, slanting inward to form a crimped skin. Quadrangular panels are covered with slate, and triangular ones contain tracery fitted with colored glass; the effect is so striking as to deny attention to the chancel. The Air Force Academy Chapel, which is also triangular in cross section, is more restless in form despite its precision (306). One hundred prefabricated tetrahedrons of welded steel pipe were assembled on a rectangular plan and the resultant cage was sheathed in silvery aluminum and set with strips of colored glass. But the effect remains intellectual; it is a chapel without ceremonial space and unresponsive to its mountainous setting.[4]

In contrast to this fragile geometry, the 190-foot-high sweeping roof of St. Mary's Cathedral, formed by four hyperbolic paraboloids in concrete, seems exactly suited to its hilltop site (307). The interior is equally dramatic. A wire sculpture by Richard Lippold serves as a baldacchino for the altar, which is placed off-center instead of, as one might have expected, at the crossing of the bisymmetrical structure, itself a giant canopy over the entire volume of space.

Large dimensions are usually demanded to sustain the unique shapes of Neo-Expressionism; there are few Neo-Expressionist houses and very few successful ones. The most memorable was built in Lincoln, Massachusetts, in 1965, by Thomas McNulty and his architect-wife. Simply constructed of plain concrete exposed inside and out, it is given life by its plan, comprising a single continuous space, 150 feet long, shaped by segments of curved walls. With each alternating enclosure and release come changing patterns of light across pale gray, textured walls (308).

Related to Expressionism in its outward form but evolved from a rational, sociotechnological system is the extraordinary project called Arcosanti, under construction in central Arizona. Designed as a small (3,000 inhabitants) prototype for a city of the future, Arcosanti is a demonstration of "Arcology," a concept of Italian-born Paolo Soleri, who was briefly a student-apprentice of Wright. The antithesis of Wright's Broadacre City, Soleri's ideal city is an extremely compact one because compactness in his view is necessary to offset the increased complexity of modern life. Although Arcosanti is a laboratory for studying environmental problems, the individual structures that have appeared on the barren landscape are sculptured designs in

307
St. Mary's Cathedral,
San Francisco, California.
Pietro Belluschi and Pier
Luigi Nervi, 1971.
Exterior.

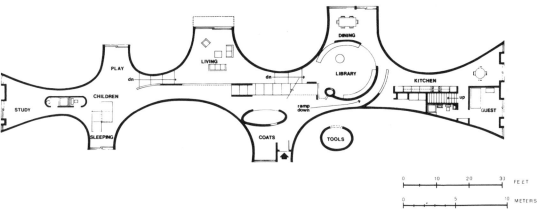

308
Thomas McNulty House,
Lincoln, Massachusetts.
Thomas McNulty and
Mary Harkness, 1965.
Plan.

concrete with segmental forms, reminiscent of those used by Soleri earlier in his Cosanti Foundation near Phoenix (begun in 1955). As the latter was, Arcosanti is being built by mostly unskilled, young apprentices who form Soleri's following.

The New Formalism

The movement variously called Neo-neo-Classicism or New Formalism had many more adherents than Neo-Expressionism ever did. Conspicuous among them were Edward Durell Stone, Minoru Yamasaki, Philip Johnson, Wallace Harrison, and Max Abramovitz; even Walter Gropius in his designs with TAC for Athens and Baghdad succumbed to its power of attraction. The respectable and perhaps bland presence that could be given to buildings of skeletal frame construction, whether of steel or reinforced concrete, was in its favor. Clients readily accepted the superficial elegance of the New Formalism as an artistic achievement and a worthy symbol of their culture, government, or business enterprise. Some architects were quick to flatter themselves that they had restored long-exiled beauty to architecture. In fact the New Formalism lacked vigor and had little real importance; it was a minor episode in the reaction against the programmed severities of the International Style.

The classical attributes of symmetry, enclosed form, and regular structure were never wholly absent from modern architecture. It is possible to regard Mies's Seagram Building as a pointer of the New Formalism, but the building in which all the salient characteristics of the movement were first manifested was Edward Stone's American Embassy at New Delhi (1954). Here was the temple reclaimed: a suave pavilion with gilded steel supports in front of a seductive screen of openwork terrazzo blocks to filter out sunlight. (Wright used similar block in the Millard House of 1923.) Stone reused the formula of the New Delhi embassy in the Stuart Pharmaceutical Company in Pasadena (1956), the Stanford University Hospital (1959), and the Kennedy Center for Performing Arts in Washington (1959) (309). He himself lived in a remodelled New York brownstone (1956) whose facade was replaced by a screen of concrete blocks.[5]

Yamasaki joined in the pursuit of delight after a visit to New Delhi. His neoformalist designs are more lively in their detail than Stone's and often contain a suggestion of Gothic mixed with classicism. In the McGregor Memorial Conference Center for Wayne State University in Detroit (1958) Yamasaki bisected the length of a rectangular building with a two-story lobby recalling a Victorian conservatory. Its faceted glass reflects the bevelled motif of triangular concrete box-beams. This formal yet delicate building, set among water gardens such as Stone had used at New Delhi, was hailed as

309
*Stuart Pharmaceutical
Company, Pasadena, Cal-
ifornia. Edward D. Stone,
1956. Exterior.*

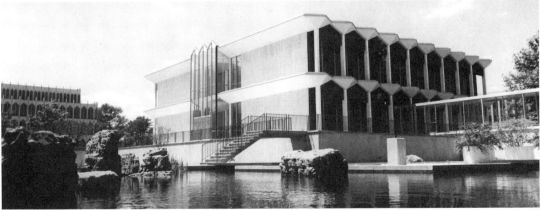

310
*McGregor Memorial Con-
ference Center, Wayne
State University, Detroit,
Michigan. Minoru Yama-
saki and Associates, 1958.
Exterior.*

311
Sheldon Memorial Art Gallery, University of Nebraska, Lincoln, Nebraska. Philip Johnson, 1963. Exterior.

312
Lincoln Center for the Performing Arts, New York City. Harrison and Abramovitz and Philip Johnson, 1962–68. View.

a timely loosening of esthetic strictures (310). Yamasaki followed the conference center with the Reynolds Aluminum Building of 1959, also in Detroit. This is basically a Miesian structure of three stories with a skylit interior court and the upper stories fitted with exterior screens of gold-anodized aluminum, a metallic version of Stone's openwork concrete block. Miesian austerity was apparent at a distance, but close at hand was the sensuous sight of a golden veil over a water-lilied moat and a plush purple carpet overlaid on an expanse of polished white terrazzo. Yamasaki took the final step toward the temple form in the Northwestern Life Insurance Company in Minneapolis (1962–64). A six-story office building inset with dark-green marble and gray glass to minimize floor levels, it is wrapped in an ethereal screen of tall, slender white concrete arches, reflected in pools of water.

Philip Johnson's formalist buildings are distinguished from those of Yamasaki and Stone by a more intellectual monumentality both within and without. With his scholarly mind, especially open to the influence of Schinkel and Soane, Johnson was an anomaly among the rank-and-file architects who viewed themselves as futurists or at least fully contemporary practitioners and him as a dilettante, although his sizable commissions soon led them to revise this opinion. In particular, Johnson's sympathy with the Beaux-Arts and his awareness of the processional element in design and siting gave his work an altogether more serious character.

Once a self-proclaimed disciple of Mies, Johnson turned from his Lieber Meister's principles in 1956, ironically the very year he was asked to associate with Mies on the Seagram Building. The Kneses Tifereth Israel Synagogue at Port Chester, New York, a steel-framed box enclosed with white concrete panels with only staggered slits of colored glass in between, was the first work of his apostasy. Although largely opaque, it has a sense of airiness and unreality, an illusion sustained within by a scalloped canopy suspended underneath the length of the structural ceiling.

Such delicate effects do not appear in Johnson's later formalist buildings: the Amon Carter Museum in Fort Worth, Texas (1961), and the Sheldon Memorial Art Gallery for the University of Nebraska at Lincoln (1963) (311). Both museums are arcaded in sculptured stone; their unbroken curves and tapered lines suggest a giant frame molded in one piece. Juxtaposed with these arcades are Miesian elements of curtain wall and, in the Sheldon Art Gallery, a Miesian stairway. The small and shallow plan of the Carter Museum behind the presumptuous facade is further dwarfed by Johnson's conception of the building as a viewing platform for the axial sequence of descending terraces and the skyline beyond. In both the museum and the art gallery a new visual vocabulary was being tested without abandoning the proven usefulness of the old.

That America never regained the ease with monumentality of the McKim years is proved by the assortment of auditoriums in New York called the Lincoln Center for the Performing Arts, completed in 1968 (312). The Campidoglio-like plan is focused on Wallace Harrison's Metropolitan Opera House (1966), flanked by Max Abramovitz's Philharmonic (now Avery Fisher) Hall (1962), and Philip Johnson's New York State Theater (1964), each with a variation on the theme of the monumental colonnade. The various provincial culture centers that Lincoln Center spawned, with their plazas and colonnades, did not improve upon the center's quality, and before the end of the sixties enthusiasm for the New Formalism ran out.

The Influence of Le Corbusier

Simultaneously with the rise of the New Formalism another generation, disenchanted with Mies and Gropius, was turning to the third patriarch of the International Style, Le Corbusier (Charles-Edouard Jeanneret). Unlike the two emigrés Le Corbusier was never favorably disposed to American values or opportunities. But the intensity and primitivism of his postwar buildings, notably the Unité d'Habitation in Marseilles, the Maisons Jaoul at Neuilly, and the Monastery of La Tourette, had a strong appeal for architects to whom the quite different qualities of his earlier works had become insufficient. The feature common to all the three buildings is the exposed concrete with the imprint of the wooden forms left upon it—"béton brut," as Le Corbusier called it, supplying a convenient derivation for the term Brutalism, commonly used to designate the work of his followers, even if it originated in another context.[6]

The only building by Le Corbusier in the United States is the Carpenter Visual Arts Center (1961–64) at Harvard University (313). An iconoclastic building of raw concrete snugly inserted between Neo-Georgian buildings of fastidious brick, the Carpenter Center would at first seem to represent an outright rejection of the kind of respect for locale shown by Richardson's Sever Hall across the street. But Le Corbusier provided connective tissue with the campus by means of an oblique pathway through the building, a pathway that begins with entrance ramps at street level, front and back, and rises to the third level within. On each side the ballooning shapes of studios, in which light is monitored by the deep reveals of brise-soleils, cushion the genteel neighbors. It is a building that engages the emotions; one cannot remain indifferent to it. Unfortunately, Le Corbusier never saw the center.

313
Carpenter Visual Arts Center, Harvard University, Cambridge, Massachusetts. Le Corbusier, 1961–64. Exterior.

314
Boston City Hall, Boston,
Massachusetts. Kallmann,
McKinnell and Knowles,
1963–68. Exterior.

José Luis Sert, a follower of Le Corbusier since the thirties, was dean of the Harvard Graduate School of Design when the Carpenter Visual Arts Center was built and supervised its construction. In his own work for Harvard, Married Student Housing (1964) and Holyoke Center (1965), Sert remained loyal to Le Corbusier's philosophy, balancing a modular rationale with visual diversity and maintaining a high density of occupation to secure the amenities of urban life.

The year the Carpenter Center was designed a competition for a new city hall for Boston was announced. It drew 256 entries. A much publicized event in professional circles, it brought recognition to a trio of architects who had never built a major building, Kallmann, McKinnell and Knowles. Their winning design, executed in 1963–68, is the closest emulation of Le Corbusier's late style in the United States (314). Besides repeating the free-standing, slablike supports and cellular divisions of the upper floors of La Tourette, the architects have, more importantly, followed Le Corbusier's thinking. They have conceived their city hall not as a static, isolated monument but as an active form embedded in the matrix of the city, drawing upon the movement of people across the square, into and through the building. The red brick paving is a traditional Bostonian feature; it is used here not only for that reason but also as a means of uniting building and square and of symbolizing the breaking down of barriers between the people and their city government, which was the central philosophical aim of the architects. The council chamber, with a large window directly over the main entrance, is linked with the square by a stair tower faced with the same red brick.

Rudolph and Breuer

The movement away from linear order and transparency was joined by some who had only recently completed their Bauhaus-oriented training. The best-known of these apostates is Paul Rudolph, former pupil of Walter Gropius. In the Sarasota Senior High School in Florida (1960) Rudolph turned to the spatial complexities possible with reinforced concrete, yet the essentials of his design forms were based on the integration of structural and mechanical systems. Here, and in most of his other works, Rudolph avoids direct borrowings from Le Corbusier; an exception is the Married Student Housing for Yale University (1961), with its obvious debts to the Maisons Jaoul.

The Art and Architecture Building at Yale, begun in 1958 and completed in 1964 (years when Rudolph was chairman of the department), was perhaps the most provocative American building of the decade (315, 316). Free of any Bauhaus constraints, Rudolph caused a collision of forms and interlocking spaces with cavernous

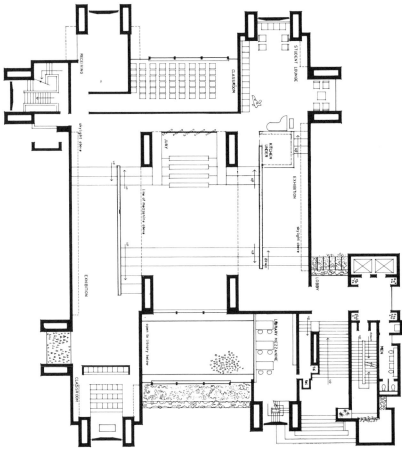

shadows, imparting a Piranesian element of mystery. The opaque, hollow piers for services, the windmill positioning of stairways, and a central skylighted space take us back to Wright's Larkin Building and Unity Temple. The sliding movement of horizontal beams past vertical supports, however inefficient structurally, recall Rietveld's de Stijl esthetics. The building is of a fascinating complexity. It contains a multiplicity of levels (thirty-seven in all) with crossing bridges and traylike spaces that may disorient the visitor but are arranged to separate various functions; there is even a penthouse suite for visiting critics. The contrived texture of the building stirred as much argument as more basic considerations. The vertical corrugations of concrete were the result of special formwork and were later hand-hammered to expose the inner aggregate and achieve an instant patina of age. Thus came the passing of an architectural ideal: a perpetual shining newness gave way to the weathered look.

Paul Rudolph survived the celebrity of the Yale building. Subsequent commissions of larger scale and with more demanding requirements tested his abilities, and the results enhanced his reputation. Characteristic of his work is a sense of onward rush, a compulsive drive toward a crescendo—exhausting to those who prefer architecture of a more tranquil tempo. Yet by virtue of its intrinsic principle, it is never merely exhibitionistic. Rudolph could produce architecture of distinction even within the stringent cost limits of public housing. Crawford Manor in New Haven (1962–66), consisting of high-rise apartments for the aged, is a case in point. Here the deeply fluted shadows created by the indented plan of the tower are repeated in more delicate fashion in the ribbing of the specially molded concrete block that covers the entire surface, including the cylindrically curved balconies.

Rudolph's Government Center in Boston (1962–68) is an urban complex of considerable size, executed with the cooperation of four other architectural firms. The splayed arrangement and stepped forms of the buildings on their triangular site suggest the influence of Alvar Aalto but are more declamatory in expression. In other urban projects Rudolph welcomed the difficult problem of combining pedestrian use with automobile access by devising buildings that are virtually miniature cities, or megastructures. The unexecuted Graphic Arts Center (1967), to be built over the West Side Drive in Manhattan, is an example. Here offices and apartments were to be combined with other services, including schools and a marina. Believing that the trailer-home is "the brick of twentieth-century technology," Rudolph stacked prefabricated apartment units in a manner similar to Moshe Safdie's Habitat housing built for the Montreal Exposition of the same year.

The qualities of design provided by Rudolph would have been totally incomprehensible had they appeared a decade earlier: walled forms, harsh textures, inward orientations, and a directional quality of space, not to mention an interest in monumentality and ceremony. These qualities, while conspicuous in Rudolph, were not his sole possession. In the unmistakable shifting of values in the mid-1950s others embraced them too, including a European expatriate, who, second to Mies, had the most illustrious and patronized career as a practicing architect in America: Marcel Breuer. Breuer, who came to the Bauhaus as an eighteen-year-old student in 1920, later to be an instructor, had been an intimate and constituent figure in German architectural development of the twenties and early thirties. Yet his innately pliable approach to design enabled him, as early as 1936, to temper the asceticism of the Bauhaus style, as seen in an exhibition pavilion in Bristol, England (designed in association with F. R. S. Yorke). The Gane's Pavilion was Breuer's turning point toward a more weighty and variable esthetic: uncoursed masonry wall-planes contrasted with large sheets of glass. Breuer was seemingly without the latent guilt about individuality common to many German modernists. From the very beginning his American work showed an open sympathy toward the visual craftsmanship of construction, toward a tactile language of building that reminds us of the muscularity of early Schindler. Furthermore, Breuer is the one German-trained architect who benefited from Le Corbusier, following his sense of individuality and primitiveness as well as adapting his planning and architectural motifs, particularly the pilotis and the brise-soleil.

Breuer's design for St. John's Monastery and College in Minnesota shows how he acknowledged the necessity for a broader esthetic and a considerably enlarged vocabulary of architecture (317). The Benedictines of St. John's, aware of their historic tradition of artistic patronage, interviewed five architects, including Gropius, Byrne, and Neutra—Belluschi and Saarinen declined—before choosing Breuer as their master architect for a comprehensive plan for a century of building. First constructed were a monastic wing and the great abbey church (1953–61). Breuer had never before built a ceremonial building of any kind, although he was working concurrently on the UNESCO Headquarters in Paris. For both projects he enlisted the talents of the Italian engineer-architect, Pier Luigi Nervi. It was Nervi who provided the folded-plate concrete shell design for the roof and walls of the church, similar to that of the UNESCO conference hall. As in the Romanesque and Gothic styles, one feels the

317
St. John's Abbey Church,
Collegeville, Minnesota.
Marcel Breuer, 1953–61.
Exterior.

flow of stresses through the structure; the structure itself becomes the architecture. And for the equivalent of the skyward thrust of medieval towers, Breuer conceived a free-standing bell banner, a pierced trapezoidal slab of raw concrete whose base supports also serve as an archway entrance to the church. Individuality and discipline, once opposites in Bauhaus doctrine, were united.

In Breuer's subsequent deflections from European modernism it became evident that the oldest of materials, wood and masonry, rather than the newest, steel and plate glass, held greater fascination for him. Breuer preferred the walled effects of masonry—in reinforced concrete, to be sure—over the skeletal frame. The lecture hall at New York University, one of a group of four buildings for University Heights in New York City (1956–61), is lifted above the ground by three supports. The textured patterns of formwork left in the concrete are contrived in trapezoidal areas to dramatize further the oblique angles of its side elevations.

Given the great number and variety of museums built in the third quarter of the century, one could easily write a synoptic architectural history of these years based on this single building type. Included would be the Whitney Museum in New York (1963–66) where Breuer, as in the NYU lecture hall, formed the building as a sculpture—one with serious functional requirements, said Breuer, as if to defend his design. The cantilevered, inverted stepped form of the lecture hall is repeated at the Whitney Museum with perhaps more reason because an entrance and a sunken sculpture court are provided on the small site. Although the inversion suggests the Guggenheim Museum, the Whitney is without Wright's dramatic interior, but in compensation it satisfies the more conventional requirements of flexible exhibition space. In the Whitney Museum and in all his commissions from the mid-1950s and beyond, in both the United States and Europe—his practice was a markedly international one—Breuer sought an enrichment of architectural forms rather than a substantial redirection in point of view. He might well be labelled a moderate iconoclast.

Radical Proposals   A far more radical architecture of dissent than any we have considered hitherto was proposed by the English Archigram group in the late sixties. It challenged all fixed assumptions, proposed expendability and change, and favored designs of seemingly random assemblies of parts arranged solely for flow and movement. Le Corbusier's thinking was revived with the forecast of a wholly machine-made architecture, not the hand-made one, which, despite superficially radical appearances, all so-called modern architecture continued to

Mummers Theater, Oklahoma City, Oklahoma. John M. Johansen, 1966–70. Exterior.

be. Engineering and the mechanical services were no longer to be the "shameful secret of the architectural family" but a visible and expressive part of the whole. Theoretically, components as large as a room or a house could be plugged in, moved to another location, or exchanged for an updated model.

While no Archigram building ever materialized in England, one that could be accepted as such appeared in Oklahoma, in the Mummers Theater in Oklahoma City (318). It was designed in 1966 by John Johansen, who, like Rudolph, was a student of Gropius. The building comprises three separate theaters of different types in raw concrete, loosely tied together by brightly painted, lightweight metal stairs and walkways. A conspicuous feature is the exposed air-conditioning tower, which rises above a central courtyard space, sprouting visible ducts leading to the various components of the design. No attempt was made to adjust disparate elements into the patterned logic of conventional design or a preconceived form. Instead, the architect took pride in creating a nonarchitecture of pure content. For him this visually chaotic design, a literal translation, so to speak, of the functional program, expressed honesty and "reality."

A similar approach was taken by the architects of Hardy Holzman Pfeiffer Associates, for example, in the Occupational Health Center in Columbus, Indiana (1969–73). The program was analyzed without preconceptions, and the result is very different from the stereotypical clinic: an openly planned and unregimented interior, decidedly provisional to the traditional eye, is decorated with structural steelwork

319
Guild House, Philadel-
phia, Pennsylvania. Ven-
turi and Rauch, 1960–63.
Exterior.

320
Sea Ranch Condominium,
Sea Ranch, California.
Moore, Lyndon, Turnbull,
Whitaker, 1964–66.
Exterior.

painted in bright green and exposed ducts in blue, all inside an exterior envelope of silver and black glass.

The indirect influence of Archigram and similar groups sustains the pattern of the European avant-garde in providing the ideas and archetypes needed to nourish the mainstream of American architectural development. The basic conservatism of America over the years—and centuries—has resulted in a lack of generative ideas but not of technology or desire to carry them out.

Another expression of iconoclasm, this time American-generated, was contained in a manifesto entitled *Complexity and Contradiction in Architecture*, written in 1962, published in 1966. The author was the practicing Philadelphia architect Robert Venturi, who formulated his argument in the late fifties. Claiming to be writing from the personal view of an architect rather than that of a theoretician or objective critic, Venturi stated his preference for "messy vitality" over imposed visual order, for "the difficult unity of inclusion" over "the easy unity of exclusion." He also stated that the International Style had failed because of its cool disregard of those hybrid impurities of the real world. In Venturi's view this was not the age for grand architecture; his "reality" lay in the images of everyday America, of Main Street and the highway strip.

Of Venturi's limited number of executed works, Guild House in Philadelphia (1960–63) may stand as a representative (319). By no means as radical as one might expect from his dicta, this intelligently planned housing for the elderly, with its unassuming brick walls and functional window pattern, could not express its purpose more directly or fit its neighborhood better. Guild House is quite without rhetoric, save a nonfunctioning replica of a television antenna ceremonially placed on top as an ironic symbol of the lives of its inhabitants. Yet in the understatement of his designs Venturi, who claims to appreciate popular taste, surely ignores what the public really likes, for example, the Fontainebleau Hotel in Miami Beach (1952), designed by the master of modern kitsch, Morris Lapidus.

The ordinariness of vernacular building advocated by Venturi was artfully transposed at Sea Ranch, a development of second homes in Sonoma County north of San Francisco, built in 1964–66 (320). Designed by Moore, Lyndon, Turnbull, Whitaker (MLTW) in association with the landscape architect Lawrence Halprin, the condominium cluster of ten units could be mistaken for abandoned mine buildings in Utah if it were not for the rugged coastal cliff that forms its perch. The units are assembled to minimize their similarity, although each has a shed roof and unpainted vertical siding. The serious unpretentiousness of the Sea Ranch Condominium—once

321
Kresge College, University of California, Santa Cruz, California. MLTW (Charles Moore and William Turnbull), 1972–74. Exterior.

fresh, now cloying—suggests a twentieth-century *hameau*, a rustic weekend retreat for city folk. Even if Sea Ranch Condominium provided no answer to pressing problems of architecture, its stark and irregular silhouette supplied a memorable image that has filtered down into housing tracts and shopping centers—a very different vernacular from the one from which Sea Ranch sprang.[7]

In the course of time the work of MLTW became freer and more imaginative, with conscious attempts to incorporate historical and cultural symbolism. Two commissions for the University of California, the Faculty Club on the Santa Barbara campus (1966–68) and Kresge College for the Santa Cruz campus (1972–74) illustrate this trend (321). Everyone, including the architects (Charles Moore and William Turnbull in these two cases), acknowledged theatrical and irreverent qualities in these designs. There was much dispute as to whether such qualities were appropriate in buildings that were to serve the serious purposes of university life. In the Santa Barbara Faculty Club baronial allusions in the whimsical furnishings are mocked by banners made of neon tubing; at Santa Cruz a noninstitutional character was obtained by erecting a cardboardlike village street set in a redwood forest. In both projects the ephemeral nature of stage scenery is suggested by angled plans, paint, and layered effects obtained by superimposing cut-out screen walls. (The last device was first used by Ralph Rapson in the Tyrone Guthrie Theater in Minneapolis in 1963.)

Influences of History

The dissenters and apostates of the fifties and sixties adopted a range of attitudes too multifarious to be identified by a common title. The once accepted values of modern architecture, anonymity and conformity, a commitment to structure, and a spartan view of function, no longer provided common ground. Sensibilities shifted. In ascendancy were allusion and symbolism, cultivation of a personal style and a more sensory involvement, and respect for vernacular architecture and the past. The value of modernity itself was challenged by the rise of the historical preservation movement. That the old could be beautiful, relevant, and still useful was acknowledged by the annual awards (starting in 1976) given by the American Institute of Architects for the adaptive reuse of buildings.

Acceptance of historical preservation, a cause originating with the public rather than with architects, produced still another response: a revived electicism founded on tradition and regionalism and regard for the genius loci. Years earlier, when it was completed in 1958, Rudolph's Jewett Arts Center for Wellesley College in Massachusetts perplexed a wary profession with its echoes of the pseudo-Gothic of adjacent campus buildings. Rudolph dared to relate his design not only by extending the crescentlike siting of James Gamble Rogers's work but by evoking Gothic forms with concrete columns of quatrefoil section and a spiky rhythm of pointed skylights.[8] Again flirting with history, Rudolph recalled the Greek Revival plantation houses of the South for the Wallace House in Athens, Alabama (1961–64), with a grid of stately columnar supports in white-painted brick. Although more interesting for their intent than for absolute achievement, such examples nonetheless indicate a substantial reevaluation of and a willingness to reconsider the past. One of the most discussed projects now is Philip Johnson's design for the American Telephone and Telegraph Building in New York (1978), which deliberately recalls the McKim, Mead and White era of the 1890s. Johnson has adopted the column formula of skyscraper design so popular in that decade; the base of his skyscraper was suggested by Brunelleschi's Pazzi Chapel; and a giant broken pediment adorns its top. Once again history has infiltrated the practice of architecture.

"Architecture is the masterly, correct and magnificent play of volumes brought together in light." Not only was Le Corbusier's post-World War II work the inspiration of the Brutalists, the classic definition in his book of 1923 describes a concept of architecture embodied in many of the most notable American buildings of the sixties and seventies. In these decades a growing number of American architects became absorbed with the arrangement of geometrical forms and patterns and the exploration of the possibilities of light and reflecting surfaces, and precisely curved shapes and oblique, faceted planes, often suggesting the structure of crystals, turned buildings into geometrical sculpture.

Europe anticipated this development. Two skyscrapers, one in Milan and the other in Dusseldorf, built after the Second World War when skyscrapers appeared for the first time abroad, demonstrated that the high-rise office block could be shaped and treated as a piece of sculpture. The Pirelli Tower, Gio Ponti's slender prism rising 400 feet above the skyline of Milan, is a reinforced concrete structure based on a lenticular plan, subtly bevelled so that its bulk is disguised by tapered ends. A sculptured effect of a different sort was obtained by Hentrich and Petschnigg in the Phoenix-Rheinrohr Building. Its composite form is of three layered, staggered slabs, the center one higher by three floors. These two buildings, both completed by 1960, caught the restless eyes of American architects seeking a release from the rectangular parallelepiped, and once again, as in the *Chicago Tribune* competition, Europe set a new course for the American skyscraper.

Thus it came about that in the sixties and seventies skyscrapers were designed for effects of sculptural form, and the expression of structure and function, once held to be accountable values, were subordinated. This new architecture of appearances gave license to arbitrary design. To obtain the unbroken and scaleless unity of form, entrances, floor levels, and individual windows were suppressed, often with a loss of convenience. Rather than communicating living functions within, such buildings celebrate an abstract ideal. Eero Saarinen was a master of this kind of simplification, as he proved in the CBS Building in New York, completed in 1965 after his death. The closely spaced supports of the square plan are seen as dark granite piers, which are triangular in section; between them are recessed windows of dark glass. When viewed at an angle, the windows become invisible and the flank appears as a monolithic wall of stone. The effect is one of great density, unity, and sobriety. The same brooding quality pervades Philip Johnson's Kline Biology Tower at Yale (1966), where round piers in brick replace the angular granite ones of the CBS Building.

Saarinen's granite stela marked the waning of the Miesian tradition: in the CBS Building the primary motivation was not to express the structure but to dramatize the surface with accordionlike facets, emphasizing the skin rather than the bones of the building. Saarinen's Law Library for the University of Chicago (1960) was similarly faceted, but with blue-green glass. Tinted glass was soon exchanged for mirrored glass in gold, silver, and copper tones, which has improved solar properties and allows one to see out but not to see in. The latter advantage permitted the architect to extend the glass over the solid walls and relieved him of the necessity of acknowledging interior relationships, which were only revealed when lights were turned on at dusk. By day such buildings were giant mirrored images of the immediate environment; chameleonlike, they changed color with the sky and weather. As mullions became more slender, almost pencil-thin—in some cases, butt-jointed glass sealed with epoxy glue or vinyl tubing dispensed with mullions altogether—all sense of architectonic construction was dispelled.[1]

The dematerialization of mass achieved with even grids of panes of mirrored glass became the prevailing characteristic of the new vernacular for office buildings; a random example is the Equitable Building in St. Louis (1971) by Hellmuth, Obata and Kassabaum. In such a design all edges, corners, top, and bottom are given no greater weight than the narrow mullions that elsewhere divide the sheets of mirrored glass, so one can only guess how many stories high the building is. The same is true of the reflective glass cube that contains offices for the Blue Cross-Blue Shield of Maryland (1970–72) in Towson, Maryland (322). The architects Peterson and Brickbauer have retained its purity of form by placing the entrance and parking below a grass-covered platform; for the sake of contrast, mechanical equipment is placed within a separate, smaller cube covered in bright red glazed brick. In Atlanta John C. Portman, Jr.'s, Peachtree Center Plaza Hotel, completed in 1976 as the tallest reinforced concrete structure in the world, is a seventy-story cylinder sheathed in bronze reflective glass, sending forth in all directions fractured images of the city. In Los Angeles the Great Western Savings Center (1972) by William L. Pereira & Associates is wrapped in a more conventional curtain wall; it is unusual for its elliptical plan, a shape antithetical to a rectangular structural grid. Seen in the light of history, these experiments represent a return to earlier proposals that emphasize the glass skin, for example, Mies van der Rohe's two projects for all-glass skyscrapers of 1919–22. Indeed, the latter one was the direct

322
*Blue Cross-Blue Shield of
Maryland, Towson,
Maryland. Peterson and
Brickbauer, 1970–72.
Exterior.*

inspiration for the curvilinear plan of Lake Point Tower (1968), a Chicago apartment building designed by two of his former pupils, George Schipporeit and John Heinrich.

The merging of architecture and sculpture was reciprocated by contemporary minimalist sculptors, such as Donald Judd and Larry Bell, whose purely geometrical works could well serve as model projects for buildings. The monotonous, boxlike skyline that threatened larger cities was averted by the rise of elegant prisms in taut, shiny skins, such as I. M. Pei's Hancock Building in Boston (1972), which stands across from Richardson's Trinity Church. The attenuated trapezoidal plan of the Hancock Building is notched at its narrow end to emphasize its slenderness. The device of offsetting various planes was often used to accelerate the vertical rhythms of a tall building, and with striking success. This staggered treatment benefited the interior plan of the recent Minneapolis landmark, the Investors Diversified Services Building (1968–73) by Philip Johnson and John Burgee, where the serrated ends of the lozenge plan provide multiple corner offices (always considered the most desirable) instead of only four (323). Both the Boston and Minneapolis buildings are glazed with mirrored glass.

How to design the enclosure of a skeletal building had long been a major problem of modern architecture. Certainly an all-glass exterior expressed perfectly the nonstructural character of a skin; yet it might be undesirable for practical or esthetic reasons. An unusual experiment of 1952 is the Alcoa Building in Pittsburgh by Harrison and Abramovitz, which is sheathed in thin sheet aluminum, formed in 6-by-12-foot prefabricated panels incorporating both window and spandrel. The precision of factory parts, the sensibly rounded corners of the windows, and the rapidity of installation demonstrated the advantages of a fully technological curtain wall. This bold example was neglected for two decades until the idea reappeared, with equally convincing results, in the Bronx Developmental Center in New York, designed by Richard Meier & Associates and completed in 1976 (324). Without the crimped pattern of the Alcoa Building, its reflective aluminum panels have a smooth, machined appearance. A very different effect is achieved by the curtain walls of the Beinecke Rare Book Library at Yale (1964) (325). These are constructed of translucent marble slabs, one and one-quarter inches thick, set in huge Vierendeel trusses. Gordon Bunshaft of Skidmore, Owings & Merrill was the designer. Different again is the envelope of opaque blue glass of the Pacific Design Center in Los Angeles (1971–76), designed by Cesar Pelli for Gruen Associates. Nicknamed the "blue

323
*Investors Diversified
Services Building, Minne-
apolis, Minnesota.
Johnson/Burgee, 1968–73.
Exterior.*

324
*Bronx Developmental
Center, New York City.
Richard Meier & Associ-
ates, 1970–76. Exterior
detail.*

325
Beinecke Rare Book Li-
brary, Yale University,
New Haven, Connecticut.
Skidmore, Owings &
Merrill, 1964. Exterior.

326
Marina City, Chicago, Il-
linois. Bertram Goldberg
Associates, 1961–63.
Plan.

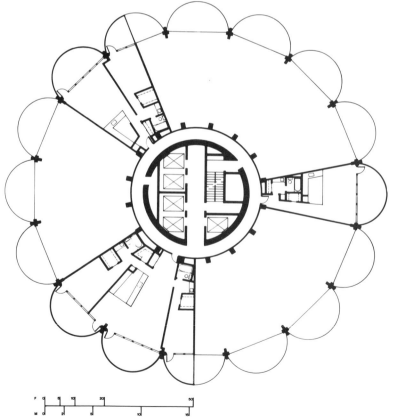

whale," this swollen building, practically windowless although it is completely sheathed in glass, brings the development of the curtain wall full circle.

Chicago after Mies   It is not surprising that Chicago should have been the source of the new geometries that evolved primarily from structural rather than esthetic considerations. It was, after all, the city that gave birth to skyscraper construction and became the adopted home of Mies van der Rohe. Chicago architects in general were uncomfortable with the permissive fashions that engaged the attention of much of the country during these decades, and the presence of Bertram Goldberg, Fazlur Kahn, Myron Goldsmith, and other disciples of Mies was insurance against the Chicago tradition being overturned by any merely cosmetic style.

Faithfulness to structural ethics yielded several remarkable buildings by Bertram Goldberg. Once a student of Mies, in practice Goldberg found both more freedom and more logic in reinforced concrete than in steel. However outwardly rhapsodic, his designs are in essence rigorously controlled by engineering and cost factors. In Chicago three of the most important designs employ curved forms in concrete: Marina City (1961–63), the Raymond Hilliard Housing (1964–66), and the Prentice Women's Hospital (1970–75).

The Marina City complex is dominated by twin sixty-story cylindrical towers. The lower third of each contains helical parking ramps, and the upper two-thirds consists of forty floors of apartments, divided on plan into sixteen petallike segments (326). The ramp and apartment floors are cantilevered from a central core with an outer ring of secondary supports; on the apartment floors curved balconies project from each segment. The splayed walls of the apartments are unconventional but suggest a joyous outward release of space. The use of formwork of molded plastic left the concrete surfaces smooth, requiring only a coat of paint. Goldberg made intensive use of the three-and-a-half-acre site: in addition to the apartment towers there are a ten-story office block and a theater (of markedly sculptural form) as well as a public skating rink, restaurant, and shops at a lower level and boat-docking facilities at the water's edge. It was no small achievement to have dramatized a neglected river, realized an intensely urban design, and demonstrated a viable alternative to the steel frame of Chicago tradition.

What might at first sight seem arbitrary in the Hilliard Housing is justified by economical structural forms that have the advantage of creating interior spaces as well (327). The curved segments of the bearing walls of these four high-rise apartment buildings—two cir-

327
Raymond Hilliard Housing, Chicago, Illinois. Bertram Goldberg Associates, 1964–66. Exterior.

cular towers for the elderly and two crescent-shaped ones for families—were chosen for their strength and the oval windows for minimum stress in puncturing the walls. With the use of slip forms, concrete was poured at the rate of one vertical foot an hour. Technology and economics, Mies's determinants, set the design for the un-Miesian end result. Washington officials initially objected to Goldberg's proposal as being too good for the poor; bleak and regimented designs had become the accepted standard in public housing.

The Prentice Women's Hospital, with its giant quatrefoil of nursing wards billowing out nearly fifty feet beyond a central mastlike support, is equally vulnerable to misjudgment as a mere tour de force, but it too demonstrates Goldberg's belief in the efficiency of the circle. Liberation from the right angle came as a corollary of Goldberg's search for optimal structure and useful space in one form.

An upswing in the construction of 'tall buildings starting in the sixties produced skyscrapers rising well beyond the thirty- to forty-story height set as the economical limit for the rigid frame, a basic idea initiated by William LeBaron Jenney. A jump to sixty to a hundred stories was facilitated by certain technological advances, and made the added stories economically feasible. The Chicago office of Skidmore, Owings & Merrill developed new structural systems for very tall buildings by using the tubular concept, applicable to reinforced concrete as well as steel. Recognizing that the horizontal stress caused by wind is the decisive factor rather than the vertical load, this concept regards the tall building as a cantilevered tube anchored in the ground. By allocating the major structural role to the periphery, interiors could be free of columns and transverse shear walls, with substantial cost savings. Often the inner service core is treated as a structural tube as well so that the whole building becomes a tube within a tube. Early examples of this, both in reinforced concrete, are Saarinen's CBS Building and the Brunswick Building in Chicago (1966) by the local office of Skidmore, Owings & Merrill, with Myron Goldsmith in charge. In both, the closely spaced mullions are structural; the visual result is a dense surface grid rather than a linear framework merely holding the glass in place.

This transfer of the structure to the surface of the building is obvious in the John Hancock Center in Chicago with its huge X-pattern of bracing, recalling the wall trusses of Mies van der Rohe's Chicago Convention Center project (328). In the age of Jenney, skyscrapers had been stiffened with knee bracing and cross bracing, but these were always hidden from view. In the Hancock Center the diagonal geometry essential to stability forms a rigid tube structure to resist the wind. The tapering profile resulted from a program requiring a lesser volume of apartments above a greater volume of offices, shops and parking. Like Marina City, the multiple-function Hancock Center is in effect a small town, a place to live and work, with commercial and recreational facilities within the city. Completed in 1968, it was designed by Bruce Graham of Skidmore, Owings & Merrill, with Fazlur Kahn as the structural engineer.

The same designers were responsible for the Sears Tower in Chicago, completed in 1976 (329). Rising 1,450 feet, this is the world's tallest structure, 100 feet taller than the twin towers of the World Trade Center in New York by Minoru Yamasaki and Associates and more than 300 feet higher than the Hancock Center. The tubular concept was repeated: nine structural tubes, each 75 feet square in plan, are bundled together and terminate at various levels; only two rise to the building's full height. The staggered silhouette recalls Adler and Sullivan's proposal for the Fraternity Temple; the building as a whole bears a striking resemblance to a visionary skyscraper for Moscow projected by the Russian Constructivist architect Lopatin in 1923.

Meanwhile the Chicago office of Skidmore, Owings & Merrill was experimenting with the suspension principle. The central building for Baxter Laboratories in Deerfield, Illinois (1976), was the result. The designers, again Graham and Kahn, suspended the entire roof of a double-square building (144 by 288 feet) with cables hung from two masts, one in the center of each square. Additional cables placed inside the building and along the periphery prevent any twisting or

328
*John Hancock Center,
Chicago, Illinois. Skid-
more, Owings & Merrill,
1966–68. Exterior.*

329
Sears Tower, Chicago, Illinois. Skidmore, Owings & Merrill, 1974–76. Aerial view.

330
*Federal Reserve Bank
Building, Minneapolis,
Minnesota. Gunnar Birk-
erts, 1968–72. Exterior.*

deflection of the roof—a crucial consideration because excessive movement would crack the aluminum and glass curtain wall.

The suspension principle, common in long-span bridges, was rarely justified in architecture but on occasion was used for a theatrical effect, as the Minneapolis Federal Reserve Bank Building (1968–72) shows (330). To meet the requirement of a column-free basement, Gunnar Birkerts suspended the ten-story office building from two inverted catenary arches, constructed of cables and welded steel plates. The arches drop downward from a pair of concrete towers spaced 275 feet apart and braced from toppling inward by a deep truss at roof level. The complicated structural relationships are summarized on the facade, with the mirrored glass set on the inner face of the mullion within the curve and on the outer face elsewhere. The play of light and shadow on this detail makes for a facade that is photogenic, certainly, but its self-consciousness and scale prevent it from harmonizing with its neighbors.

Glazed Atriums

In the standard histories of modern architecture, Peter Behrens and his German factory buildings are credited with advancing straightforward design, and emphasizing structural clarity and spacious, transparent enclosures. Behrens's American counterpart in this respect is Albert Kahn. Kahn's factories, such as the much admired Dodge Half-Ton Truck Plant in Detroit (1938), however, were regarded as having a special drama too categorical to be assimilated into architecture proper. But this changed. Starting rather timidly in the early work of Yamasaki, skylighted spaces were revived when the client's program allowed for such extravagances. These spaces recalled not only the factory esthetic but also light courts in office buildings before the days of electricity and Victorian greenhouses. Architects had long admired Paxton's Crystal Palace, and the sheltered *gallerie* of Italy still proved their worth as urban amenities; the Providence Arcade Building (1828) and the Cleveland Arcade (1890) are surviving American examples of the latter. In this spirit Johnson and Burgee attached a skylighted concourse to their IDS Tower in Minneapolis, linking shops and a hotel and thereby providing an impressive retreat from Minnesota winters. Earlier, in 1967, John Portman revolutionized hotel design by providing the Hyatt Regency Hotel in Atlanta with an immensely high skylighted lobby or atrium with shops and restaurants, which, though completely enclosed and air-conditioned, suggests an open-air plaza. Portman successfully followed the same formula in his other Hyatt hotels, one at the Chicago O'Hare Airport (1971) and another in San Francisco (1974). In Harvard's Gund Hall by John Andrews (1968–

331
Gund Hall, Harvard University, Cambridge, Massachusetts. John Andrews, 1968–72. Exterior.

72), a saw-tooth, factory-type roof is carried by deep tubular trusses to shelter four hundred design students (331). Ten times as many people will congregate in the star-shaped Crystal Cathedral for the Garden Grove Community Church in California (1978–80), by Philip Johnson and John Burgee. This space-frame structure entirely enclosed with glass recalls the proposals of another German pioneer, Bruno Taut.

A revival of the Victorian obsession with horticulture made its contribution. The Ford Foundation in New York (1963) is an L-shaped building fitted to a vertical greenhouse planted with tall trees around a tiny pool, which most of the offices overlook. Roche and Dinkeloo were the architects, Dan Kiley the landscape architect. With more commercial interests in mind, Cesar Pelli's Rainbow Center Mall and Winter Garden in Niagara Falls, New York (1976–78), successfully combines shopping with botanical pleasures. An earlier design, the Commons-Courthouse Center for Columbus, Indiana (1974), also by Cesar Pelli for Gruen Associates, prepared the way.[2]

The Le Corbusier Revival

The evidence of geometry is everywhere in Le Corbusier's work, in plans and elevations, in the composition of forms and the spaces within. The late sixties saw the beginning of what amounted to a revival of the earlier *style Corbu*, inspired by his poetic handling of space in his two masterpieces of the late twenties, the Stein House at Garches and the Villa Savoye at Poissy. At the center of this revival was a mandarin group of young, New York-based architects, which included Peter Eisenman, Charles Gwathmey, and Richard

332
House in Old Westbury,
Long Island, New York.
Richard Meier & Associ-
ates, 1971. Exterior.

Meier. Of these Eisenman was the most provocative, independent, and theoretical; Gwathmey was the most ingratiating and the least theoretical; Meier's work came closest to the spirit of Le Corbusier's buildings of the twenties. Meier consciously repeated the master with his white-painted geometrical forms poignantly contrasting with the green surroundings, his grid system of columns that freely interrupted the open plan or sometimes raised the house above the ground, and his two-story living space with interior balconies. In a house by Meier at Old Westbury, Long Island (1971), the nautical forms, the ramps, and the circular stair of the Villa Savoye all reappear, together with a comparable serenity and precision (332). The absence of domesticity is compensated by the satisfactions of a distilled, pure-white construction, meticulously executed, forming an abstract sculpture of space.

Similar sharp edges and unbroken planes characterize the houses of Charles Gwathmey, but his designs are less indebted to Le Corbusier. His use of an oblique plane set at a 45-degree angle and a half-circle are more likely to establish spatial measure than a grid of structural supports. Gwathmey's frequent use of natural cedar siding and slate floor paving recalls Breuer's similar choice of materials in the late forties. Yet Gwathmey's way of cutting into an overall geometrical form to create space, as seen in his residence and nearby studio built at Amagansett, New York (1965–68), is clearly derived from Le Corbusier.

The minimalist tendencies in Meier and Gwathmey are more pronounced in Eisenman. More important, the theoretical character of his work, mostly small houses, results from a proportional system that in application severely limits the functional ordering of spaces. Instead of comfort or convenience, Eisenman offers delight in a cerebral esthetic order; unlike Palladio, he disdains to reconcile geometry and proportion with human needs.

Netsch and Pei

The most ambitious combination of theory and geometry ever attempted by a modern architect was proposed by Walter Netsch of the Chicago office of Skidmore, Owings & Merrill. He called it "field theory." Its objective was an arrangement of spaces more varied than those obtained with a conventional grid pattern, yet still compact. Characteristic of field-theory plans is the unit of a square rotated 45 degrees to form a star-shaped module. A repetition of such modules, each with its own subdivisions, yields designs of intense formal complexity, as seen in the Behavioral Science Center (1968–70) and other buildings on the Chicago Circle Campus of the University of Illinois (333). Outwardly these designs retain the fascination of snowflake patterns; indoors, for all the claims of efficiency and flexibility made for the field-theory system, substantial problems of orientation arise from introverted mazes of angular rooms and oblique corridor intersections. Netsch's field theory, with its controlled system of spaces, was one of the results of a widespread quest for a more emphatic and permanent shaping of space, a quest begun in the fifties by Louis Kahn.

The triangulations, knife edges, and opaque, skylighted forms of the Chicago Circle Campus buildings were found elsewhere in the designs of others, though without Netsch's rigorous geometry. An example is the East Building of the National Gallery of Art in Washington, D.C. (1974–78), by I. M. Pei who, in the balance between intellect and imagination ever present in architecture, leaned towards the latter (334). Pei elaborated on the trapezoidal site set by L'Enfant's city plan by designing a fluid and poetic geometry of pale pink marble triangles to counterpoint the static, classical form of John Russell Pope's building. The result displays all the reserve and urbanity that had long been characteristic of Pei's work, heeding as he does the caution that "strength is born of restraint and dies in freedom"; yet the central, three-story triangular lobby achieves a spatial animation that is rare in his work. Outside, as well as within, the building is sheathed in marble, fastidiously detailed, to achieve some degree of harmony with its neighbors on the Mall, although its success in this regard is counterbalanced by a sculptural assertiveness that—as in Wright's Guggenheim—is something of a threat to the modern art it was designed to contain.

333
*Behavioral Science
Center, Circle Campus,
University of Illinois,
Chicago, Illinois. Skid-
more, Owings & Merrill,
1968–70. Aerial view.*

334
*East Building, National
Gallery of Art, Washing-
ton, District of Columbia.
I. M. Pei and Partners,
1974–78. Exterior.*

335
Christian Science Center,
Boston, Massachusetts.
I. M. Pei and Partners,
1968–74. Exterior.

Much of Pei's success derives from his ability to design in the urban context and within limits of economic investment. Many of his earlier large schemes were done in association with William Zeckendorf, president of the real estate firm of Webb and Knapp. Among them are Mile High Center in Denver (1955), Place Ville Marie in Montreal (completed 1961), Kips Bay Plaza in New York City (1960), and Society Hill Towers in Philadelphia (1964). In all of these Pei adopted the clear forms and site planning of Mies van der Rohe and applied the lessons of Rockefeller Center. For apartment buildings he developed a reinforced concrete exterior wall with relatively narrow window openings that eliminate the need for submullions. The most ceremonial of all his designs is the Christian Science Center, completed in 1974, a major urban renewal project for Back Bay in Boston (335). Here Pei turned from the reductionism of Mies to the massive, sculptural presence of Le Corbusier's late buildings, the High Courts Building at Chandigarh in particular. The colonnaded structure connecting the Mother Church (1894 and 1904) with new administrative buildings forms an architectural boundary to a vast, rectangular reflecting pool that terminates in a giant circular fountain. The controlled bravura of Pei's conception injects an alien character into the Boston cityscape, unexpected but welcome.

Pei's work, like Johnson's, cannot be identified by a single stylistic label: it is neither avant-garde in a doctrinaire manner nor impulsive in a personal one. He has advanced with measured and adroitly placed steps, making intelligent use of others' work, not only of Mies but also, in the National Center for Atmospheric Research near Boulder, Colorado (1964–66), of Kahn's.

Post-Modern
Architecture

Time will tell whether the architecture of the sixties and seventies is a transformation of the themes of the twenties or whether entirely new developments have supplanted a moribund International Style. Certainly post-modern architecture, as it has been called, is diverse; it ranges from reactionary, which includes an extraordinary reappearance of the arbitrary geometry of Beaux-Arts composition, once the *bête noire* of modernists, to radical.

Clarity of an overall *parti* and firmness of volumes are Beaux-Arts qualities well suited to large-scale commissions and bring focus to diverse requirements. In the work of Saarinen's former associates, Kevin Roche and John Dinkeloo, these qualities were joined with regularity of structure. An example is the Richard C. Lee High School in New Haven (1967). Conceptually it is the exact opposite of the dispersed, fingerlike school plans first seen in the forties, such as those by Ernest Kump in California, in which the various functions were clearly articulated. Roche and Dinkeloo's school is compact and formal, with four large square modules of classroom clusters separated by Greek-cross corridors and an entrance in the center of each side of the overall square plan. Ceremonial axes and powerful shadows created by overhangs, together with rough concrete surfaces, contribute to an intensely formidable character. Although the school has the diagrammatic clarity of a Beaux-Arts solution, there is none of the use of appropriate detail to give it scale that Beaux-Arts theory required.

The effect is livelier in Roche and Dinkeloo's Knights of Columbus Building and Veterans Memorial Coliseum in New Haven, designed as a complementary pair and begun in 1965. In both, structure is paraded in a self-conscious way. (In Goldberg's buildings the outward appearance of the structure, however flamboyant, is a byproduct of economy and efficiency). It is apparent that in designing the twenty-three-story Knights of Columbus tower Roche and Dinkeloo had more of an eye than a mind for structure, which can be taken in a glance by the speeding motorist on the highway: four cylindrical corner legs of concrete sheathed in purplish-brown tile support visible girders of Cor-Ten steel, which darkens to a similar color (336).[3] The corner "silos" contain stairs and toilets and function as supports; the center elevator core is also structural. The adjacent Coliseum is more successful because, by its very complication, the structure enriches the design. Eighteen 70-foot-high rectangular concrete piers are arranged in a double row to support four levels of parking constructed of open-work trusses, also in Cor-Ten steel (337). This parking element forms a giant roof over the arena and the services below. Two circular auto ramps provide access to the parking levels. The greater forcefulness of the Coliseum points up the affected simplicity of the Knights of Columbus Building. In both buildings there is something that reminds us of Mies's last designs as well as his practice of arranging buildings in groups.

Roche and Dinkeloo's tendency toward the ostentatiously dramatic was reinforced by the search for a distinctive corporate image for the headquarters of the College Life Insurance Company in Indianapolis, Indiana (1967–71). Like their Knights of Columbus Building in New Haven, it seems to be designed for the passing motorist (338). Three identical office buildings, each square in plan and ten stories high, are formed by two adjacent vertical stone walls and two sloping greenhouse walls of blue reflecting glass. These deformed pyramids, half glass, half wall, linked by bridges and underground passages, are aligned on a skew and will eventually be complemented by six

336
*Knights of Columbus,
New Haven, Connecticut.
Kevin Roche, John Dinke-
loo & Associates, 1965–
69. Exterior.*

337
Veterans Memorial Coliseum, New Haven, Connecticut. Kevin Roche, John Dinkeloo & Associates, 1965–72. Exterior detail.

338
*College Life Insurance
Company, Indianapolis,
Indiana. Kevin Roche,
John Dinkeloo & Associ-
ates, 1967–71. Exterior.*

others to form a three-by-three grid. Such mute and wholly abstract geometry, with the highest refinement in detail and execution although uncommunicative and seemingly uninhabited, has been a major theme in Roche and Dinkeloo's architecture.

Louis Kahn

The greatest architect to appear since the mid-1900s was Louis I. Kahn. Already fifty when he was given the commission for his first major building, the Yale University Art Gallery (1951–63), he soon became a hero to a younger generation of architects, many still in school.[4] Curiously, his views were conservative. Believing that architecture was an art—a sore point with the Bauhaus-trained generation—he impressed upon his work strong, essential forms, arranged in an almost Renaissance manner but more vigorously rhythmical in the final result. He presented anew the timeless architectural elements of column, wall, beam, and truss. Most of Kahn's conceptions were expansive in nature. He was as eager to design cities as buildings, as his inventive redesign of historic Philadelphia, his home city, shows. But to see Kahn's largest and most awesome works one must travel abroad: to Bangladesh for his government buildings in the capital city of Dacca and to India for those at Ahmedabad.

Kahn's major buildings, crowded into scarcely more than a dozen years—he died in 1974—form a lucid and complete statement of his architectural theory, which is remarkable because of his apparent lack of a consistent approach to design before 1950. He had been both a student and employee of Paul Cret and, by temperament, was unsympathetic to the tenets of the International Style. The open, flowing plan did not interest him. Instead he sought well-ordered and defined spaces, proposing containment and separation of volumes and reasserting the wall and pier to achieve these ends. He favored definition and weight over fluidity and transparency. His plans, always more expressive than his elevations—as were those of the Beaux-Arts architects—were composed of additive spatial units, often axially arranged. Although he was not committed to axiality as such, every building of Kahn's is rooted in axis and geometrical form. Although he did not attend the Ecole, his work is in the tradition of Durand, Choisy, and Guadet, whose expository treatises guided an earlier age of discipline.

Kahn swept aside the accretions of modernism and asked simply: What does the building want to be? His design for the Richards Medical Research and Biology Buildings at the University of Pennsylvania (1957–61) was his answer to this basic question (339, 340). The building consists of six separate but linked towers, each floor limited to a 47-foot square to retain the intimacy of a laboratory workspace. Dominating the composition are windowless brick towers, some of them nostrils for the intake and exhaust of air and others for stairways, which cluster around the sides of the laboratories and rise above their roofline. They look like supports, but in reality the structure is a less obvious precast concrete skeleton with complicated Vierendeel trusses, arranged so that the corners are open and without support. Kahn called his giant brick tubes "servant spaces." In his wish to separate and articulate function he necessarily discarded the simple envelope and surface unity. Paradoxically his elementary question produced answers that were, esthetically, visually assertive rather than minimal. Although picturesque effect was not what he sought, the Richards Medical Research and Biology Buildings present an animated group of towers on the skyline. For those ready for a change, this richness of form articulated with such authority was particularly welcome. Kahn's work, as this building predicted, was to be quite different in kind from what all others had done before, despite his conservative bias.

At the Salk Institute of Biological Studies at La Jolla, California (1959–65), Kahn had an opportunity to express his ceremonial predilections, which had been inhibited by the limited site on the Philadelphia campus (341). Again he chose differentiated architectural forms to express different functions: access, research work, and study. The parallel pair of large laboratory buildings is augmented by a bold file of projecting stair towers on the outer flanks and a rhythmic series of individual studies for scientists on the courtyard side. Kahn repeated the reinforced concrete frame and Vierendeel truss of his Philadelphia laboratory—August Komendant was the structural engineer for both buildings—but here the long-span and thus story-high trusses more easily accommodate the numerous ducts and services in their ample openings. (Kahn preferred concrete and after 1950 never used a steel frame.) For all the openness that the site on a bluff overlooking the Pacific allowed, he kept the plan symmetrical. The wide, travertine-paved courtyard between the laboratories suggests the nave of a roofless church: serene, ceremonial, and timeless. Its axis is marked by a slot of water in the paving, streaming towards a magnificently simple fountain at the seaward end.

A laboratory, however, did not lend itself to the full realization of the poetic quality that Kahn could achieve in interior spaces, interweaving elements of structure and light; Kahn believed that "structure is the maker of light." This special quality can be seen in the First Unitarian Church in Rochester, New York (1956–64), and

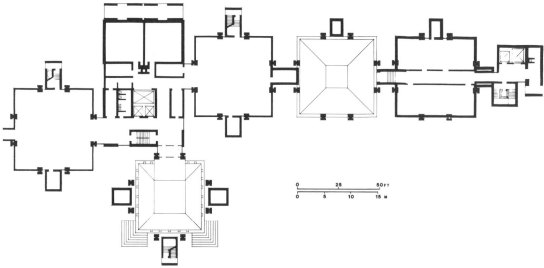

339
Richards Medical Research and Biology Buildings, University of Pennsylvania, Philadelphia, Pennsylvania. Louis I. Kahn, 1957–61. Exterior.

340
Richards Medical Research and Biology Buildings, Philadelphia, Pennsylvania. Plan.

341
Salk Institute of Biological Studies, La Jolla, California. Louis I. Kahn, 1959–65. Central courtyard.

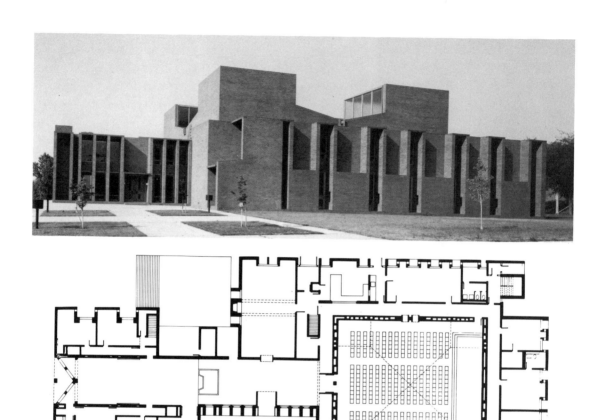

342
*First Unitarian Church,
Rochester, New York.
Louis I. Kahn, 1959–64.
Exterior.*

343
*First Unitarian Church,
Rochester, New York.
Plan.*

the Kimbell Art Museum in Fort Worth, Texas (1967–72). The meeting room of the church is a stern and frugal cubelike space that would satisfy any Gothic revivalist's call for "truth" (342, 343). Devoid of trivia and any kind of distracting element, meticulously detailed though never sleek, its space extends upward in the corners, in which partially concealed clerestories provide the only source of light. The inverted, keellike ceiling of concrete, a cross in plan, is supported by a concrete column at the center of each side. The meeting room is double-walled by cinder block with discrete slots to provide for the circulation of air; its cool gray interior suggests a Cistercian rigor or the spirit of the American Quakers. Around it Kahn has placed the "servant spaces" of classrooms, offices, and a library, with outer walls folded inward at intervals to sustain the introverted nature of the design.

Kahn's art is infused with a meditative quality that is an extension of his own introspective personality. His buildings are tranquil and resolute. They often unexpectedly mix traditional compliance with radical assertiveness. The library of Phillips Exeter Academy in New Hampshire (1967–72) is a case in point. Without esthetic injury to older campus buildings, Kahn designed a well-mannered cubic form with chamfered edges and identical elevations. The library's outer structure, simple but handsome red brick bearing walls with piers that grow progressively narrower as they rise and windows spanned by flat voussoired arches that grow progressively wider (recalling the identical structural logic of Richardson's Marshall Field Wholesale Store), is married to an inner structure of bare reinforced concrete. The central court, skylighted and six levels high, is framed by four walls, each pierced with a single, huge circular opening revealing bookstacks behind (344). The usual bland and bureaucratic quality of libraries is not evident here, and one instinctively grasps Kahn's purpose: to express the stimulation and intimacy of learning from books. Ascending the levels one discovers study spaces arranged around the periphery, with a coziness reminiscent of window seats in Shingle Style houses, and an inner ring of bookstacks conveniently near. Kahn's combination of the heroic and the humane is a rare achievement.

A measure of the admiration so quickly accorded Kahn by his peers is his influence on their work. The Boston Public Library Annex designed by Johnson and Burgee (1965–73) derives its plan and forms from Kahn. The bisymmetrical plan of nine equal squares divided by squared clusters of supports enlarges upon Kahn's Bath House for the Jewish Community Center at Trenton, New Jersey (1956), in which Kahn first effected the separation between the served

344
*Library, Phillips Exeter
Academy, Exeter, New
Hampshire. Louis I.
Kahn, 1967–72. Interior.*

345
Kimbell Art Museum,
Fort Worth, Texas. Louis
I. Kahn, 1967–72.
Interior.

and servant spaces. The segmental arched forms of Johnson's elevations, sheathed in granite, recall Kahn's governmental buildings in Ahmedabad, which are in structural brick.

Kahn's warmth and reverence toward culture—he had once considered becoming a concert violinist—is nowhere more strongly sensed than in the Kimbell Art Museum in Fort Worth, Texas (345). Here Kahn was inspired by Roman vaulting to use a vaultlike reinforced concrete beam, which needed support only at the ends of its 100-foot length. These cycloid-curved vaults are arranged in parallel rows in sets of three and form the entire structure of the building. Each vault section is slotted to admit natural light, which then is evenly distributed by reflective baffles. The visual harmony of light and structure combined with a sense of permanence appropriate to its function makes the Kimbell Art Museum perhaps the most quietly satisfying museum ever built.

Kahn's buildings epitomize the major shift in contemporary architecture toward geometrical order and the celebration of the wall after many decades of ascendancy of the metal skeleton. Even more important, he reaffirmed the architect as an artist—a position taken by Richardson, Sullivan, Wright, and Mies van der Rohe. Kahn recognized that "the architect builds primarily not for need but for Art. Art is the only language of Man."

Notes

Foreword 1. W. F. Deknatel, quoted by B. Zevi, *Towards an Organic Architecture* (London: Faber & Faber, 1950), p. 126.

1 1. Forman, *The Architecture of the Old South*, p. 28.

2. In the English colonies piazza (Italian for an open space or square in a town) was the common designation of any kind of porch—in the South it still is. This was a result of Inigo Jones's giving to the great square he planned for the Earl of Bedford in 1631 the name of Covent Garden Piazza. Londoners transferred the outlandish new term from the square to what was for them the most novel feature of the development, the arcaded walks under the houses bounding it on two sides.

3. The *galerie* seems to have come into general use in the 1740s. In 1751 the plantation owner Jean de Pradel wrote to his brothers in France of his new house, Monplaisir: "It will be one hundred and sixteen feet in length by forty-eight in width, including the galleries which will surround the house. What a great convenience these galleries are in this country!"

4. See J. Evans, *Monastic Architecture in France from the Renaissance to the Revolution* (Cambridge: Cambridge University Press, 1964), figs. 388, 390, 541. The resemblance between the stair at New Orleans and the one at Auberive is striking but can only be coincidental, since the former was retained from the building of 1727–34 and Auberive was not built until circa 1750.

5. The resemblance was more marked before 1847, when the balustrades over the cornices of the Cabildo and Presbytère were removed and mansard roofs added.

2 1. J. A. Baird, Jr., *The Churches of Mexico 1530–1810* (Berkeley and Los Angeles: University of California Press, 1962), p. 5.

2. The present woodwork of the *portal* dates from a restoration in 1909.

3. When the friar's house was in the usual position its flat roof could be used as a halfway platform for hoisting the materials for the roof of the church.

4. In 1776, when Fray Dominguez visited and reported on the church, there were three windows in the south wall.

5. Today the effect can still be experienced at Isleta, Trampas, and Ranchos de Taos. Most transverse clerestories have been blocked up at one time or another because of their tendency to leak.

6. The *presidio* church of San Miguel, Santa Fe, is one of the few with eastern sanctuaries; the church at Pecos was another.

7. The *retablo* is dated 1780 in an inscription on the back; the decoration of the walls of the sanctuary is presumably coeval. The murals in the nave must be much later. Similar but less extensive paintings in the nave at Acoma were whitewashed over circa 1970.

8. H. de la Croix, *Military Considerations in City Planning: Fortifications* (New York: Braziller, 1972), p. 44.

9. The churches of the other two missions near San Antonio, San Francisco de la Espada and San Juan Capistrano, have been too thoroughly reconstructed to count as eighteenth-century buildings. The Moorish arch of the

doorway of San Francisco is not without interest, although its voussoirs were "incorrectly reassembled in a restoration." P. Goeldner, *Texas Catalog: Historic American Buildings Survey* (San Antonio: Trinity University Press, 1976), p. 193.

10. For example, the *portadas* of La Valenciana near Guanajuato and of the parish church of Lagos de Moreno in Jalisco; see Baird, *The Churches of Mexico 1530–1810,* plates 153 and 146.

11. It was rebuilt once before, incorrectly, in 1884.

3 1. The best brief account of these books is in R. Wittkower, *Palladio and Palladianism* (New York: George Braziller, 1974), chapter 7.

2. The area had been settled in the seventeenth century by planters from Barbados.

3. For what it really was, see Wittkower, *Palladio and Palladianism,* pp. 79–85.

4. The plan of Coleshill must have crossed the Atlantic be some other means than a book, for it was not published in one until 1771, when it appeared in the continuation of *Vitruvius Britannicus* by J. Woolfe and J. Gandon.

4 1. The portico was not built until 1785–87, and then of wood instead of stone; Harrison's design is said to have been followed faithfully. The balustrade was originally continued around the roof of the nave.

2. The Swanenburch House, Halfweg.

3. "The Capitol is a light and airy structure, with a portico in front of two orders, the lower of which, being Doric, is tolerably just in its proportions and ornaments, save only that the intercolonnations are too large. The upper is Ionic, much too small for that on which it is mounted, its ornaments not proper to the order, nor proportioned within themselves. It is crowned with a pediment, which is too high for its span." (*Notes on the State of Virginia,* p. 152).

4. A "penitentiary house" containing sixteen cells for solitary confinement was built to the rear of Smith's building in 1791

5. Mount Airy was gutted by fire in 1844.

6. The craftsmen who did the decorations in the dining room at Mount Vernon were Lamphier and Sears; they were probably from Philadelphia.

5 1. The detailed treatment of Monticello I was Palladian. The uninterrupted templelike roof between the pediments, its most Neo-Classical feature, had Anglo-Palladian precedent in Colen Campbell's Wanstead, built in 1715–20.

2. Jefferson may also have been influenced by seeing a painting by Hubert Robert ("Robert des Ruines"), *La Réunion des Plus Célèbres Monuments Antiques de la France,* with the Maison Carrée in the foreground, which was exhibited in the Salon du Louvre when he was in Paris in 1785.

3. In 1807 Bulfinch had rebuilt the spire of Old North, blown down in a gale three years before, reducing the total height of the steeple from 191 feet to 175 feet.

4. So called because the first operation with ether used as an anaesthetic was performed in it on October 6, 1846.

6   1. He won the Gold Medal at the Royal Academy Schools in 1781 and in 1790 received the first Travelling Scholarship in Architecture awarded by the Academy.

2. As in the Walnut Street Prison, Philadelphia.

3. When it was dedicated in 1821, Baltimore Cathedral lacked its portico, and its east end terminated in an apse, flanked by square rooms, abutting the piers under the dome. The present portico was completed in 1865 by Latrobe's son, John H. B. Latrobe, and the domed choir was added in 1890, in accordance with Latrobe's plan, which had been truncated for reasons of economy. (The choir being equal in length to the nave is one of the clearest evidences of the relationship to Wren's St. Paul's.) The onion domes on the belfries date from 1832 and were not designed by Latrobe.

4. H.-R. Hitchcock, *Architecture: Nineteenth and Twentieth Centuries*, p. 7.

5. The interior was altered radically in 1893.

6. He went first to London, where he spent seven years; his only building there, as well as another in which elements of a competition design by him were incorporated, has been destroyed. In 1827 he returned to France, where he ended his career as Architect of the Department of Mayenne.

7. Mills already had independent commissions when he joined Latrobe, and it was in connection with one of them that Latrobe wrote him a letter which contains a classic description of the situation of the professional architect in America at the time: "The profession of architecture has been hitherto in the hands of two sorts of men. The first, of those, who from travelling or from books have acquired some knowledge of the theory of the art, but know nothing of its practice; the second, of those who know nothing but the practice, and whose early life being spent in labor, and in the habits of a laborious life, have had no opportunity of acquiring the theory. The complaisance of these two sets of men to each other, renders it difficult for the Architect to get in between them, for the building mechanic finds his account in the ignorance of the *Gentleman-architect*, as the latter does in the submissive deportment which interest dictates to the former" (T. F. Hamlin, *Benjamin Henry Latrobe*, p. 586).

7   1. Under the head of curvature, only the entasis of the columns of the Parthenon had yet been observed, for the first time in 1810; their inclination—inward, so that their vertical axes meet about a mile above the earth's surface—went unnoticed until 1829, and the curvature of the stylobate and entablature until 1837.

2. An explanation is offered by R. G. Carrott, *The Egyptian Revival*, pp. 120–21.

8   1. Assuming that the traditional but apparently undocumented attribution is correct.

2. In the history of architecture as an art, that is. Upjohn also has an important place in the history of the architectural profession. In his office on February 23, 1857, the meeting that led to the founding of The American Institute of Architects was held. Including Upjohn and his son Richard M. Upjohn, fourteen architects were present; twelve more were invited to subsequent meetings, and the institute was incorporated two months later. Upjohn was President of the AIA for its first eighteen years.

3. The most important nineteenth-century technical innovation in building in wood, the balloon frame, was first used for St. Mary's Church, Chicago, by the Connecticut architect and builder A. D. Taylor in 1833. It was unknown in the East until the end of the fifties, when it was described first in a New York newspaper in 1857 and then, with illustrations, in *Carpentry Made Easy* by William Bell (Philadelphia, 1858). In the sixties it was called "Chicago construction." It would be hard to exaggerate the importance of the part that the balloon frame, which required only know-how (as distinct from skill) and lent itself to the prefabrication of buildings, played in the westward movement and the urbanization of the Middle West. But its effect on architectural design was negligible.

4. The first iron-fronted building in America was erected on Washington Street, Boston, in 1842 by Daniel Badger. The Miners' Bank at Pottsville, Pennsylvania, built in 1829 to Haviland's design, was a masonry structure faced with iron plates, like the Narva Triumphal Arch in St. Petersburg, which was completed in 1816, the year in which Haviland left Russia for America. Russia was a leader in iron technology; there was an all-iron house in St. Petersburg by 1765, when it was visited by Casanova (Giacomo Casanova, *History of My Life*, translated and edited by W. R. Trask (New York: Harcourt, Brace & World, 1966–71), X, p. 132). The earliest known iron columns in America are (as already noted) in Christ Church, Washington, completed to Latrobe's design in 1808; in 1820 Strickland used iron columns in the Chestnut Street Theatre, Philadelphia. The first iron roof was also, it would seem, due to Latrobe, who covered Nassau Hall, Princeton, with one in 1803 when he renovated the building after a fire. Iron was also used for fire-proofing. A building in which it proved its worth for this purpose was Mills's Record Office in Charleston, whose window frames, sashes, and shutters of iron, combined with the brick vaults supporting the floors and the copper sheathing of the wooden roof structure, enabled it to survive the fire at the beginning of the Civil War.

9 1. Owen Jones published two volumes on the Alhambra (1842 and 1845) before his *Grammar of Ornament* (1856). In 1850–51 he served as color consultant for Paxton's Crystal Palace, whose supports and girders were painted red, yellow, and pale blue.

2. Ruskin's architectural Lamp of Truth did "not admit iron as a constructive material," although, like other mid-Victorians, Ruskin vaguely prophesied "the time is probably near when a new system of architectural laws will be developed, adapted entirely to metallic construction."

3. Charles Eliot Norton, a key member of the building committee, was the first professor of fine art at Harvard (1875–98), just as Ruskin, whom Norton knew well, had been at Oxford. Norton's belief in the idea of collegiate architecture as an influence on youth has its parallel in Jefferson's thoughts in designing the University of Virginia. Despite the enduring effects of architecture, the selected competitors for Memorial Hall were given only twenty-five days in which to prepare their designs. Norton, without giving specific reasons, did not like the final building. Wight and Russell Sturgis would have been more sympathetic architects, but then they were not graduates of Harvard College.

4. Later, in 1864, William Robert Ware opened an *atelier* of his own in Boston. The following year he was asked to form an architectural department at MIT. Actual instruction did not begin until 1868, in Rogers Hall in Boston. The second school of architecture was founded at the University of Illinois in 1867. Subsequently schools were established at Cornell in 1871, Syracuse in 1873, Michigan in 1876, and Columbia in 1880, the last also under Ware.

5. Durand, professor of architecture at the Paris Ecole Polytechnique, published two volumes summarizing French theory and practice (1802–1805). His emphasis on repetition of elements forced a joint clarity of plans and elevations.

10

1. The term skyscraper first appeared in print in 1890: "A new system has found much favor here, and is being generally followed now in the construction of mammoth buildings known as 'Sky-scrapers,' which has given Chicago a new celebrity." John J. Flinn, *Chicago: A History, an Encyclopedia and a Guide*, p. 129.

2. The firm name Burnham and Root was not changed until 1894 when it became D. H. Burnham and Co., which it remained until Burnham's death in 1912. In his *Autobiography* Wright tells of Burnham's offer to him of an expense-paid Beaux-Arts training, which Wright refused.

3. Raft foundations proved unreliable. Portions of the Monadnock have settled more than twenty inches. Today's practice is to sink concrete caissons down to bedrock, which in Chicago lies more than 100 feet below ground level. The first use of caissons in Chicago building was under the west party wall of the Chicago Stock Exchange, completed in 1894. William Sooy Smith was the engineer; Adler and Sullivan were the architects. Pneumatic caissons were first developed by English and French engineers in the mid-nineteenth century.

4. The first use of terra-cotta for sheathing a facade was in 1889–90 in Burnham and Root's second Rand McNally Building. It soon became popular for tall buildings everywhere, the Woolworth Building in New York being the largest example.

5. Interior courts were frequent delights in nineteenth-century buildings of all sorts. Some examples are the Palace Hotel in San Francisco (1874–75), the second John Shillito Store in Cincinnati (1878), the Old Pension Building in Washington, D.C. (1883), the thirteen-story Chamber of Commerce Building in Chicago (1888–89), the Brown Palace Hotel in Denver (1892), and the Bradbury Building in Los Angeles (1893).

6. Even before the building was completed Adler and Sullivan moved into the tower, the loftiest office suite in Chicago at that time. Here Frank Lloyd Wright assisted Sullivan on the final decorative details of the Auditorium Building.

7. Holabird and Roche received the 1898 Gage commission for a trio of buildings on South Michigan Avenue, of eight, seven, and six stories. For the tallest, at the north, a millinery establishment, Sullivan was asked to design the facade, which included a four-foot band of translucent glass above the clear glass windows of each grouping to diffuse the glare for the benefit of close needlework. Sullivan's facade was increased in 1902 by the addition of four stories, which were according to the same design as the lower stories.

8. The first use of Chicago construction in New York was in the Tower Building by Bradford Gilbert (1888–89).

9. Prior to 1916 the building code of New York City merely limited the weight of a building on rock foundation to fifteen tons per square foot. On this basis it would have been theoretically possible to erect on a 200-foot square plot an office building 2,000 feet high.

11 1. To Wells it was "inconceivable . . . how any civilized architect [could] design in the Romanesque or Gothic styles." The story goes that Wells declined a partnership in the firm saying, with sly humor, that he could not with self-respect sign his name to such mediocre work. Wells served as a draftsman in the firm for ten years. He died in 1889.

2. The French educational model was so highly esteemed that in the following year McKim instigated plans for an architectural study center in Rome. After a trial, the American Academy was founded in 1898 to provide a graduate experience for architects, sculptors, and painters.

3. This vaulting method was introduced to America in 1881 with the arrival of the Spaniard Rafael Guastavino. He had perfected the traditional Catalan tile vault with an improved mortar, essential because the principle of adhesion rather than compression is the source of its strength. Tiles are laid in horizontal layers; centering is not required. McKim, Mead and White used Guastavino vaulting in the Boston Public Library, Madison Square Presbyterian Church, and the rebuilding of Jefferson's library at the University of Virginia.

4. Vaughan never returned to England. From his Boston base he continued to receive commissions for ecclesiastical work, notably St. Paul's School Chapel in Concord, New Hampshire, completed in 1888 (except for the tower), and the Cathedral Church of St. Peter and St. Paul in Washington, D.C., a joint commission received with Bodley in 1907. The cathedral was incomplete at the time of Vaughn's death in 1917 and remains so.

5. Cram was perhaps more the antiquarian than the modern medievalist he claimed to be. He was quite proud that the hammer-beam trusses of his Princeton dining hall had no hidden steel. He advocated, to no avail, Latin for the services in the Princeton chapel and boasted that on his estate he built a chapel first, a garage second.

6. Although never enunciated, there seems to have been an understood apportionment of styles to various sects. Gothic and Colonial were acceptable for Protestants of all types; earlier medieval styles, both Lombard and Tuscan, with a permitted touch of Byzantine, were principally for Roman Catholics; synagogues opted for Moorish and Byzantine combinations. Newer, freer cults were a problem. The Christian Scientists seemed to find most inspiration under a Pantheon-like dome.

12 1. Wright was born in 1867 but claimed 1869 in *An Autobiography*, published in 1943. The willful error is perpetuated on his grave marker at Spring Green, Wisconsin.

2. Wright had equal admiration for Dankmar Adler and went out of his way to make known the injustice of underrating Adler's contribution to the firm. (See "Recollections," 10 July 1940, letter from Wright to The Art Institute

of Chicago. Burnham Library, The Art Institute of Chicago.) Wright believed that Adler, not Sullivan, deserved the credit for the dictum form follows function.

3. Wright to Ashbee, 26 September 1910: "Do not say that I deny my love for Japanese art has influenced me—I admit that it has but claim to have digested it—"

4. The discipline of Wright's interlocking forms and geometrical massing has been traced to the Froebel "gifts." These were constructive games of maple blocks and colored papers to be arranged against a linear grid that encouraged an instinctive order in the creative act. See Grant Manson, "Wright in the Nursery: The Influence of Froebel Education on the Work of Frank Lloyd Wright," *Architectural Review* CXIII (June 1953): 114–123.

5. When Wright returned to the United States in 1911, he established himself at Spring Green and began to build Taliesin. He revived his architectural practice using a downtown Chicago office but this ended when he sailed for Japan in the winter of 1915–16 to begin work on the Imperial Hotel.

6. The West Coast, unlike the Midwest, was not given to pronouncements on architecture or essays in print. An exception is the modest book by Charles A. Keeler, *The Simple Home*, San Francisco, 1904. Illustrated were various Berkeley houses, including his own by Maybeck.

13 1. Louis Sullivan, "The Chicago Tribune Competition," *Architectural Record* LIII (February 1923): 151–157. Saarinen's proposal was not wholly new; his Helsinki Railroad Station, designed in 1904, incorporated a tower of similar design.

2. In the midst of the Depression most Americans could not afford a Streamline Moderne house, but they might content themselves with household items designed by Raymond Loewy, Russel Wright, Donald Deskey, and Henry Dreyfus.

3. A likely source for the PSFS Building is the Tagblatt Turm in Stuttgart (1927–28) by E. Otto Osswald, which was published in the February 1929 issue of *Architectural Record*.

4. The exhibition and the accompanying catalog did include Wright's work and that of other Americans because a numerical balance between Europeans and Americans was a condition of the museum trustees' approval.

5. A symptom of an impending academic phase of the modern movement was the founding in 1928 of the Congrès Internationaux d'Architecture Moderne (CIAM). Through its meetings and publications it began to codify the loose theories of the twenties.

14 1. Promontory Apartments was the first of numerous projects done in association with the developer Herbert Greenwald, whose dedication to Mies places him among the important patrons of modern architecture. He died in 1959 in a plane crash.

2. At a time when temperate glances backward were inadmissible, Johnson freely confessed in print a number of historical sources of inspiration for his glass house. See "House at New Canaan . . ." *Architectural Review* CVIII (September 1950): 152–160.

3. Mies van der Rohe, "Frank Lloyd Wright," 1940. An appreciation written for the unpublished catalog of the Frank Lloyd Wright Exhibition held at the Museum of Modern Art, New York. Reprinted in P. Johnson, *Mies van der Rohe* (New York, 1947): 195–196.

4. In 1913 Wright's son John recommended the sculptor Alfonso Iannelli as an assistant for the Midway Gardens project. Iannelli accepted Wright's offer, leaving San Diego, where he had been working with John Wright, and spent eight months in Chicago alongside of Richard W. Bock, who had previously done sculpture for Wright's Oak Park studio. Together they executed Wright's designs for sculptured figures and four large stair towers for Midway Gardens. Iannelli later regretted that he did not accept Wright's offer to continue with the Imperial Hotel project in Japan, but he did return to the Midwest to collaborate with Purcell and Elmslie and also with Barry Byrne.

5. Wright's solution for urban problems was to eliminate the city altogether by substituting a decentralized, agrarian society. His answer, Broadacre City, was first outlined in his book, *The Disappearing City* (William Farquhar Payson, 1932). A model of Broadacre City was exhibited at Rockefeller Center in New York in April 1935.

6. Knowing Wright's animosity and fearful of his wit, the American Institute of Architects, which Wright had dubbed the "Arbitrary Institute of Appearances," delayed awarding its Gold Medal to him until 1949.

7. The Ralph Jester House design was built in Arizona at Taliesin West in 1972 as a residence for Bruce Pfeiffer, archivist for the Frank Lloyd Wright Foundation. Concrete was substituted for the intended curved plywood walls.

15   1. "The Skyline," *New Yorker*, XXIII, October 11, 1947. Mumford's recognition of a Bay Region style was reinforced by a 1949 exhibition entitled "Domestic Architecture of the San Francisco Bay Region," held at the San Francisco Museum of Art.

2. The Eames House is one of a series that constituted the Case Study House program organized by John Entenza, editor of the Los Angeles-based *Arts and Architecture*. Between 1945 and 1962 the magazine acted as client in commissioning houses by such Californians as Pierre Koenig; Craig Ellwood; Buff, Straub and Hensman; and Killingsworth, Brady and Smith.

3. Saarinen was one of four jury members for the international competition of 1956 for the Sydney Opera House. Jorn Utzon's winning entry, while impractical structurally and functionally, was nonetheless chosen for its evocative image of billowing, saillike forms. Utzon's scheme may have influenced Saarinen, who was at work on the TWA design at the time. Yet Saarinen had long been interested in curvilinear shapes, as seen in his plastic shell chair of 1948, the Aspen music tent of 1949, and the St. Louis Jefferson Memorial Arch, designed in 1948 and completed in 1964.

4. Netsch's chapel is the exception to his Miesian architecture at the Air Force Academy. For the chapel at the Illinois Institute of Technology Mies chose to differentiate the design in a comparatively subtle way, substituting brick bearing walls for the steel frame he used elsewhere.

5. Edward Stone began his career in the thirties as an advocate of the International Style. A testimonial example of this is the Museum of Modern

Art in New York of 1939, for which Stone was associated with Philip L. Goodwin.

6. The phrase New Brutalism first appeared in print in December 1953. The first building to which it was applied was the Hunstanton School in England by Peter and Alison Smithson, designed in 1949 and completed in 1954. However, the Hunstanton School is a studiously crude version of Mies van der Rohe's work and is visually unrelated to the raw concrete and exposed brickwork of Le Corbusier's Maisons Jaoul, which became the basis of Brutalism as a style despite its proponents' regard of Brutalism as an ethic rather than an esthetic of building.

7. The beauty of primitive and vernacular buildings, particularly in their village context, was being rediscovered in the late forties and fifties. It was formally acknowledged by an exhibition sponsored by the Museum of Modern Art, the substance of which is contained in *Architecture without Architects* by Bernard Rudofsky (1964). Sympathy for nonpedigreed architecture was indicative of dissatisfaction with formal architecture. Some architects, John Johansen and Frederick Kiesler among them, proposed a revival of the primitive experience by returning to cavelike forms of shelter.

8. Rogers was a consultant and supervising architect for Wellesley College for many years. Day and Klauder were the architects of adjacent Founders and Green Hall.

16   1. The slenderizing of curtain-wall mullions together with minimized detailing of the corners and roof lines began in Denmark in two works of Arne Jacobsen: the offices for Jespersen and Sons in Copenhagen and the town hall at Rødovre, both completed in 1956.

2. The city of Columbus, Indiana, is a microcosm of recent architecture. Largely through the patronage of J. Irwin Miller, president of Cummins Engine Company, the Cummins Engine Foundation has paid architectural fees for new schools and other buildings by distinguished architects. The diversity of the sixties and seventies is illustrated by a church by Harry Weese, a library by I. M. Pei, and a school by Mitchell-Giurgola Associates.

3. Because it is largely visible, the steel structure is carefully designed. The major girder, spanning 80 feet between the "silo" supports, is five feet from the recessed glass walls. Secondary beams welded to this girder at 10-foot intervals are exposed inside as well as out. The suggestion of a trellis that shades the glass comes from the Deere and Company Administrative Center at Moline, Illinois (1962–64), designed by Saarinen and executed by Roche and Dinkeloo.

4. The Yale Art Gallery commission was secured by George Howe, who was then chairman of the Department of Architecture, for his former Philadelphia associate. Kahn first came to Yale in 1947 as a visiting critic and remained ten years before returning to Philadelphia to resume practice and hold a professorship at the University of Pennsylvania.

Sources of Illustrations

1 1. Adam Thoroughgood House, Princess Anne County, Virginia. Virginia State Library.

2. Boardman House, Saugus, Massachusetts. Marcus Whiffen.

3. Boardman House, Saugus, Massachusetts. Historical American Building Survey (HABS), Library of Congress. Redrawn by Cynthia Cobb.

4. John Ward House, Salem, Massachusetts. Sandak, Inc.

5. Bacon's Castle, Surry County, Virginia. HABS, Library of Congress.

6. Bacon's Castle, Surry County, Virginia. HABS, Library of Congress. Redrawn by Cynthia Cobb.

7. McIntire Garrison House, Scotland, Maine. HABS, Library of Congress.

8. McIntire Garrison House, Scotland, Maine. HABS, Library of Congress. Redrawn by Cynthia Cobb.

9. Second Meeting House, Sudbury, Massachusetts. Wesleyan University Press.

10. Old Ship Meeting House, Hingham, Massachusetts. Wesleyan University Press.

11. Old Brick Church (St. Luke's), Isle of Wight County, Virginia. Marcus Whiffen.

12. Old Brick Church (St. Luke's), Isle of Wight County, Virginia. HABS, Library of Congress. Redrawn by Cynthia Cobb.

13. Capitol, Williamsburg, Virginia. Colonial Williamsburg Foundation.

14. Stadthuys (City Tavern), New Amsterdam. New-York Historical Society.

15. Dyckman House, New York City. HABS, Library of Congress.

16. Dyckman House, New York City. HABS, Library of Congress. Redrawn by Cynthia Cobb.

17. The Cloister (Klosters), Ephrata, Pennsylvania. HABS, Library of Congress.

18. Cahokia Courthouse, Cahokia, Illinois. HABS, Library of Congress.

19. Parlange, Pointe Coupée Parish, Louisiana. HABS, Library of Congress.

20. Parlange, Pointe Coupée Parish, Louisiana. HABS, Library of Congress. Redrawn by Cynthia Cobb.

21. St. Louis Cathedral, New Orleans, Louisiana. Maryland Historical Society.

22. Cabildo, New Orleans, Louisiana. Marcus Whiffen.

2 23. Palace of the Governors, Santa Fe, New Mexico. Marcus Whiffen.

24. San Estevan, Acoma, New Mexico. HABS, Library of Congress.

25. San Estevan, Acoma, New Mexico. HABS, Library of Congress. Redrawn by Cynthia Cobb.

26. Santo Tomás, Trampas, New Mexico. Marcus Whiffen.

27. San Francisco, Ranchos de Taos, New Mexico. Marcus Whiffen.

28. San Francisco, Ranchos de Taos, New Mexico. HABS, Library of Congress. Redrawn by Cynthia Cobb.

29. San José, Laguna, New Mexico. Marcus Whiffen.

30. San José, Laguna, New Mexico. Marcus Whiffen.

31. Castillo de San Marcos (Fort Marion), St. Augustine, Florida. HABS, Library of Congress.

32. Castillo de San Marcos (Fort Marion), St. Augustine, Florida. HABS, Library of Congress. Redrawn by Cynthia Cobb.

33. Nuestra Señora de la Purisima Concepcion de Acuna, San Antonio, Texas. Marcus Whiffen.

34. Nuestra Señora de la Purisima Concepcion de Acuna, San Antonio, Texas. HABS, Library of Congress. Redrawn by Cynthia Cobb.

35. San Antonio de Valero (The Alamo), San Antonio, Texas. HABS, Library of Congress.

36. San José y San Miguel de Aguayo, San Antonio, Texas. Marcus Whiffen.

37. San Xavier del Bac, near Tucson, Arizona. Marcus Whiffen.

38. San Xavier del Bac, near Tucson, Arizona. HABS, Library of Congress. Redrawn by Cynthia Cobb.

39. San Xavier del Bac, near Tucson, Arizona. HABS, Library of Congress.

40. San Carlos Borromeo, Carmel, California. G. E. Kidder Smith, *A Pictorial History of Architecture in America*.

41. San Luis Rey de Francia, near Oceanside, California. Marcus Whiffen.

42. San Luis Rey de Francia, near Oceanside, California. HABS, Library of Congress. Redrawn by Cynthia Cobb.

43. Santa Barbara, Santa Barbara, California. HABS, Library of Congress.

3   44. Governor's Palace, Williamsburg, Virginia. Colonial Williamsburg Foundation.

45. McPhedris-Warner House, Portsmouth, New Hampshire. Detroit Photographic Company Collection, Library of Congress.

46. College of William and Mary, Williamsburg, Virginia. Colonial Williamsburg Foundation.

47. President's House, College of William and Mary, Williamsburg, Virginia. Colonial Williamsburg Foundation. Redrawn by Cynthia Cobb.

48. Westover, Charles City County, Virginia. Marcus Whiffen.

49. St. James's, Goose Creek, South Carolina. Marcus Whiffen.

50. Christ Church, Lancaster County, Virginia. Marcus Whiffen.

51. St. Philip's, Charleston, South Carolina. Courtesy of The Henry Francis du Pont Winterthur Museum.

52. Old North Church (Christ Church), Boston, Massachusetts. Courtesy of The Society for the Preservation of New England Antiquities.

53. Old North Church (Christ Church), Boston, Massachusetts. G. E. Kidder Smith, *A Pictorial History of Architecture in America*.

54. Old South Meeting House, Boston, Massachusetts. Courtesy of The Society for the Preservation of New England Antiquities.

55. Stratford Hall, Westmoreland County, Virginia. Courtesy of The Robert E. Lee Memorial Association.

56. Stratford Hall, Westmoreland County, Virginia. HABS, Library of Congress. Redrawn by Cynthia Cobb.

57. Whitehall, Newport, Rhode Island. Courtesy of The Preservation Society of Newport County.

58. Westover, Charles City County, Virginia. Marcus Whiffen.

59. Mulberry, St. John's Parish, South Carolina. Carnegie Survey of the Architecture of the South by Frances Benjamin Johnston, Library of Congress.

60. Drayton Hall, Charleston, South Carolina. G. E. Kidder Smith, *A Pictorial History of Architecture in America.*

61. Drayton Hall, Charleston, South Carolina. Carnegie Survey of the Architecture of the South by Frances Benjamin Johnston, Library of Congress.

62. Drayton Hall, Charleston, South Carolina. HABS, Library of Congress. Redrawn by Cynthia Cobb.

63. Old Colony House, Newport, Rhode Island. John Hopf.

64. Christ Church, Philadelphia, Pennsylvania. G. E. Kidder Smith, *A Pictorial History of Architecture in America.*

65. Christ Church, Philadelphia, Pennsylvania. G. E. Kidder Smith, *A Pictorial History of Architecture in America.*

4 66. Redwood Library, Newport, Rhode Island. Courtesy of The Preservation Society of Newport County.

67. King's Chapel, Boston, Massachusetts. Sandak, Inc.

68. Brick Market, Newport, Rhode Island. John Hopf.

69. Christ Church, Cambridge, Massachusetts. HABS, Library of Congress.

70. St. Michael's, Charleston, South Carolina. Courtesy of William H. Pierson, Jr.

71. St. Michael's, Charleston, South Carolina. HABS, Library of Congress. Redrawn by Cynthia Cobb.

72. First Baptist Meeting House, Providence, Rhode Island. Sandak, Inc.

73. Shirley Place, Roxbury, Massachusetts. *Old-Time New England.*

74. Shirley Place, Roxbury, Massachusetts. *Old-Time New England.*

75. Carter's Grove, James City County, Virginia. HABS, Library of Congress. Redrawn by Cynthia Cobb.

76. Carter's Grove, James City County, Virginia. Colonial Williamsburg Foundation.

77. Gunston Hall, Fairfax County, Virginia. Courtesy of The Board of Regents, Gunston Hall.

78. Mount Airy, Richmond County, Virginia. Marcus Whiffen.

79. Vassall-Longfellow House, Cambridge, Massachusetts. 1759. HABS, Library of Congress.

80. Whitehall, Anne Arundel County, Maryland. Sandak, Inc.

81. Miles Brewton House, Charleston, South Carolina. Marcus Whiffen.

82. Cliveden, Germantown, Pennsylvania. HABS, Library of Congress.

83. Cliveden, Germantown, Pennsylvania. J. P. Sims and C. Willing, *Old Philadelphia Colonial Details.* Redrawn by Cynthia Cobb.

84. Chase-Lloyd House, Annapolis, Maryland. HABS, Library of Congress.

85. Hammond-Harwood House, Annapolis, Maryland. HABS, Library of Congress.

115. St. Mary's Cathedral, Baltimore, Maryland. Sandak, Inc.

116. St. Mary's Cathedral, Baltimore, Maryland. Courtesy of William H. Pierson, Jr. Redrawn by Cynthia Cobb.

117. St. Mary's Cathedral, Baltimore, Maryland. Courtesy of William H. Pierson, Jr.

118. State Bank of Louisiana, New Orleans, Louisiana. HABS, Library of Congress.

119. State Bank of Louisiana, New Orleans, Louisiana. HABS, Library of Congress. Redrawn by Cynthia Cobb.

120. New York City Hall, New York. Detroit Photographic Company Collection, Library of Congress.

121. New York City Hall, New York. Sandak, Inc.

122. Unitarian Church, Baltimore, Maryland. Marcus Whiffen.

123. Unitarian Church, Baltimore, Maryland. Engraving by W. Goodacre, Maryland Historical Society.

124. Union College, Schenectady, New York. Courtesy of Union College.

125. Scarborough House, Savannah, Georgia. Carnegie Survey of the Architecture of the South by Frances Benjamin Johnston, Library of Congress.

126. Monumental Church, Richmond, Virginia. Courtesy of William H. Pierson, Jr.

7   127. Second Bank of the United States (Customs House), Philadelphia, Pennsylvania. Marcus Whiffen.

128. Second Bank of the United States (Customs House), Philadelphia, Pennsylvania. HABS, Library of Congress. Redrawn by Cynthia Cobb.

129. Second Bank of the United States (Customs House), Philadelphia, Pennsylvania. Sandak, Inc.

130. Customs House (Federal Hall National Memorial), New York City. National Park Service.

131. Customs House (Federal Hall National Memorial), New York City. HABS, Library of Congress. Redrawn by Cynthia Cobb.

132. Ohio State Capitol, Columbus, Ohio. Wayne Andrews.

133. Tennessee State Capitol, Nashville, Tennessee. G. E. Kidder Smith, *A Pictorial History of Architecture in America.*

134. Tennessee State Capitol, Nashville, Tennessee. HABS, Library of Congress. Redrawn by Cynthia Cobb.

135. St. Paul's, Richmond, Virginia. Marcus Whiffen.

136. Unitarian Church (Stone Temple), Quincy, Massachusetts. Wayne Andrews.

137. Hustings Courthouse, Petersburg, Virginia. Marcus Whiffen.

138. Girard College, Philadelphia, Pennsylvania. Sandak, Inc.

139. Patent Office (National Portrait Gallery), Washington, District of Columbia. HABS, Library of Congress.

140. Providence Arcade, Providence, Rhode Island. Marcus Whiffen.

141. Tremont House, Boston, Massachusetts. W. H. Eliot, *A Description of Tremont House.*

142. Tremont House, Boston, Massachusetts. W. H. Eliot, *A Description of Tremont House.*

143. Lee Mansion, Arlington, Virginia. Virginia State Library.

144. Judge Wilson House, Ann Arbor, Michigan. 1843. Hedrich-Blessing.

145. Judge Wilson House, Ann Arbor, Michigan. HABS, Library of Congress. Redrawn by Cynthia Cobb.

146. Uncle Sam Plantation, St. James Parish, Louisiana. Carnegie Survey of the Architecture of the South by Frances Benjamin Johnston, Library of Congress.

147. Uncle Sam Plantation, St. James Parish, Louisiana. HABS, Library of Congress. Redrawn by Cynthia Cobb.

148. New York City Halls of Justice and House of Detention (The Tombs), New York City. Metropolitan Museum of Art.

149. St. Mary's Chapel, Baltimore, Maryland. HABS, Library of Congress.

150. Eastern State Penitentiary, Philadelphia, Pennsylvania. Historical Society of Pennsylvania.

151. Lyndhurst, Tarrytown, New York. G. E. Kidder Smith, *A Pictorial History of Architecture in America.*

152. Lyndhurst, Tarrytown, New York. Metropolitan Museum of Art.

153. Kingscote, Newport, Rhode Island. Courtesy of The Preservation Society of Newport County.

154. Kingscote, Newport, Rhode Island. Upjohn Collection, Avery Architectural Library, Columbia University.

155. Kingscote, Newport, Rhode Island. Courtesy of The Preservation Society of Newport County.

156. Edward King House, Newport, Rhode Island. Courtesy of The Preservation Society of Newport County.

157. Edward King House, Newport, Rhode Island. A. J. Downing, *The Architecture of County Houses.*

158. Morse-Libby House, Portland, Maine. HABS, Library of Congress.

159. Trinity Church, New York City. Municipal Art Society of New York.

160. St. Mary's, Burlington, New Jersey. HABS, Library of Congress.

161. St. James the Less, Philadelphia, Pennsylvania. Courtesy of Phoebe B. Stanton.

162. Emmanuel Church, Cumberland, Maryland. Courtesy of Phoebe B. Stanton.

163. St. John Chrysostom's, Delafield, Wisconsin. HABS, Library of Congress.

164. The Chalet, Newport, Rhode Island. Courtesy of The Preservation Society of Newport County.

165. Old Stone Church, Cleveland, Ohio. HABS, Library of Congress.

166. Smithsonian Institution, Washington, District of Columbia. Detroit Photographic Company Collection, Library of Congress.

167. Athenaeum of Philadelphia, Philadelphia, Pennsylvania. HABS, Library of Congress.

168. Haughwout Store, New York City. Cervin Robinson.

169. Customs House (Post Office), Georgetown, District of Columbia. HABS, Library of Congress.

170. United States Capitol, Washington, District of Columbia. Sandak, Inc.

9   171. Boston City Hall, Boston, Massachusetts. HABS, Library of Congress.

172. State, War and Navy Building (Executive Office Building), Washington, District of Columbia. HABS, Library of Congress.

173. All Souls' Unitarian Church, New York City. New-York Historical Society.

174. National Academy of Design, New York City. Museum of the City of New York.

175. Museum of Fine Arts, Boston, Massachusetts. *American Architect and Building News.*

176. Nott Memorial Library (Alumni Hall), Union College, Schenectady, New York. Courtesy of Union College.

177. Church of the Holy Trinity, New York City. The Huntington Library, San Marino, California.

178. Memorial Hall, Harvard University, Cambridge, Massachusetts. Western Reserve Historical Society.

179. Pennsylvania Academy of the Fine Arts, Philadelphia, Pennsylvania. HABS, Library of Congress.

180. Provident Life and Trust Company, Philadelphia, Pennsylvania. Historical Society of Philadelphia.

181. Trinity Church, Boston, Massachusetts. G. E. Kidder Smith, *A Pictorial History of Architecture in America.*

182. Trinity Church, Boston, Massachusetts. Mrs. Schuyler Van Rensselaer, *Henry Hobson Richardson and His Works.*

183. Crane Memorial Library, Quincy, Massachusetts. Sandak, Inc.

184. Crane Memorial Library, Quincy, Massachusetts. Redrawn by Michael Riley.

185. Sever Hall, Harvard University, Cambridge, Massachusetts. The Museum of Modern Art, New York.

186. Allegheny County Court House, Pittsburgh, Pennsylvania. The Museum of Modern Art, New York.

187. Allegheny County Court House, Pittsburgh, Pennsylvania. Redrawn by Pamela Meyer.

188. Marshall Field Wholesale Store, Chicago, Illinois. Chicago Historical Society.

189. Stanford University, Palo Alto, California. Stanford University Archives.

190. Lenox Library, New York City. Museum of the City of New York.

191. W. K. Vanderbilt House, New York City. Brown Brothers.

192. Biltmore, Asheville, North Carolina. HABS, Library of Congress.

10   193. Western Union Building, New York City. New-York Historical Society.

194. Tribune Building, New York City. Museum of the City of New York.

222. Pennsylvania Station, New York City. Museum of the City of New York.

223. Pennsylvania Station, New York City. Museum of the City of New York.

224. Grand Central Terminal, New York City. Landmarks Preservation Commission, New York.

225. City Hall, San Francisco, California. Gabriel Moulin Studios.

226. New York Public Library, New York City. New-York Historical Society.

227. Castle Hill, Ipswich, Massachusetts. The Trustees of Reservations, Milton, Massachusetts.

228. Vizcaya, Miami, Florida. Courtesy of Dade County Art Museum.

229. All Saints' Church, Ashmont, Boston, Massachusetts. Courtesy of Boston Public Library, Print Department.

230. Cadet Chapel, United States Military Academy, West Point, New York. Boston Public Library, Print Department.

231. St. Thomas's Church, New York City. Museum of the City of New York.

232. St. Catherine's Church, Somerville, Massachusetts. Courtesy of Kennedy and Kennedy, Architects.

233. Competition Drawing: Nebraska State Capitol. Courtesy of American Institute of Architects.

234. Nebraska State Capitol, Lincoln, Nebraska. G. E. Kidder Smith, *A Pictorial History of Architecture in America.*

235. Indianapolis Public Library, Indianapolis, Indiana. Art Alliance Press, Philadelphia.

12 236. Watts Sherman House, Newport, Rhode Island. Wayne Andrews.

237. Isaac Bell House, Newport, Rhode Island. Sheldon, *Artistic Country Seats.*

238. Isaac Bell House, Newport, Rhode Island. Redrawn by Todd Heringer.

239. Richard Ashurst House, Overbrook, Pennsylvania. Sheldon, *Artistic Country Seats.*

240. William Kent House, Tuxedo Park, New York. Sheldon, *Artistic Country Seats.*

241. Mrs. F. M. Stoughton House, Cambridge, Massachusetts. Mrs. Schuyler Van Rensselaer, *Henry Hobson Richardson and His Works.*

242. W. H. Winslow House, River Forest, Illinois. Marcus Whiffen.

243. Warren Hickox House, Kankakee, Illinois. Courtesy of the Archives of the Frank Lloyd Wright Memorial Foundation.

244. Ward Willits House, Highland Park, Illinois. Sandak, Inc.

245. Ward Willits House, Highland Park, Illinois. *Frank Lloyd Wright: Ausgeführte Bauten.*

246. Darwin D. Martin House, Buffalo, New York. *Frank Lloyd Wright: Ausgeführte Bauten.*

247. Avery Coonley House, Riverside, Illinois. *Frank Lloyd Wright: Ausgeführte Bauten.*

274. Walter Gropius House, Lincoln, Massachusetts. Sandak, Inc.

275. Robinson House, Williamstown, Massachusetts. Sandak, Inc.

276. Robinson House, Williamstown, Massachusetts. Redrawn by Delbert Shotwell.

277. Harvard Graduate Center, Cambridge, Massachusetts. Robert Damora.

278. Baker House, Massachusetts Institute of Technology, Cambridge, Massachusetts. MIT Historical Collections.

14 279. Promontory Apartments, Chicago, Illinois. Hedrich-Blessing.

280. 860–880 Lake Shore Drive Apartments, Chicago, Illinois. Hedrich-Blessing.

281. 860–880 Lake Shore Drive Apartments, Chicago, Illinois. Redrawn by Robert Westerhoff.

282. Seagram Building, New York City. Esto, Ezra Stoller.

283. Illinois Institute of Technology, Chicago, Illinois. Hedrich-Blessing.

284. Edith Farnsworth House, Plano, Illinois. Hedrich-Blessing.

285. Crown Hall, Illinois Institute of Technology, Chicago, Illinois. Balthazar Korab.

286. Project for Convention Center, Chicago, Illinois. Hedrich-Blessing.

287. Lever House, New York City. Museum of the City of New York.

288. General Motors Technical Center, Warren, Michigan. Sandak, Inc.

289. Philip Johnson House, New Canaan, Connecticut. Esto, Ezra Stoller.

290. McCormick Place, Chicago, Illinois. Hedrich-Blessing.

291. Midway Gardens, Chicago, Illinois. The Museum of Modern Art, New York.

292. Herbert Jacobs House, Madison, Wisconsin. Redrawn by Noe Valle.

293. Goetsch-Winkler House, Okemos, Michigan. Hedrich-Blessing.

294. Fallingwater, Kaufmann House, Bear Run, Pennsylvania. Hedrich-Blessing.

295. Price Tower, Bartlesville, Oklahoma. Courtesy H. C. Price Co.

296. Guggenheim Museum, New York City. Solomon R. Guggenheim Museum.

297. Taliesin West, Scottsdale, Arizona. Marcus Whiffen.

298. Wayfarers' Chapel, Palos Verdes, California. G. E. Kidder Smith, *A Pictorial History of Architecture in America.*

299. Gene Bavinger House, Norman, Oklahoma. Photo by Gene Bavinger. Courtesy of Bruce Goff.

15 300. Dymaxion House. Buckminster Fuller, 1927. Buckminster Fuller Archives.

301. Charles Eames House, Pacific Palisades, California. Julius Shulman.

302. Kresge Auditorium, Massachusetts Institute of Technology, Cambridge, Massachusetts. MIT Historical Collections.

303. Ingalls Hockey Rink, Yale University, New Haven, Connecticut. Esto, Ezra Stoller.

304. Trans World Airlines Terminal, New York City. Esto, Ezra Stoller.

305. Dulles International Airport, Chantilly, Virginia. Courtesy Revere Copper and Brass.

306. Chapel, United States Air Force Academy, Colorado Springs, Colorado. Courtesy Skidmore, Owings & Merrill.

307. St. Mary's Cathedral, San Francisco, California. Gabriel Moulin Studios.

308. Thomas McNulty House, Lincoln, Massachusetts. Redrawn by Oscar Burgueno.

309. Stuart Pharmaceutical Company, Pasadena, California. Julius Shulman.

310. McGregor Memorial Conference Center, Wayne State University, Detroit, Michigan. Courtesy of Wayne State University.

311. Sheldon Memorial Art Gallery, University of Nebraska, Lincoln, Nebraska. Esto, Ezra Stoller.

312. Lincoln Center for the Performing Arts, New York City. Courtesy of Lincoln Center for the Performing Arts, Inc. Photograph by Bob Serating.

313. Carpenter Visual Arts Center, Harvard University, Cambridge, Massachusetts. Julius Shulman.

314. Boston City Hall, Boston, Massachusetts. G. E. Kidder Smith, *A Pictorial History of Architecture in America*.

315. Art and Architecture Building, Yale University, New Haven, Connecticut. Julius Shulman.

316. Art and Architecture Building, Yale University, New Haven, Connecticut. Courtesy Paul Rudolph.

317. St. John's Abbey Church, Collegeville, Minnesota. Hedrich-Blessing. Courtesy of Marcel Breuer Associates.

318. Mummers Theater, Oklahoma City, Oklahoma. Balthazar Korab.

319. Guild House, Philadelphia, Pennsylvania. Courtesy Venturi and Rauch.

320. Sea Ranch Condominium, Sea Ranch, California. © Morley Baer, from *Bay Area Houses.*

321. Kresge College, University of California, Santa Cruz, G. E. Kidder Smith, *A Pictorial History of Architecture in America.*

16   322. Blue Cross-Blue Shield of Maryland, Towson, Maryland. G. E. Kidder Smith, *A Pictorial History of Architecture in America.*

323. Investors Diversified Services Building, Minneapolis, Minnesota. Courtesy Johnson and Burgee, Photograph by Richard W. Payne.

324. Bronx Developmental Center, New York City. Esto, Ezra Stoller.

325. Beinecke Rare Book Library, Yale University, New Haven, Connecticut. G. E. Kidder Smith, *A Pictorial History of Architecture in America*.

326. Marina City, Chicago, Illinois. Redrawn by Alan Maglaughlin.

327. Raymond Hilliard Housing, Chicago, Illinois. Orlando Cabanban.

328. John Hancock Center, Chicago, Illinois. Hedrich-Blessing.

329. Sears Tower, Chicago, Illinois. Orlando Cabanban.

330. Federal Reserve Bank Building, Minneapolis, Minnesota. Balthazar Korab.

331. Gund Hall, Harvard University, Cambridge, Massachusetts. Steve Rosenthal.

332. House in Old Westbury, Long Island, New York. Retoria, Y. Futagawa.

333. Behavioral Science Center, Circle Campus, University of Illinois, Chicago, Illinois. Orlando Cabanban.

334. East Building, National Gallery of Art, Washington, District of Columbia. National Gallery of Art.

335. Christian Science Center, Boston, Massachusetts. G. E. Kidder Smith, *A Pictorial History of Architecture in America.*

336. Knights of Columbus, New Haven, Connecticut, New Haven. G. E. Kidder Smith, *A Pictorial History of Architecture in America.*

337. Veterans Memorial Coliseum, New Haven, Connecticut. G. E. Kidder Smith, *A Pictorial History of Architecture in America.*

338. College Life Insurance Company, Indianapolis, Indiana. Retoria, Y. Futagawa.

339. Richards Medical Research and Biology Buildings, University of Pennsylvania, Philadelphia, Pennsylvania, John Lautman.

340. Richards Medical Research and Biology Buildings, University of Pennsylvania, Philadelphia, Pennsylvania. Redrawn by Henry C. Mahlstedt.

341. Salk Institute of Biological Studies, La Jolla, California. Jim Cox.

342. First Unitarian Church, Rochester, New York. John Ebstel.

343. First Unitarian Church, Rochester, New York. Redrawn by Jeffrey Sessions.

344. Library, Phillips Exeter Academy, Exeter, New Hampshire. Photograph by Herndon Associates with permission of the Trustees of Phillips Exeter Academy.

345. Kimbell Art Museum, Fort Worth, Texas. Courtesy of Kimbell Art Museum. Photograph by Bob Wharton.

Select Bibliography

Books published before 1895 are not included in this bibliography. Refer to H.-R. Hitchcock, *American Architectural Books: A List of Books, Portfolios and Pamphlets Published in America before 1895 on Architecture and Related Subjects* for a complete bibliographical listing of these books. A comprehensive bibliography of writings on the period covered in part I is F. J. Roos, Jr., *Bibliography of Early American Architecture: Writings on Architecture Constructed Before 1860 in Eastern and Central United States* (Urbana: University of Illinois Press, 1968). For part II there are the guides to information sources by L. Wodehouse, *American Architects from the Civil War to the First World War* (Detroit: Gale Research Company, 1976) and *American Architects from the First World War to Present* (Detroit: Gale Research Company, 1977).

Adams, E. B., and Chavez, F. A., editors. *The Missions of New Mexico, 1776: A Description by Fray Francisco Atanasio Dominguez with Other Contemporary Documents.* Albuquerque: University of New Mexico Press, 1956. Reprinted in 1975.

Adams, W. H., editor. *Jefferson and the Arts: An Extended View.* Washington, D.C.: National Gallery of Art, 1976.

Alexander, R. *The Architecture of Maximilian Godefroy.* Baltimore: Johns Hopkins University Press, 1975.

American Philosophical Society. *Historic Philadelphia from the Founding until the Early Nineteenth Century.* Issued as Vol. XLIII, Part 1, of the *Transactions* of the American Philosophical Society, 1953.

Andrews, W. "Alexander Jackson Davis." *Architectural Review* CIX (May 1951): 307–312.

Andrews, W. *Architecture, Ambition, and Americans.* New York: Free Press, 1947. Revised edition, 1978.

Architectural Book Publishing Company. *A Monograph of the Work of McKim, Mead and White.* 4 vols. New York, 1915–25.

Baigell, M. "James Hoban and the First Bank of the United States." *Journal of the Society of Architectural Historians [JSAH]* XXVIII (May 1969): 135–136.

Baigell, M. "John Haviland in Philadelphia 1818–1826." *JSAH* XXV (October 1966): 197–208.

Baldwin, C. C. *Stanford White.* New York, 1931. Reprinted by Da Capo Press, New York, 1971.

Banham, R. *The Architecture of the Well-Tempered Environment.* Chicago: University of Chicago Press, 1973.

Beirne, R. R., and Scarff, J. H. *William Buckland, 1734–1774, Architect of Virginia and Maryland.* Annapolis: Maryland Historical Society, 1958.

Bridenbaugh, C. *Peter Harrison: First American Architect.* Chapel Hill: University of North Carolina Press, 1949.

Briggs, M. S. *The Homes of the Pilgrim Fathers in England and America.* London and New York: Oxford University Press, 1932.

Brooks, H. A. *The Prairie School: Frank Lloyd Wright and His Midwest Contemporaries.* Toronto: University of Toronto Press, 1972.

Brown, G. *History of the United States Capitol.* 2 volumes. Washington: Government Printing Office, 1900, 1902.

Burchard, J., and Bush-Brown, A. *The Architecture of America: A Social and Cultural History.* Boston: Little, Brown and Co., 1961.

Burnham, A. "The New York Architecture of Richard Morris Hunt." *JSAH* XI (May 1952): 9–14.

Cardwell, K. H. *Bernard Maybeck: Artisan, Architect, Artist.* Santa Barbara and Salt Lake City: Peregrine Smith, 1977.

Carrott, R. G. *The Egyptian Revival: Its Sources, Monuments, and Meaning.* Berkeley: University of California Press, 1978.

Carter, P. *Mies van der Rohe at Work.* New York: Praeger, 1974.

Chicago Tribune. The International Competition for a New Administration Building for the Chicago Tribune MCMXXII. Chicago, 1923.

Christ-Janer, A. *Eliel Saarinen.* Chicago: University of Chicago Press, 1948. Reprinted in 1979.

Condit, C. W. *American Building: Materials and Techniques from the Beginning of the Colonial Settlements to the Present.* Chicago: University of Chicago Press, 1969.

Condit, C. W. *The Chicago School of Architecture.* Chicago: University of Chicago Press, 1964.

Cook, J. *The Architecture of Bruce Goff.* New York: Harper and Row, 1978.

Cook, J. W., and Klotz, H. *Conversations with Architects.* New York: Praeger, 1973.

Coolidge, J. *Mill and Mansion: A Study of Architecture and Society in Lowell, Massachusetts, 1820–1865.* New York: Russell and Russell, 1942.

Coolidge, J. "Peter Harrison's First Design for King's Chapel, Boston." In *De Artibus Opuscula XL: Essays in Honor of Erwin Panofsky,* edited by M. Meiss, pp. 64–75. New York: New York University Press, 1961.

Cortissoz, R. *Monograph of the Work of Charles A. Platt.* New York: Architectural Book Publishing Company, 1913.

Cummings, A. L. "The Foster-Hutchinson House." *Old-Time New England* LIV (January–March 1964): 59–76.

Cummings, A. L. *The Framed Houses of Massachusetts Bay, 1625–1725.* Cambridge: Harvard University Press, 1979.

Danz, E. *Architecture of Skidmore, Owings & Merrill, 1950–1962.* New York: Praeger, 1963.

Donnelly, M. C. *The New England Meeting House of the Seventeenth Century.* Middletown, Conn.: Wesleyan University Press, 1968.

Dorsey, S. P. *Early English Churches in America 1607–1807.* New York: Oxford University Press, 1952.

Downing, A., and Scully, V. J., Jr. *The Architectural Heritage of Newport, Rhode Island.* Cambridge: Harvard University Press, 1952. Second edition published by Clarkson N. Potter, New York, 1970.

Drexler, A., editor. *The Architecture of the Ecole des Beaux-Arts.* New York: Museum of Modern Art, 1977.

Early, J. *Romanticism and American Architecture.* New York: A. S. Barnes, 1965.

Eaton, L. K. *Landscape Artist in America: the Life and Work of Jens Jensen.* Chicago: University of Chicago Press, 1964.

Edgell, G. H. *The American Architecture of Today.* New York: C. Scribner's Sons, 1928. Reprinted by AMS Press.

Ferriss, H. *The Metropolis of Tomorrow.* New York: I. Washburn, 1929.

Fitch, J. M. *American Building: The Historical Forces that Shaped It.* Boston: Houghton Mifflin Co., 1966. Second edition published by Schocken Books, New York, 1973.

Fitch, J. M. *Walter Gropius.* New York: George Braziller, 1960.

Floyd, M. H. "A Terra-Cotta Cornerstone for Copley Square: Museum of Fine Arts, Boston, 1870–1876, by Sturgis and Brigham." *JSAH* XXXII (May 1973): 83–103.

Forman, H. C. *The Architecture of the Old South.* Cambridge: Harvard University Press, 1948. Reprinted by Russell and Russell, 1969.

Frary, I. T. *Early Homes of Ohio.* Richmond: Garrett and Massie, 1936.

Frary, I. T. *Thomas Jefferson, Architect and Builder.* Richmond: Garrett and Massie, 1950.

Y. Futagawa, editor. *Kevin Roche, John Dinkeloo and Associates 1962–1975.* New York: Architectural Book Publishing Company, 1977.

Gallagher, H. M. P. *Robert Mills, Architect of the Washington Monument.* New York: Columbia University Press, 1935. Reprinted by AMS Press, 1975.

Garvan, A. N. B. *Architecture and Town Planning in Colonial Connecticut.* New Haven: Yale University Press, 1951.

Gebhard, D. *Schindler.* New York: Viking Press, 1971.

Giedion S. *Space, Time and Architecture.* Cambridge: Harvard University Press, 1946. Fifth revised and enlarged edition, 1979.

Gilchrist, A. A. "Additions to *William Strickland, Architect and Engineer, 1788–1854.* Supplement to *JSAH* XIII (October 1954).

Gilchrist, A. A. "John McComb, Sr. and Jr., in New York, 1784–1799." *JSAH* XXXI (March 1972): 10–21.

Gowans, A. *Images of American Living: Four Centuries of Architecture and Furniture as Cultural Expression.* Philadelphia: Lippincott, 1964.

Granger, A. H. *Charles Follen McKim: A Study of His Life and Work.* Boston: Houghton Mifflin Company, 1913.

Grube, O. W.; Pran, P. C.; and Schultz, F. *One Hundred Years of Architecture in Chicago.* Chicago: Follett, 1976.

Hamlin, T. F. *Benjamin Henry Latrobe.* New York: Oxford University Press, 1955.

Hamlin, T. F. *Greek Revival Architecture in America.* New York: Oxford University Press, 1944.

Heyer, P. *Architects on Architecture.* New York: Walker & Co., 1966.

Hines, T. S. *Burnham of Chicago: Architect and Planner.* New York: Oxford University Press, 1974.

Hitchcock, H.-R. *American Architectural Books: A List of Books, Portfolios and Pamphlets Published in America before 1895 on Architecture and Related Subjects.* Minneapolis: University of Minnesota, 1965.

Hitchcock, H.-R. *The Architecture of H. H. Richardson and His Times.* New York: Museum of Modern Art, 1936. Revised edition published by Anchor Books, Hamden, 1961.

Hitchcock, H.-R. *Architecture: Nineteenth and Twentieth Centuries.* London and Baltimore: Penguin Books, 1958. Fourth edition, 1977.

Hitchcock, H.-R. *Rhode Island Architecture.* Providence: Rhode Island Museum Press, 1939.

Hitchcock, H.-R. "Ruskin and American Architecture, or Regeneration Long Delayed." In *Concerning Architecture,* edited by J. Summerson, pp. 166–208. London and Baltimore: Allen Lane, 1968.

Hitchcock, H.-R., and Johnson, P. *The International Style: Architecture since 1922.* New York: W. W. Norton and Company, 1932.

Hitchcock, H.-R., and Seale, W. *Temples of Democracy: The State Capitols of the U.S.A.* New York: Harcourt Brace Jovanovich, 1976.

Hoffmann, D. *The Architecture of John Wellborn Root.* Baltimore: Johns Hopkins University Press, 1973.

Jacobus, J. *Twentieth-century Architecture: The Middle Years 1940–65.* New York: Praeger, 1966.

Jencks, C. A. *The Language of Post-Modern Architecture.* New York: Rizzoli, 1977.

Johnson, P. *Mies van der Rohe.* New York: Museum of Modern Art, 1947.

Johnson, P. *Writings.* New York: Oxford University Press, 1979.

Johnston, N. B. "John Haviland, Jailor to the World." *JSAH* XXIII (May 1964): 101–106.

Hunter, W. H., Jr., editor. *The Architecture of Baltimore: a Pictorial History.* Baltimore: Peale Museum, 1953.

Jordy, W. H. *American Buildings and Their Architects: The Impact of European Modernism in the Mid-Twentieth Century,* Vol. 4. Garden City, N.Y.: Doubleday & Co., 1976.

Jordy, W. H. *American Buildings and Their Architects: Progressive and Academic Ideals at the Turn of the Century,* Vol. 3. Garden City, N.Y.: Doubleday & Co., 1976.

Jordy, W. H. "Veterans Memorial Coliseum, New Haven, Connecticut." *Architectural Review* CLIII (April 1973): 228–232.

Kaufmann, E., Jr., editor. *The Rise of an American Architecture.* New York: Praeger in association with the Metropolitan Museum of Art, 1970.

Kelly, J. F. *Early Connecticut Meetinghouses.* New York: Columbia University Press, 1948.

Kelly, J. F. *The Early Domestic Architecture of Connecticut.* New Haven: Yale University Press, 1924.

Kimball, S. F. *American Architecture.* Indianapolis and New York, 1928.

Kimball, S. F. *Domestic Architecture of the American Colonies and of the Early Republic.* New York: C. Scribner's Sons, 1922. Reprinted by Dover Publications, 1966.

Kimball, S. F. "Gunston Hall." *JSAH* XIII (May 1954): 3–8.

Kimball, S. F. "Jefferson and the Public Buildings of Virginia: I—Williamsburg, 1770–1776." *Huntington Library Quarterly* XII (February 1949): 115–120.

Kimball, S. F. "Jefferson and the Public Buildings of Virginia: II—Richmond, 1779–1780." *Huntington Library Quarterly* XII (May 1949): 303–310.

Kimball, S. F. *Mr. Samuel McIntire, Carver, Architect of Salem.* Portland: The Southworth-Anthoensen Press, 1940.

Kimball, S. F. *Thomas Jefferson, Architect.* Boston: Riverside Press, 1916.

Kirker, H. *The Architecture of Charles Bulfinch.* Cambridge: Harvard University Press, 1977.

Komendant, A. E. *Eighteen Years with Architect Louis I. Kahn.* Englewood, N.J.: Aloray, 1975.

Kramer, E. W. "Detlef Lienau, An Architect of the Brown Decades." *JSAH* XIV (March 1955): 18–25.

Krinsky, C. H. *Rockefeller Center.* New York: Oxford University Press, 1978.

Kubler, G. *The Religious Architecture of New Mexico in the Colonial Period and Since the American Occupation.* Colorado Springs: Taylor Museum, 1940. Fourth edition published by the University of New Mexico Press, 1972.

Lancaster, C. *The Japanese Influence in America.* New York: W. H. Rawle, 1963.

Lancaster, C. "New York City Hall Stair Rotunda Reconsidered." *JSAH* XXIX (March 1970): 33–39.

Landy, J. *The Architecture of Minard Lafever.* New York: Columbia University Press, 1970.

Lehmann, K. *Thomas Jefferson, American Humanist.* New York: Macmillan Co., 1947.

Lockwood, C. "The Italianate Dwelling House in New York City." *JSAH* XXXI (May 1972): 141–151.

Maginnis, C. *The Work of Cram and Ferguson.* New York: Pencil Points Press, 1929.

Manson, G. C. *Frank Lloyd Wright to 1910: The First Golden Age.* New York: Reinhold, 1958.

Makinson, R. L. *Greene and Greene: Architecture as a Fine Art.* Salt Lake City and Santa Barbara: Peregrine Smith, 1977.

McCallum, I. R. M. *Architecture, U.S.A.* London: Architectural Press, 1959.

McCoy, E. *Five California Architects.* New York: Reinhold, 1960.

McCoy, E. *Richard Neutra.* New York: George Braziller, 1960.

McHale, J. *Buckminster Fuller.* New York: George Braziller, 1962.

McKee, H. J. "St. Michael's Church, Charleston, 1752–1762: Some Notes on Materials and Construction." *JSAH* XXIII (March 1964): 39–42.

Meeks, C. L. V. "Henry Austin and the Italian Villa." *Art Bulletin* (June 1948): 145–149.

Meeks, C. L. V. *The Railroad Station.* New Haven: Yale University Press, 1956.

Meeks, C. L. V. "Romanesque before Richardson in the United States." *Art Bulletin* XXXV (March 1953): 17–33.

Mendelsohn, E. *Amerika: Bilderbuch eines Architekten.* Berlin: R. Mosse, 1926.

Metcalf, P. "Boston Before Bulfinch: Harrison's King's Chapel." *JSAH* XIII (March 1954): 11–14.

Michels, E. "Late Nineteenth Century Published American Perspective Drawing." *JSAH* XXXI (December 1972): 291–308.

Middleton, W. D. *Grand Central . . . The World's Greatest Railway Terminal,* San Marino, Calif.: Golden West Book, 1977.

Miller, J., II. "The Designs for the Washington Monument in Baltimore." *JSAH* XXIII (March 1964): 19–28.

Moholy-Nagy, S. *The Architecture of Paul Rudolph.* New York: Praeger, 1970.

Moore, C. *The Life and Times of Charles Follen McKim.* Boston: Houghton Mifflin, 1929.

Moore, C.; Allen, G.; and Lyndon, D. *The Place of Houses.* New York: Holt, Rinehart & Winston, 1974.

Morrison, H. S. *Early American Architecture from the First Colonial Settlement to the National Period.* New York: Oxford University Press, 1952.

Morrison, H. S. *Louis Sullivan: Prophet of Modern Architecture.* New York: Museum of Modern Art, 1935. Reprinted by Greenwood Press, Westport, 1971.

Mujica, F. *History of the Skyscraper.* New York: Archaeology and Architecture Press, 1930.

Mumford, L. *The Brown Decades.* New York: Harcourt, Brace and Company, 1931. Second revised edition published by Dover Publications, New York, 1955.

Mumford, L. *Roots of Contemporary American Architecture.* New York: Reinhold, 1952. Second edition republished with updated biographical sketches by Dover Publications, New York, 1972.

Mumford, L. *The South in Architecture.* New York: Harcourt, Brace and Company, 1941.

Mumford, L. *Sticks and Stones.* New York: Boni and Liveright, 1924. Second revised edition published by Dover Publications, New York, 1955.

Museum of Modern Art. *Modern Architecture: International Exhibition.* New York, 1932.

Nelson, G. *The Industrial Architecture of Albert Kahn.* New York: Architectural Book Publishing Company, 1939.

Neutra, R. *Wie Baut Amerika.* Stuttgart: J. Hoffman, 1927.

Newcomb, R. *Architecture in Old Kentucky.* Urbana: University of Illinois Press, 1953.

Newcomb, R. *Architecture of the Old North-West Territory*. Chicago: University of Chicago Press, 1950.

Newcomb, R. *The Old Mission Churches and Historic Houses of California*. Philadelphia and London: J. B. Lippincott Company, 1925.

Newton, R. H. *Town & Davis, Architects*. New York: Columbia University Press, 1942.

Nichols, F. D. *The Early Architecture of Georgia*. Chapel Hill: University of North Carolina Press, 1957.

Noffsinger, J. P. *The Influence of the Ecole des Beaux-Arts on the Architects of the United States*. Washington: Catholic University of America Press, 1955.

Norton, P. F. *Latrobe, Jefferson, and the National Capitol*. New York: Garland Publishing, 1977.

O'Gorman, J. F. *The Architecture of Frank Furness*. Philadelphia: Philadelphia Museum of Art, 1973.

O'Gorman, J. F. *Henry Hobson Richardson and his Office*. Cambridge: MIT Press, 1974.

Orr, C. *Addison Mizner: Architect of Dreams and Realities*. Palm Beach: The Gallery, 1977.

Park, H. *A List of Architectural Books Available in America Before the Revolution*. Los Angeles: Hennessey & Ingalls, 1973.

Perrin, R. W. E. "'Fachwerkbau' Houses in Wisconsin." *JSAH* XVIII (March 1959): 29–33.

Peterson, C. E., editor. *Building Early America*. Radnor: Chilton Book Company, 1976.

Pickens, B. "Mr. Jefferson as a Revolutionary Architect." *JSAH* XXXIV (December 1975): 257–279.

Pickens, B. "Wyatt's Pantheon, the State House in Boston and a New View of Bulfinch." *JSAH* (May 1970): 124–131.

Pierson, W. H., Jr. *American Buildings and Their Architects: The Colonial and Neo-Classical Styles*, Vol. 1. Garden City, N.Y.: Doubleday & Co., 1970.

Pierson, W. H., Jr. *American Buildings and Their Architects: The Corporate and Early Gothic Styles*, Vol. 2. Garden City, N.Y.: Doubleday & Co., 1978.

Place, C. A. *Charles Bulfinch, Architect and Citizen*. Boston and New York: Houghton Mifflin, 1925.

Portman, J. C., Jr., and Barnett, J. *The Architect as Developer*. New York: McGraw-Hill Book Co., 1976.

Pratt, R. *David Adler: The Architect and his Work*. New York: M. Evans & Co., 1971.

Randall, F. A. *A History of the Development of Building Construction in Chicago*. Urbana: University of Illinois Press, 1949.

Robinson, C., and Bletter, R. H. *Skyscraper Style: Art Deco*. New York: Oxford University Press, 1975.

Roper, L. W. *FLO: A Biography of Frederick Law Olmsted.* Baltimore: Johns Hopkins University Press, 1974.

Rose, H. W. *The Colonial Houses of Worship in America.* New York: Hastings House, 1963.

Roth, L. M. *The Architecture of McKim, Mead and White, 1870–1920, A Building List.* New York: Garland Publishing, 1978.

Rutledge, A. W. "The Second St. Philip's, Charleston, 1710–1835." *JSAH* XVIII (October 1959): 112–114.

Saarinen, A. B., editor. *Eero Saarinen on His Work.* New Haven: Yale University Press, 1962.

Schless, N. H. "Dutch Influence on the Governor's Palace, Williamsburg." *JSAH* XXVIII (December 1969): 254–270.

Schless, N. H. "Peter Harrison, the Touro Synagogue, and the Wren City Church." *Winterthur Portfolio 8* (1973): 187–200.

Schuyler, M. *American Architecture and Other Writings.* W. H. Jordy and R. Coe, editors. 2 vols. Cambridge: Harvard University Press, 1961.

Scully, V. J., Jr. *American Architecture and Urbanism.* New York: Praeger, 1969.

Scully, V. J., Jr. *Frank Lloyd Wright.* New York: George Braziller, 1960.

Scully, V. J., Jr. *Louis I. Kahn.* New York: George Braziller, 1962.

Scully, V. J., Jr. *Modern Architecture: The Architecture of Democracy.* New York: George Braziller, 1961.

Scully, V. J., Jr. "Romantic Rationalism and the Expression of Structure in Wood: Downing, Wheeler, Gardner, and the 'Stick Style,' 1840–1876." *Art Bulletin* XXXV (June 1953): 121–142.

Scully, V. J., Jr. *The Shingle Style.* New Haven: Yale University Press, 1955.

Shurtleff, H. R. *The Log Cabin Myth.* Cambridge: Harvard University Press, 1939.

Smith, G. E. K. *A Pictorial History of Architecture in America.* 2 vols. New York: W. W. Norton & Co., 1976.

Smith, N. K. *Frank Lloyd Wright: A Study in Architectural Content.* Englewood Cliffs: Prentice-Hall, 1966.

Stanton, P. B. *The Gothic Revival and American Church Architecture.* Baltimore: Johns Hopkins University Press, 1968.

Stebbins, T. E., Jr. "Richardson and Trinity Church: The Evolution of a Building." *JSAH* XXVII (December 1968): 281–298.

Stern, R. A. M. *George Howe: Toward a Modern American Architecture.* New Haven: Yale University Press, 1975.

Stickley, G. *Craftsman Homes.* New York: The Craftsman Publishing Company, 1909.

Stillman, D. "New York City Hall: Competition and Execution." *JSAH* XXIII (October 1964): 129–142.

Stoddard, R. "A Reconstruction of Charles Bulfinch's First Federal Street Theater, Boston." *Winterthur Portfolio 6* (1970).

Stoney, S. G. *Plantations of the Carolina Low Country.* Charleston: The Carolina Art Association, 1938.

Sturges, W. K. "Arthur Little and the Colonial Revival." *JSAH* XXXII (May 1973): 147–163.

Sullivan, L. H. *The Autobiography of an Idea.* New York: W. W. Norton and Company, 1924. Reprinted by P. Smith, New York, 1949.

Sullivan, L. H. "The Chicago Tribune Competition." *Architectural Record* LIII (February 1923): 151–157.

Sullivan, L. H. *Kindergarten Chats and Other Writings.* New York: Wittenborn, Schultz, 1947.

Summerson, J. N. *Architecture in Britain 1530 to 1830.* London and Baltimore: Penguin Books, 1953. Sixth revised edition, 1977.

Sweeney, R. L. *Frank Lloyd Wright: An Annotated Bibliography.* Los Angeles: Hennessey & Ingalls, 1978.

Tallmadge, T. E. *Architecture in Old Chicago.* Chicago: University of Chicago Press, 1941.

Tallmadge, T. E. *The Story of Architecture in America.* New York: W. W. Norton and Company. Enlarged and revised edition, 1936.

Tatum, G. B. *Penn's Great Town: 250 Years of Philadelphia Architecture.* Philadelphia: University of Pennsylvania Press, 1961.

Taut, B. *Modern Architecture.* London: The Studio, 1929.

Torres, L. "Federal Hall Revisited." *JSAH* XXIX (December 1970): 327–338.

Torres, L. "John Frazee and the New York Custom House." *JSAH* XXII (October 1964): 143–150.

Tselos, D. "The Enigma of Buffington's Skyscraper." *Art Bulletin* XXVI (March 1944): 3–12.

Tselos, D. "Exotic Influences in the Architecture of Frank Lloyd Wright." *Magazine of Art* XLVI (April 1953): 160–169, 184.

Tunnard, C., and Reed, H. H. *American Skyline.* Boston: Houghton Mifflin, 1955.

Turner, P. V. *The Founders and the Architects: The Design of Stanford University.* Palo Alto: Department of Art, Stanford University, 1976.

Upjohn, E. M. *Richard Upjohn, Architect and Churchman.* New York: Columbia University Press, 1939.

Van Brunt, H. *Architecture and Society: Collected Essays of Henry Van Brunt.* Cambridge: Harvard University Press, 1969.

Van Derpool, J. G. "The Restoration of St. Luke's, Smithfield, Virginia." *JSAH* XVIII (March 1958): 12–18.

Van Zanten, D. T. "Jacob Wrey Mould: Echoes of Owen Jones and the High Victorian Styles in New York, 1853–1865." *JSAH* XXVIII (March 1969): 41–57.

Venturi, R. *Complexity and Contradiction in Architecture.* New York: Museum of Modern Art, 1966. Revised edition, 1977.

Waterman, T. T. *The Dwellings of Colonial America.* Chapel Hill: University of North Carolina Press, 1950.

Waterman, T. T. *The Mansions of Virginia.* Chapel Hill: University of North Carolina Press, 1946.

Waterman, T. T., and Barrows, J. A. *Domestic Colonial Architecture of Tidewater Virginia.* New York: C. Scribner's Sons, 1932.

Weisman, W. "The Commercial Architecture of George B. Post." *JSAH* XXXI (October 1972): 176–203.

Weisman, W. "Commercial Palaces of New York: 1845–1875." *Art Bulletin* XXXVI (December 1954): 285–302.

Weslager, C. A. *The Log Cabin in America: From Pioneer Days to the Present.* New Brunswick: Rutgers University Press, 1969.

Whiffen, M. *American Architecture Since 1780: A Guide to the Styles.* Cambridge: MIT Press, 1969.

Whiffen, M. "The Early County Courthouses of Virginia," *JSAH* XVIII (March 1959): 1–10.

Whiffen, M. *The Eighteenth-Century Houses of Williamsburg, Colonial Capital of Virginia.* Williamsburg: Colonial Williamsburg, 1960.

Whiffen, M. *The Public Buildings of Williamsburg, Colonial Capital of Virginia.* Williamsburg: Colonial Williamsburg, 1958.

Whiffen, M. "Some Virginia House Plans Reconsidered." *JSAH* XVI (May 1957): 17–19.

Whitaker, C. H., editor. *Bertram Grosvenor Goodhue, Architect and Master of Many Arts.* New York: Press of the American Institute of Architects, 1925.

White, T. B. *Paul Philippe Cret: Architect and Teacher.* Philadelphia: Art Alliance Press, 1974.

White, T. B., editor. *Philadelphia Architecture in the Nineteenth Century.* Philadelphia: University of Pennsylvania Press, 1953.

Wight, P. B. "Reminiscences of Russell Sturgis." *Architectural Record* XXVI (August 1909): 123–131.

Wilson, S., Jr. "Louisiana Drawings by Alexandre de Batz." *JSAH* XXII (May 1963): 75–89.

Wilson, S., Jr. "Religious Architecture in French Colonial Louisiana." *Winterthur Portfolio 8* (1973): 63–106.

Wilson, S., Jr., and Huber, L. V. *The Cabildo on Jackson Square.* New Orleans: Friends of the Cabildo, 1970.

Withey, H. F., and Rathburn, E. *Biographical Dictionary of American Architects (Deceased).* Los Angeles: New Age Publishing Company, 1956.

Wodehouse, L. "Alfred B. Mullett and his French Style Government Buildings." *JSAH* XXXI (March 1972): 22–37.

Wodehouse, L. "Ammi Burnham Young, 1798–1874." *JSAH* XXV (December 1966): 268–286.

Woodbridge, S., editor. *Bay Area Houses.* New York: Oxford University Press, 1976.

Wrenn, G. L. "'A Return to Solid and Classical Principles,' Arthur D. Gilman, 1859." *JSAH* XX (December 1961): 191–193.

Wright, F. L. *Ausgeführte Bauten und Entwürfe von Frank Lloyd Wright*. Berlin: Wasmuth, 1910. Reprinted as *Buildings, Plans and Designs*, Horizon Press, 1963. Also as *Studies and Executed Buildings by Frank Lloyd Wright*, Prairie School Press, 1975.

Wright, F. L. *An Autobiography*. London and New York: Longmans, Green and Company, 1932. Second edition published by Duell, Sloan and Pearce, New York, 1943.

Wright, F. L. *Frank Lloyd Wright: Ausgeführte Bauten*. Berlin: Wasmuth, 1911. Reprinted as *Frank Lloyd Wright: The Early Work*, Horizon Press, 1968.

Index